P9-ARV-534

Figleafing Through History:

The Dynamics of Dress

ALBERT9
DVRER
NORICVS
FACIEBAT
1504

Figleafing Through History:
The Dynamics of Dress

Christie Harris and Moira Johnston

illustrated by Moira Johnston

Atheneum 1971 New York

Library of Congress catalog card number 79-134811
Published simultaneously in Canada by McClelland & Stewart, Ltd.
Manufactured in the United States of America
by Halliday Lithograph Corporation
West Hanover, Massachusetts
First Edition

To the three men of action
—T.A. HARRIS, D.R. JOHNSTON, *and little* WOOLSEY—
who fought their way through a storm of fig leaves
to survive this book

Acknowledgements

Our warmest thanks to some of the many people who have helped us during two and a half years of researching, writing, and illustrating this book.

The resources of the Metropolitan Museum of Art in New York have been invaluable—the advice of director Thomas P. F. Hoving on the Carolingian era and the help of Costume Institute librarian Gordon Stone and of individual department curators.

Virginia Borland, research librarian, and Marie Duffee, both of the Marin County Library System, California, have shown an enthusiasm and generosity of spirit that have gone far beyond professional duty.

Among the scholars who have given freely of their knowledge and ideas are the director of the Lowie Museum, Dr. William Bascom, African specialist Kenneth G. Goode, and political scientist Dr. Norman Uphoff, all of the University of California at Berkeley; Dr. Marjorie Grene, Chairman of Philosophy Department, University of California at Davis; Stanford University historians Dr. Philip Dawson and Dr. Gavin Langmuir, and Dr. B. Gerow, professor of anthropology; Dr. Hanna Kassis, Department of Religious Studies at University of British Columbia; and Dr. Douglas Fraser and Dr. Ann Farkas, scholars on African and Steppes art respectively, at Columbia University.

We are grateful to the libraries of the Metropolitan Museum of Art, New York Public, Women's Wear Daily, Marin County (California), San Francisco Public, University of California at Berkeley, Stanford University, and the Library of the Center of Asian Art and Culture, the Avery Brundage Collection, San Francisco.

Barbara Simpson and Rebecca Galdeano were efficient production assistants on the artwork. Family and friends have been encouraging and patient. Without them all we would never have persisted.

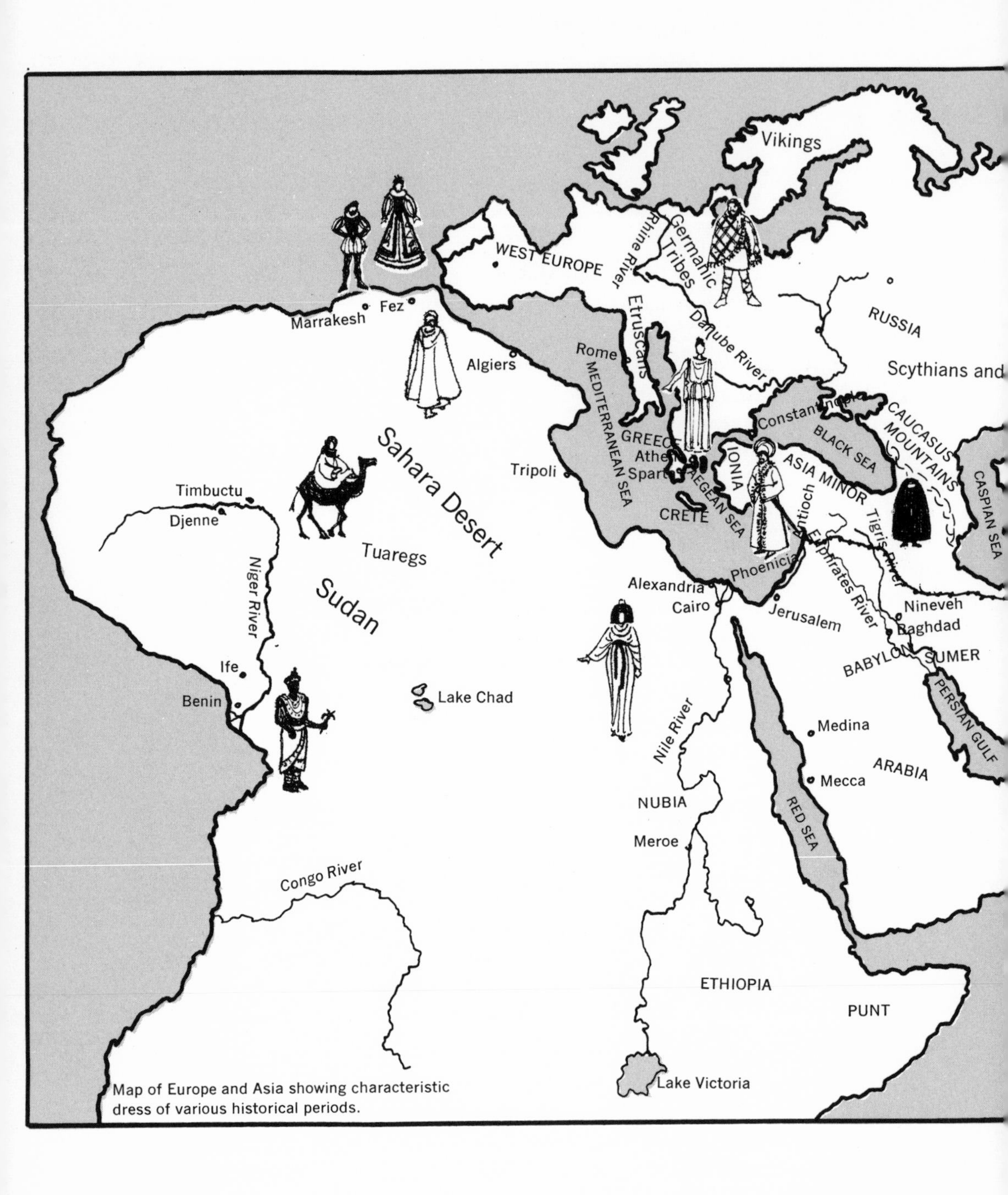

Map of Europe and Asia showing characteristic dress of various historical periods.

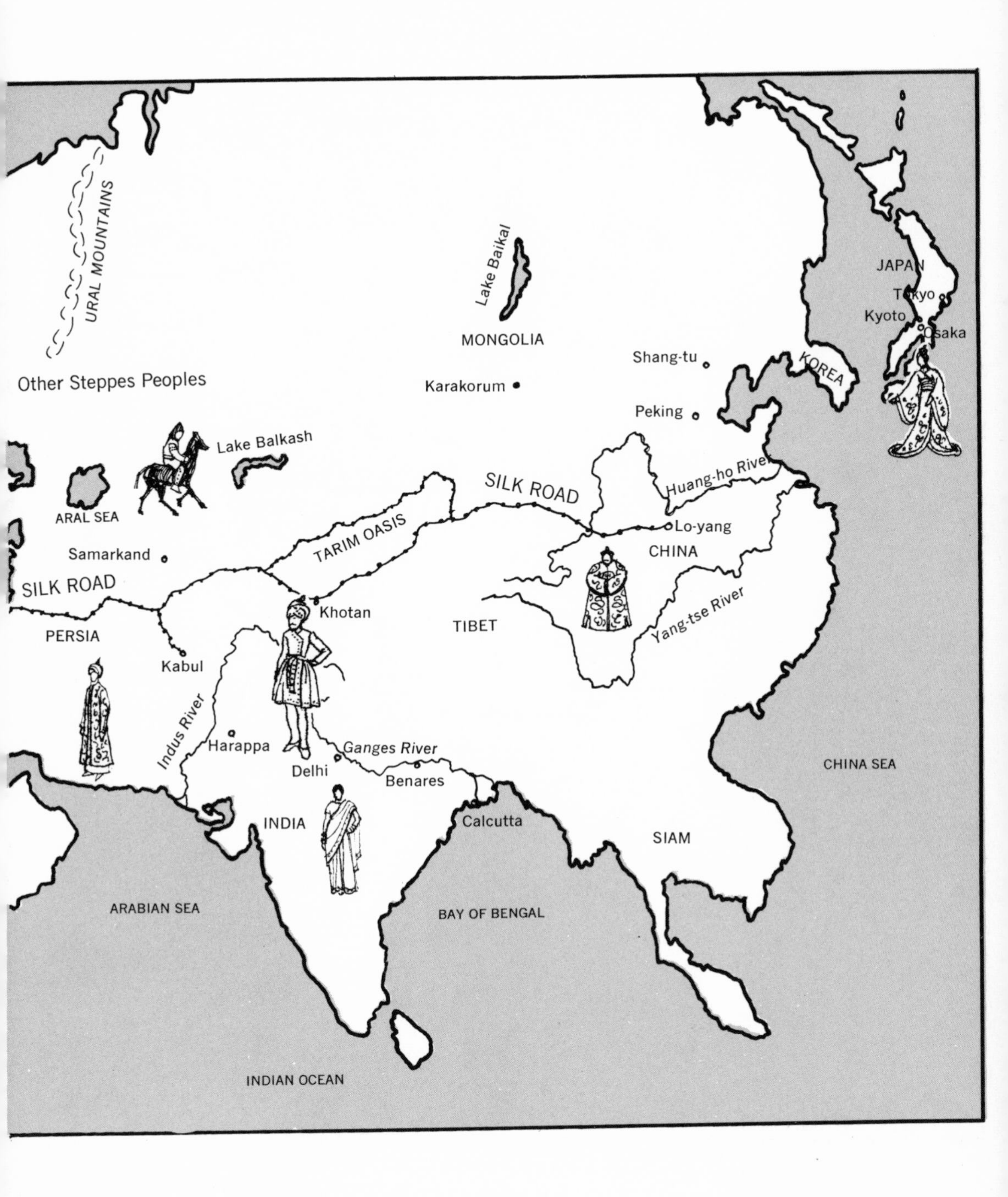
URAL MOUNTAINS
Lake Baikal
MONGOLIA
JAPAN
Tokyo
Kyoto
Osaka
Shang-tu
KOREA
Karakorum
Other Steppes Peoples
Peking
Lake Balkash
Huang-ho River
SILK ROAD
ARAL SEA
TARIM OASIS
Lo-yang
CHINA
Samarkand
SILK ROAD
Khotan
Yang-tse River
TIBET
PERSIA
Kabul
Indus River
Harappa
Ganges River
Delhi
Benares
CHINA SEA
INDIA
Calcutta
SIAM
ARABIAN SEA
BAY OF BENGAL
INDIAN OCEAN

Figleafing Through History:
The Dynamics of Dress

Before You Start—
Why Should You?

If ever there was a time to get interested in clothes, this is it. For clothes have become a powerful weapon in a major social revolution.

American Negroes are wearing African patterns and frizzly hair as if they were warpaint in a fight for black identity in a white world.

Men and women are invading each other's territory, knocking down traditional sex images with pant suits and male beauty parlors. They're stripping down to their skin in public, wrecking a code of sexual modesty that dates back thousands of years.

Rebels and Establishment attack and counterattack with the hemline. Even priests and nuns are tearing off encumbering robes and getting into the action.

And the western business suit is the focus of the attacks. Its survival or its death in this decade may be a reliable clue to the real outcome of the social revolution.

The suit is a symbol of everything western progress is based on. Taking its shape from the riding clothes of the barbarian horseman, the suit has been dulled and depersonalized over the past two centuries by the impersonal disciplines of Science and Reason. It has eliminated poetry and romance and individual expression from male dress. It has conditioned men to the regimentation of the Army without the satisfactions of its gold braid, drums, and banners. And it has swept over the world like a gray wash, dimming native color and ornament.

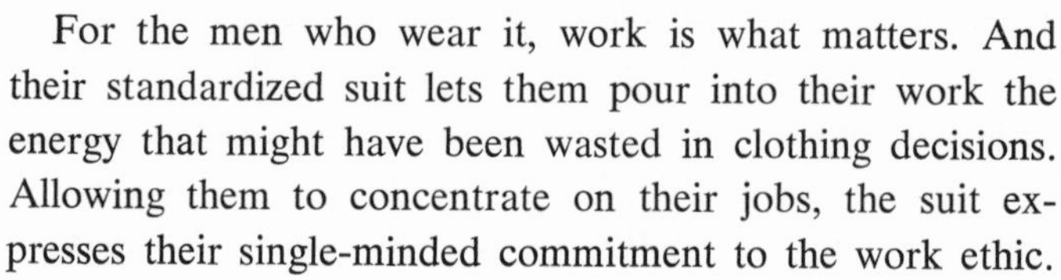

For the men who wear it, work is what matters. And their standardized suit lets them pour into their work the energy that might have been wasted in clothing decisions. Allowing them to concentrate on their jobs, the suit expresses their single-minded commitment to the work ethic.

The power of the suit has been obvious only in places like Turkey, where Kemal Ataturk imposed it in 1925 to move his people into the modern world.

At home in the West it was taken for granted. Dark and unobtrusive, it was accepted as the natural, proper way for men to dress.

Until the hippies came along.

In flagrant rejection of their fathers' values, hippies stopped showering and shaving and working. They let their hair grow. They scrounged through old trunks and second-hand stores to dress themselves for roles that seemed more worthwhile than their fathers'—the frontier loner, the Indian child of nature, the Asian mystic.

Hippies disturbed people. Somehow, those undisciplined rummages of ponchos and beads and attic finery were a threat to the American way. They were a breakdown of the rules you lived by.

Long hair was part of the hippie cult. And the intensity of family battles over hair showed that people instinctively knew appearance involved the whole person. Parents' fury over a son's hair was actually terror over what the hair represented. Was he going to throw out everything that was tried and true? Was he going to drop out of school? Was he going to embarrass the family? Was he on drugs? And WHY did he hate what his parents were?

Adults less directly threatened by granny shawls and headbands might dismiss the hippies as dirty dropouts littering the roads and beaches with beer cans. But the dropouts had found a way to hit society. They had discovered a weapon more effective than rocks or pamphlets. CLOTHES.

Obviously dress was such a deep expression of a society that to attack its dress was to attack the society itself. Clothes were much, much more than fashion.

Fashion, because of its apparent commitment to a consumer society and to designers' whims, had given clothes a very superficial reputation. In fact, the average man had felt that clothes were neither importantly useful, like a machine, nor culturally enriching, like a painting. He had felt guilty about admitting they were important to him.

A noted authority, James Laver, saw sex as the main force behind clothes. His three principles of seduction, hierarchy and utility, discussed in his book, *Modesty in Dress,* meant that women dressed to attract men by stimulating them sexually; men dressed to attract women by a display of status symbols; and everybody—especially the poor—dressed for practical reasons like warmth and work. And these principles did seem to hold true for much of history.

But now, explorations into human and animal behavior are showing how limiting the sex-based psychology was.

For seduction depends on keeping the body sufficiently forbidden and concealed to make even a bit of exposed flesh sexually stimulating. The frank, uncoy miniskirt and public nudity are undermining the power of a plunging neckline to drive men mad.

During the late 1960s, the dress of rebellion began to eliminate the sex stereotype, which had conditioned girls from birth to a pink, coy, submissive image, and had conditioned boys to a blue, practical, dominant he-manliness. The free flow of satins and beads and perfumes and trousers across sexual lines began knocking down the walls that have kept the sexes confined to their traditional roles.

Angry young women stormed up and down the Atlantic City boardwalks outside the Miss America contest protesting the marketing of sex under a phony packaging of swim suits, piano playing, social graces, fixed smiles, and lofty ideals. They fought for political equality with men and organized to ban the bra—another prop to seduction.

Attacks were spirited. But the Establishment was fighting back. The 70s began with attempts to slow the momentum of revolt on all fronts. The American president began a revival of white tie and tails and long gowns at White House parties, and introduced palace guard uniforms for White House police. The *longuette* or *midi*—the ma-

tronly, mid-calf skirt length—swung away from the youthful liberation of the miniskirt. And a vote of confidence was given the suit wearing men when they produced the most spectacular achievement in history—the walk on the moon.

The *moon suit* was a triumph for science and technology, industry, finance, and the military. But it bristled with all the things the alienated young didn't like about the society. It replaced sense-pleasing color and texture and form with robot efficiency, a micro meteorite-proof synthetic skin, urine transfer fittings, a biomedical data transmission belt, and a portable life support backpack. It was impersonal and physically restricting; the wearer could walk on the moon, but he could not easily have bent down to tie a child's shoelace. It manipulated him, isolated him from his fellow men, and insulated him from his environment. It gave him absolutely no scope for personal self expression. Its discreet American flag marked him as just another expensive product Made in U.S.A. And it gave him the power to mess up even more of his environment.

To the young, the moon suit was function at the expense of human values.

Oddly enough, a group of European scientists had already been protesting the obsession with function as the purpose of all animal "dress." Dr. Adolf Portmann, of the Zoological Institute of Basle, Switzerland, had challenged, in his book, *Animal Forms and Patterns,* the accepted theory that all color and form and pattern in the animal world must contribute directly to the survival of the species; that if a survival function was not immediately apparent, one must be found.

Dr. Portmann believes that much of the magnificence in the animal world cannot be explained by usefulness as we usually define it (sex attraction, camouflage, signalling, protection). And it can't all be explained by chance mutations or growth markings. The grandeur of a stag's antlers, he says, goes far beyond weaponry and signs of maturity and rank. The glory of a peacock's train goes far beyond sex attraction, unless a peahen is an art connoisseur. Animal pattern is incredibly ordered, rythmic, harmonious and beautiful.

But why so much genetic energy has been poured into this excessive display of shimmer, whorls, stripes, rings, spots and brilliant color is a mystery that is tantalizing him. There has to be a reason, he thinks, beyond the elementary functions of survival.

Dr. Portmann has come to the conclusion that animals have an organic compulsion to make a visual statement of what they are, to their world—like the visual statement of a grand piano, which goes far beyond the functions of housing the works and accomodating the sound. A stag's antlers and a lion's mane, he thinks, "belong to the many organs through which a high-ranking organism expresses its intrinsic worth."

In other words, the antlers and the mane are saying, "Look! This is what I am."

Is it possible that the human animal has an inner compulsion, too, to express himself visually to his world?

Antler and mane are the expression of a limited self.

But man is not so limited. His big brain gives him a potential for change and variety and cultural richness and self-delusion and calculated effect that no predictable set of antlers could express. Perhaps he needs a changeable display. Like clothes.

The minute you begin to speculate seriously about clothes, their most obvious functions—like warmth—come under attack.

Instead of perishing in the cold without clothes, men have survived on the stormy tip of South America with only a tiny, moveable patch of hide between them and the Antarctic gales that froze sleet on their bodies. Darwin found these Fuegians coping with their frigid world with bold streaks of body paint, a clatter of shell and birdbone necklaces, and white feathers in headbands. And when he gave them red cloth, they did not wrap it around themselves for warmth. They tore it into strips for more ornament.

Why?

Historians have ignored clothes, or have tossed them in for a little local color, like scenery.

But now there is a new climate that invites research. The revolt that hurled clothes at society like rotten eggs

The 1970 frontiersman undermines the somber uniformity of the suit. His textures and color reject pure function.

Ruffles and cut velvet break down the myth that dull dress is instinctive in men.

The assault on the suit. Growing irreverence for the suit, and for the suit-wearer's values, may lead to its extinction before the year 2000.

Long hair, beards and casualness of the young attack the clipped, shaved, white-shirted grooming basic to the suit's image of stripped-down efficiency.

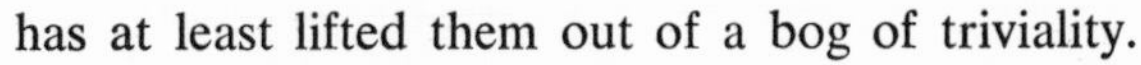
has at least lifted them out of a bog of triviality.

Now, historians note the similarity between the scruffy unorthodoxy of the hippies and the early Christians, who outlasted their decadent Roman Empire as a vital force in the world.

Political observers are beginning to watch the burnoose and the hemline as clues to what's really going on in the Arab world or in our world.

Sociologists watch the desexualizing of clothes as a clue to shifting mores. They speculate on whether an Indian headband is an indication of a childish escape into a fantasy world, or of guilt for what the society has done to the Indian.

The Metropolitan Museum of Art, which has used its excellent Costume Institute mainly to help curators date paintings and to inspire theater costume and fashion designers, raised clothes up to the level of art with its show —Fashion as Art—in galleries more accustomed to Rembrandts and El Grecos.

And at the Architectural League in New York, James Lee Byars tried to break down human barriers by inviting people to strip off their clothes and climb into his twenty-five-foot yellow silk banana garment with him, or into his red silk room-sized Four in a Hat.

The modern world has finally sensed that clothes are important. And people are newly interested in knowing WHY.

The West has never liked being at the mercy of forces it didn't understand and couldn't control. Yet it faced the dropping hemline in 1970 the way ancient farmers faced plagues or floods—with confusion and a feeling of helplessness.

There's no need for the helplessness. We can find out about clothes.

And the obvious place to start is right back at their beginnings.

1

Half a million years ago, Africa was big game country. But the important hunters were not wearing safari jackets. They were moving through the grasses on four legs in their own permanent lionskins.

There was one newer hunter who moved on two feet. He had a bone club. But he lacked the claws and horns and canines, the size and speed and strength of the great predators. His prospects were not bright. For while his primate cousins were developing longer arms for swinging through the trees where the fruit was, this meat eater seemed to be developing only a new style of head, big buttocks, and flat feet. He was losing his hair, too. And his young were helpless.

But he survived by his wits. And as his brain enlarged, his head became a compact control center that was raised higher and higher by a lengthening neck and a more upright body. By forty or fifty thousand years ago, he looked so much like us that we could accept him without embarrassment in the family album.

Modern Man had come on the scene, a badly equiped hunter in a world of superb hunters.

Twenty-five thousand years ago, he was still pitifully inadequate, crouching through the grasses, alert for lion or leopard. But he didn't feel quite so inadequate when he glanced at the paint he had streaked on his skin. For he believed that red strengthened his lifeblood; yellow lent

him sun power; and white, the color of bleached bones and evil spirits, struck fear into his adversary. Paint made him greater than he was. So he dared to stalk his dinner.

He had sensed the universal transfer of energy in the world. And he had reasoned that like produced like. A hot sun produced a hot rock. A wet river produced wet hair. A thing transferred its essence on contact.

So it seemed reasonable to him that even part of a thing could activate this sympathetic magic, or contagious magic. Blood's red color must pulse with life force. The sun's yellow color or its reflection in a quartz rock must hold some of the sun's power.

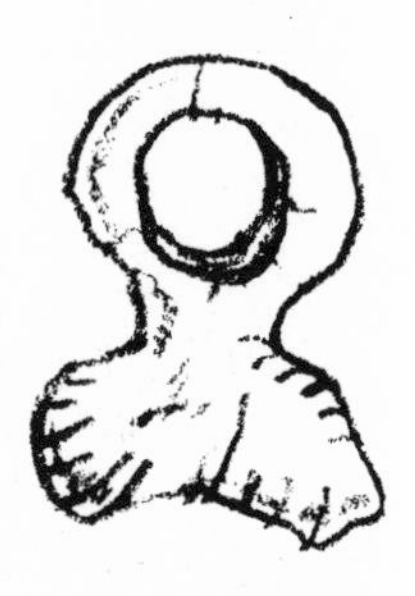

Similarly a lionskin must hold part of the skill and the strength of the lion. And it transferred that skill and that strength to a hunter when he tied it around his waist or flung it over his shoulder. The might of an elephant flowed into a man from a bit of tusk ivory hung around his neck. Ornament was a dynamo, producing power for the wearer. An amulet of bone, antler, stag's tooth, feathers, or shining rock insured a magical increase of energy.

Having faith that like produced like, a man mimicked the animals he most envied. With antlers tied to his head, he pranced like a stately buck and felt the speed and grace of that buck flowing through his body. Wearing plumes, he strutted like a mating cock and felt the virility of the cock lifting his head. Enclosing his body in a leopardskin, he borrowed the leopard's hunting power in prehunt rituals.

Since contagious magic was his source of courage and strength and skill, primitive man made the tribal magician his first chief. And this complicated the simple hierarchy of the animal world he was accustomed to.

Rank in the animal kingdom depended on one thing—the male's physical ability. There was only one way up the social ladder; and that was by a test of fighting fitness. Contenders battled until dominance was established. Both accepted the outcome.

But man had a big brain. And the fact that he often placed the witchdoctor above the great hunter, and that he tended to indicate leadership by decorating a chief's head, suggested that he suspected—or hoped—that brain outranked brawn. It was the one area in which he was superior to the beasts.

Most primitive people seem to have worn headbands. And this could be significant. By the time the simple headband had elaborated into a chief's headdress shimmering with irridescent feathers and glinting with bits of rock and shell, it had gone far beyond what it needed to be for its function of marking leadership.

Was it display of the worth of the being who could use his head and his hands to work magic and kill beasts bigger and stronger than himself?

Women weren't killing beasts. They weren't wearing grand headdresses. Small and drab beside the male, the female of any species in that animal world was dedicated to the production and protection of the young.

Lionesses hunted. But lionesses had children who could be cuffed out early and left to fend for themselves.

Human young were incredibly helpless. And they were helpless for a long time. So right from the start, women and their clothes were limited by occupation.

Their young were born only partly ready to cope with a big, dangerous world. And the mortality rate must have been terrible. But the tribe had to go on. Extra births had to make up for extra deaths. As she gathered roots and berries for her children, the woman must have eyed them with motherly alarm. What if they didn't grow up, and mate, and reproduce their kind? Perhaps it would be as well to protect and enhance her daughter's reproductive parts with the magic of seashells or a grass girdle. Her son's genitals could be protected and strengthened by a skin apron or by a magical tattoo pattern.

If there was any hiding of the genitals, it was hiding them from bad magic. In fact, the first real *figleaf* may have been proud sexual display. Biologists interested in the display theory point out that as animals rank higher and higher among the world's organisms, their reproductive area as well as their head is given visual importance. Male scrotal sacs become external instead of internal organs.

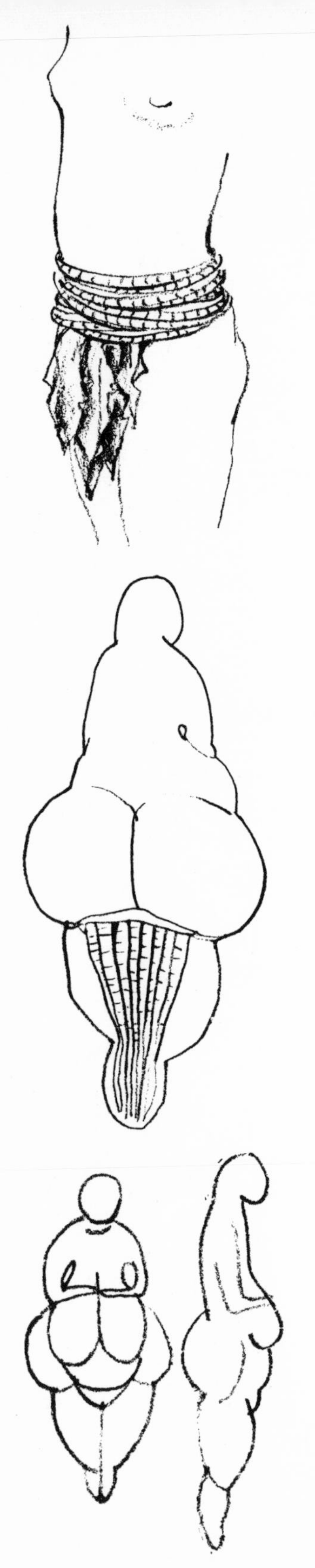

Whorls of hair and decorative tails draw attention to the anal pole of the body. So it's highly possible that the almost universal practice of covering the genitals (with tattoos, shells, leaves, grasses, girdles, breechclouts, loincloths) came from pride and not from shame.

Certainly the primitive woman, limited to her role of producing and caring for the young, would have to find much of her own worth in her fertility. She was the one who kept the race going. And why wouldn't she be proud of this great contribution? Why wouldn't she show pride, not shame, in her value to her world?

Some of the earliest known representations of women certainly flaunt fertility.

Found in Europe, and at least twenty thousand years old, tiny, squat *Venus* statuettes have such grotesquely exaggerated bosom, stomach, and buttocks that they go far beyond the needs of sympathetic magic—if their function was to produce pregnancy (in women or animals) by contact with a pregnant figure. And a string apron further focusses attention on the reproductive area. Heads are insignificant. Legs and feet often taper away to nothing.

Like the Venuses' string apron, the seashells women strung into necklaces and girdles could have been sexual display as well as fertility insurance. For seashells were thought to have life-giving magic.

Certainly shell ornaments were highly valued by women; and the value of an ornament depends on the values of its wearer.

Primitive man may not have worn much. But what he did wear showed he was responding imaginatively to his environment.

With paint and tattoos, bones and shells, feathers and animal pelts, he was reaching out into his world to take what he needed to compensate for his lack of tusks and antlers. And his adornment was as much an extension of his self as his club was an extension of his arm.

He was using furs and feathers and shells much as he found them. He was painting with earthy ochres and plant stains. And he was lifting his patterns out of his surroundings: a zebra's stripes, a leopard's spots, the swirls of a seashell.

He was one with his animal world. But he was well on his way up out of animal limitations.

He needed confidence for the climb. And if he was getting it through his faith in magical ornament, weren't his paint and his fur and his feathers as functional as a raincoat?

2

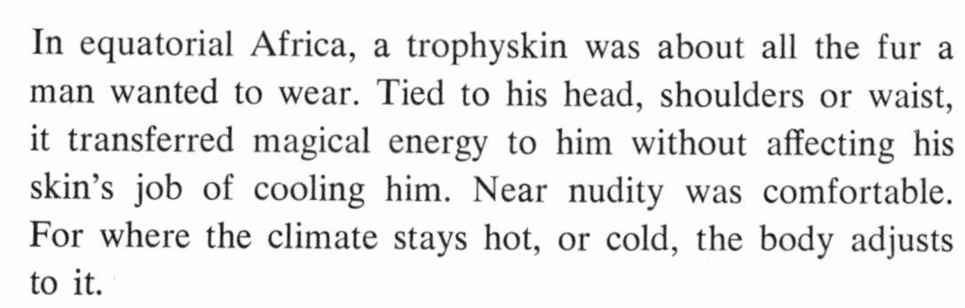

In equatorial Africa, a trophyskin was about all the fur a man wanted to wear. Tied to his head, shoulders or waist, it transferred magical energy to him without affecting his skin's job of cooling him. Near nudity was comfortable. For where the climate stays hot, or cold, the body adjusts to it.

It's change that disturbs the body. And change is what man got when he moved into northern areas. There, seasonal changes affected him, disturbing his heat control system. He began to suffer from heat and cold.

About fifteen thousand years ago, Europe was in the grip of the last Ice Age. As the ice retreated, people lived by hunting reindeer on tundra fringing the glaciers. They camped near the herds in summer, moving south into caves to escape the worst of the winter. And it was the comings and goings in winter, between a fire-warmed cave and a chilly outdoors that really bothered the caveman.

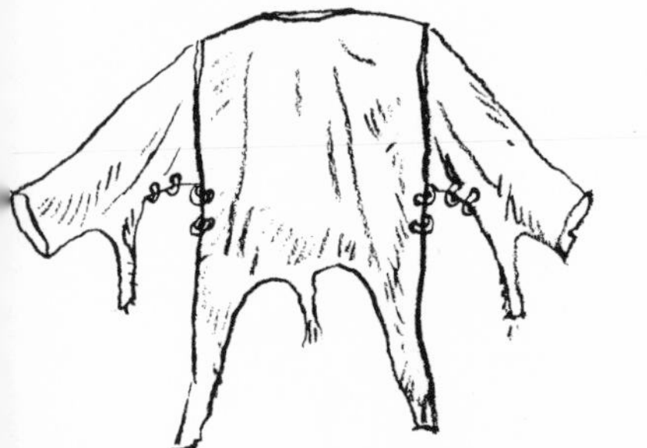

Probably his contagious magic had given him the idea of protective clothing, since cave paintings show men encased in animal skins for hunting rituals. It was an easy step from wrapping pelts for magic to wrapping pelts for warmth.

Exquisitely made needles of mammoth ivory, walrus tusk, and reindeer bone date back to about 40,000 B.C.

A cavewoman punched holes in skins and furs with a bone awl. Then, pushing her needle and reindeer sinew through with a bone plate, she sewed the edges of the skins together into crude tunics and mantles. With bone buttons and toggles to hold things on at the shoulder or waist, dress was on its halting way towards real tunics, trousers, skirts, and mantles. And the energy wasted in shivering was saved for better things. A dressed man could do more.

Cave paintings show women in longish, rather bell-shaped fur or skin skirts that resemble children's stick drawings of skirts. And the stiffness of the shape was probably just the stiffness of crudely worked skins. Hampering skirts on the women suggest that occupational difference separated male and female dress right from the beginning.

Wintering together in caves gave people the time and the incentive to elaborate their clothes and their culture. They developed their natural taste for bright, primary colors and for glitter, and their instinct for order and rhythm; and slowly magical paint and ornament grew into art.

A Stone Age necklace, found on the skeleton of a young caveman in Italy, shows the sense of order and design that could turn a collection of hunter's magic and shiny bits of shell and bone into a handsome piece of jewelry. The beads made of fish vertebrae and Nassa shells were spaced out by stag canines into a rhythmically repeated pattern.

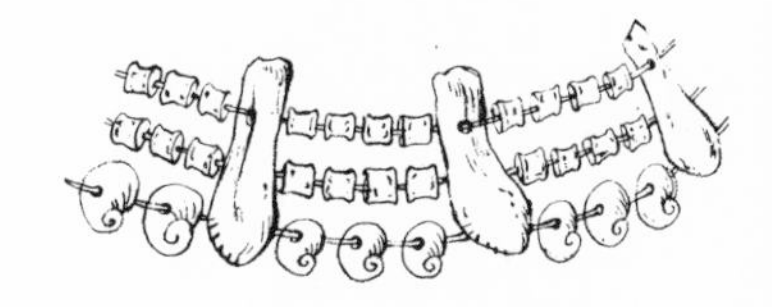

Stone Age artists had to be hunters, too.

A cave painter went from summer camp to winter cave in his working clothes, which meant going naked except for headband, amulet and skin apron. Or perhaps his body was wrapped in a primitive mantle or in a primitive tunic of skins knotted or toggled on one or both shoulders.

Letting his wife and her relatives trudge along behind with bundles of skin and the baby, he hiked ahead to search out danger and to think about the work of the winter. His mind whirled with images he had captured during the summer. And he began to select those he would paint on the rock of the ceremonial cave. He began to visualize the power of thrusting horn and muscled shoulder that must pulse through strong black lines and washes of ochre to please the animals' spirits.

Man had finally realized that there was more to his

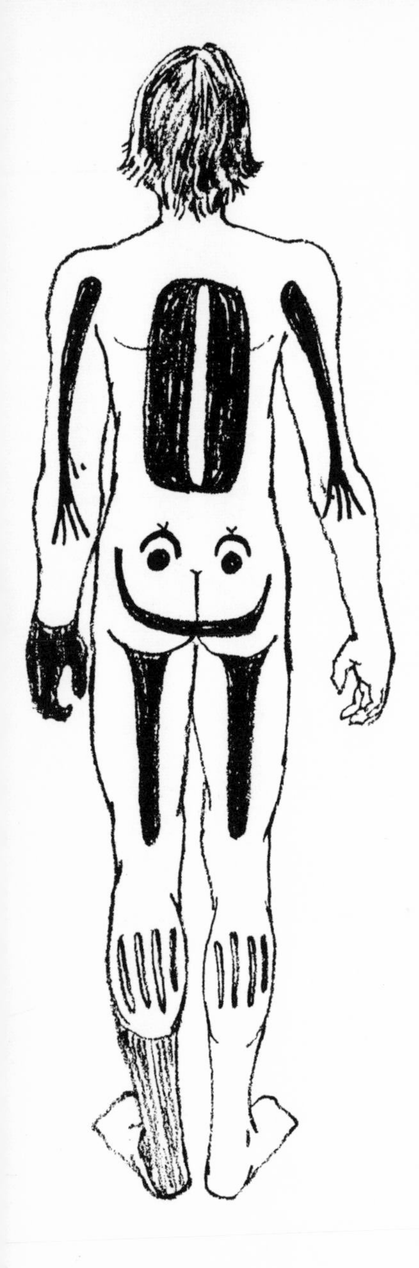

world than the simple transfer of energy. There was a universal interaction of sun and rain and grass and reindeer and man that could only be explained by spirits. Every tree, every man, every river, every reindeer had a spirit self, inside. And the spirit could be pleased or offended. If you killed too many fish, they got angry and didn't come another year. Obviously the spirit selves lived forever, to help you or punish you. So you didn't break a branch without begging a tree's pardon. You didn't kill a reindeer without appeasing its spirit. This was the hunter's religion.

There were spirits everywhere. And to be sure that at least one of them was dependably on his side, the hunter picked a friendly animal from an old family story. Storytellers built this friendly, guardian animal up into the super Stag or the super Eagle we call a *totem*. Artists made a symbolic likeness of it. And the family painted or tattooed the likeness on themselves, originating the family crest.

By branding everyone and his belongings with a crest, *totemism* sorted out relationships as well as property. People glanced at a boy's tattoo and knew his blood line. They looked at the totem painted on a girl's skin skirt and knew if marriage between her and a boy was possible, or if their blood relationship made marriage taboo.

Bloodlines gave people their belonging. But each man had to earn his rank. Status was not hereditary. As in animal societies, the ablest males topped the hierarchy, because the human hunting pack, like the animal hunting pack, needed able leadership. And each boy hoped to throw a lionskin across his shoulders, some day, as proof of his ability. Or maybe a necklace of bear claws would be his claim to high rank. Such *trophyism* was an important feature of early dress.

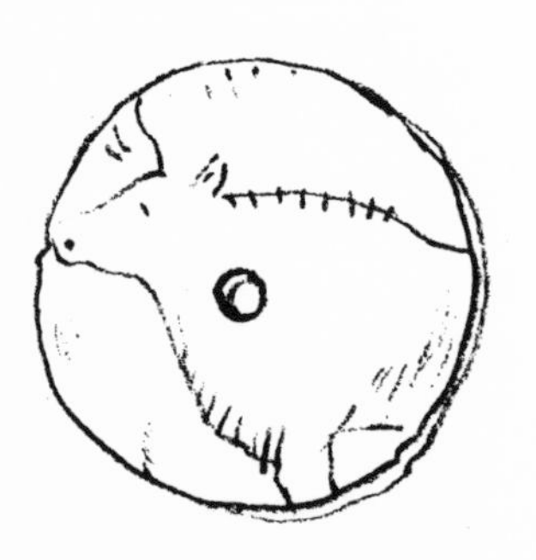

The boy's visible totem was his best security. For, just as it was his first duty to leap to the aid of others wearing the same crest, even if he had never seen them before, their first duty was to spring to his defence. Further, his totem decoration tied him firmly into his kin group. Tribal insignia tied him into the union of kin groups, the tribe. If the legendary founders of his tribe had come from the seacoast, his tribal insignia may have been traditional shells sewn in a traditional way to his mantle. And, imported through a tribe-to-tribe bucketline from the sea, such traditional dress elements must have been among the world's earliest trade goods.

The tribe's heritage was stored with its ceremonial costumes. Its values, like its regalia, had to be kept fresh by being shaken out regularly and used in ritual. Regular marking of the seasons and of the rites of passage (birth, puberty, marriage, death) with richly costumed ceremonial gave primitive life a rhythmic order that must have been deeply reassuring in a dangerous world.

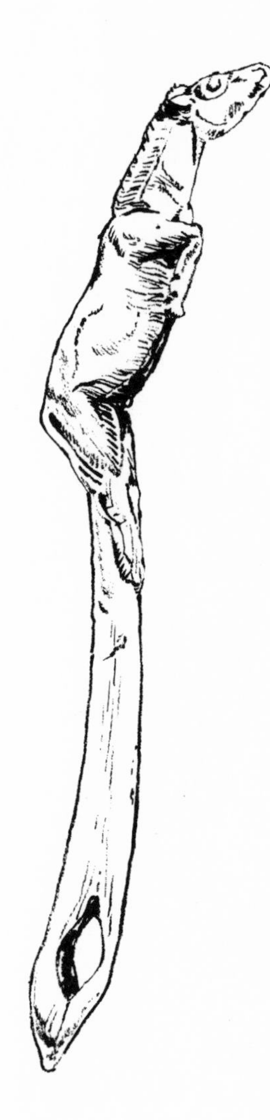

In the softening climate towards the end of the last Ice Age, the reindeer were moving north with the melting ice. And their increasing distance from the caves must have been deeply disturbing. Insecurity could have speeded the movement of shells, furs, dyes and stag teeth. For more and more insecurity demanded more and more reassuring ceremonial; more and more ceremonial demanded more and more traditional ornament.

A new excess of display and ritual may have been a desperate bid for magical help. Or it may have been a deep, subconscious assertion of the worth of the ancient way of life that was being undermined. At any rate, it gave the world its first pale golden age about 15,000 years ago. Then the caveman carved bone disc pendants with fighting mammoths. He decorated his home and his belongings, letting the forks of an antler or the bumps and stalactites of a cave collaborate in the shaping of animal bodies. He worked with nature. And his mark has lasted in his cave paintings.

But it was his wife's domestic art that got the living, evolving permanence. In her hands, the same reverence for animals, the same collaboration with natural forms led to the distinctive dress of northern man. For when she applied the natural shape of the animal skin to the natural shape of her son for a ritual dance, she made the world's first sleeves, its first trousers.

The ice receded slowly at first. Then the process

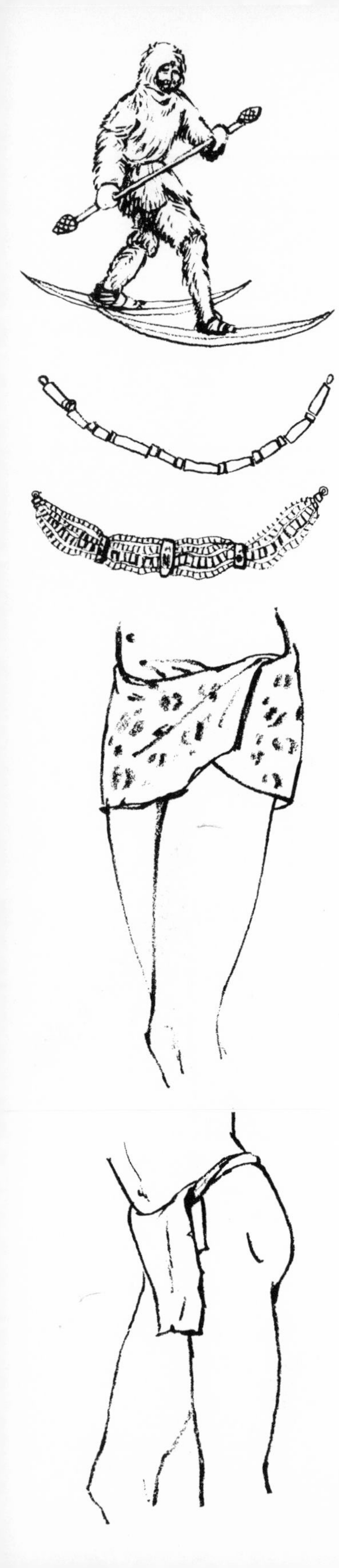

speeded. Tundra and reindeer moved north. Trees sprang up where reindeer had been grazing. And hunters were faced with the need for massive migration or for finding a new way to live.

Most moved. And for several thousand years, Europe and Asia were crisscrossed with restless hunting groups feeling their way along steppes and glacial valleys and rivers and mountain passes. Taking reassuring traditions with them, they moved dress a long way from its sources. In fact, it is possible that the unlikely tattoos and ankle bracelets of some Arctic peoples were ancient tropical traditions carried further north at this time.

Those who reached the far north continued to hunt reindeer. But the change to the longer, colder winter taxed their physical endurance. And they developed a cocoon of fur, the forerunner of the hooded sealskin jacket and trousers that provide Eskimos with perfect insulation and display their superb craftsmanship.

Primitive, hampering trousers spread only to areas where the need for warmth was acute. For men running on foot, the less clothing the better.

In Scandinavia, people discovered amber. Glowing like trapped fire, and mystifying them with its electrical properties, amber had instant appeal for superstitious people caught in a long, dark winter. It was cheering to look at, nice to handle; and obviously it was inhabited by a powerful spirit. They hung amber on their bodies so that its magic could work for them.

When the rumor spread that it could ward off the evil eye, amber was in demand all over Europe. And it began to go out along the natural trade routes with glossy northern furs, and with the reindeer skins people still needed for traditional costume. Northern amber and fur swelled the steady movement of traditional essentials like shells, furs, dyes, and stag teeth.

Reindeer hunters who had stayed behind when the reindeer left soon learned to live in a forest and hunt the red deer and wild pig. Primitive villages replaced caves and summer camps.

The women lived even safer, less exciting lives than before. Gathering wild grasses, squatting by the fire, doing jobs they could do while looking after the children, women in longish skirts had to watch men dashing around in clothes that permitted more action and colorful decoration.

Still involved with danger, men went about naked or in a minimal tunic or loinskin that freed arms and legs. Needing courage and good luck, they were streaked with paint, bright with ornament and bristling with feathers, fangs and wolfheads.

But still involved with the elements as well as with danger, a man needed a protective garment. And his mantle began to be his most important piece of clothing, serving him as blanket, windbreaker and shield. It let him range farther.

Hanging from his shoulders, straight and heavy, a mantle did something to a man. The long fall of fur made him look and feel bigger, taller. Its weight made him conscious of his unique uprightness in the world of animals. It swung heavily as he moved; and he responded to the swing with a dignified swagger, as though saying, "Look! This is what I am."

The increasing beauty and fine workmanship of the swinging mantle of fur certainly went beyond its function of protection, suggesting a growing sense of pride—probably unconscious—in the unique uprightness of man.

Though her squatting jobs kept her from much display of the unique uprightness of man, the woman was making an important breakthrough.

Using sharp flints, she was cutting animal skins for a better fit. Fingering wet, matted clumps of animal hair, she was making the first, crude felt. Experimenting with the wild flax stems she gathered for basketry, she was separating out fibers through fermentation. And the fibers were tough, yet supple. Worked in and out, like basketry, they became linen.

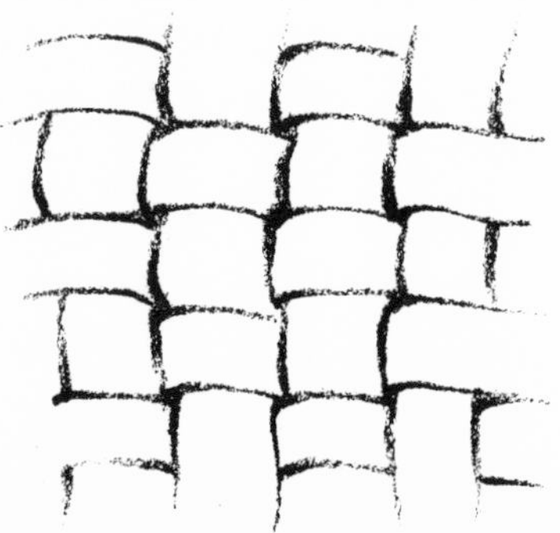

3

Deer browsed. Pigs rooted. Men and eagles hunted. Each lived his way.

Hunting was man's way, the only way he had ever known. And if his animals vanished at the end of the Ice Age, he thought he had offended them. When the old rains didn't come, he thought the rain spirits were angry.

He tried to appease angry spirits, and work magic. For the idea of turning to another way of life—farming—was as foreign to him as it would have been to an eagle.

Yet many came around to farming. And their old morale-building furs and feathers and claw necklaces were out of place.

Any who could still manage to live by hunting, hunted. Others eked out the wild meat and root supply with a little nomadic herding and with patches of grain. Some moved into settled farming, which led quickly to civilization. Different ways of life ran along side by side, with people hovering and shifting.

Clothes hovered and shifted with them.

America was deeply affected by the last Ice Age. When vast amounts of water were stored in ice sheets, the level of the sea dropped. A land bridge emerged between Siberia and Alaska. And hunting tribes crossed over from Asia, finding new homes all the way down to the tip of South America. Then the ice melted. The sea rose. And the land bridge sank, about twelve thousand years ago.

America was cut off. But the tribes didn't know it. They were alarmed by more local problems. In Mexico there was heat and drought that had never been mentioned in old tribal stories. Cool rains and reliable grasses were mysteriously disappearing. Game was vanishing.

Hunters crouched by the water holes. They killed beasts along the rivers, speeding their extinction.

Thinking they had angered spirits, people danced and drummed instead of experimenting with small, wild plants. They tried the green magic of quetzal feather headdresses before they tried the green magic of irrigation. They and their neighbors ultimately evolved a high culture based on agriculture; and they expressed it in spectacularly beautiful feather cloaks and in a blaze of gold ornament. But the initial lag proved disastrous for them later when they met Europeans who had outstripped them (in the technology of war, at least).

The end of the Ice Age hit another part of the planet—the Near East—with heat and drought like Mexico's. But there, the people turned more readily from hunting to herding and farming because the hills of the Near East were the home of easily domesticated animals and easily cultivated cereals.

Like the Mexican tribes, the Near East tribes were hunters who saw animals, not plants, as man's means of survival. And their earliest patches of wheat and barley may have been planted just to lure in wild sheep, goats and cattle. Stockbreeding, not planting, was the extension of what they knew.

Yet the change from hunting to herding was radical. Though still dependent on animals, men had lost the tension and the excitement of the old life. Confronting a proud, wild stag was one thing. Coaxing a tame sheep was another.

A stockbreeder didn't need to be streaked with paint or clattering with deer hoof fringes. And without the need, old raiment, old ritual, and old religion were empty.

Yet men clung to them. And some vestiges of them—

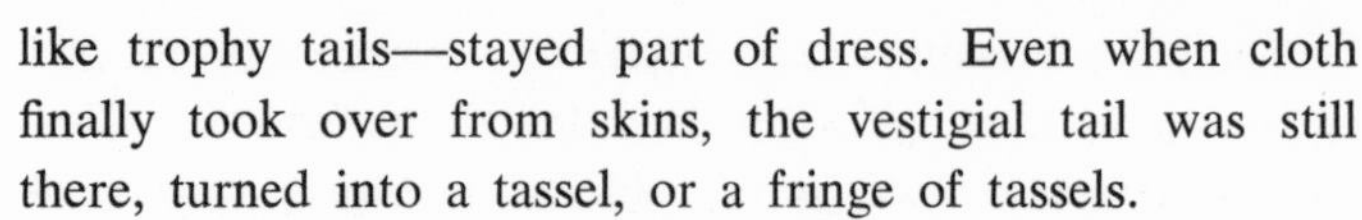

like trophy tails—stayed part of dress. Even when cloth finally took over from skins, the vestigial tail was still there, turned into a tassel, or a fringe of tassels.

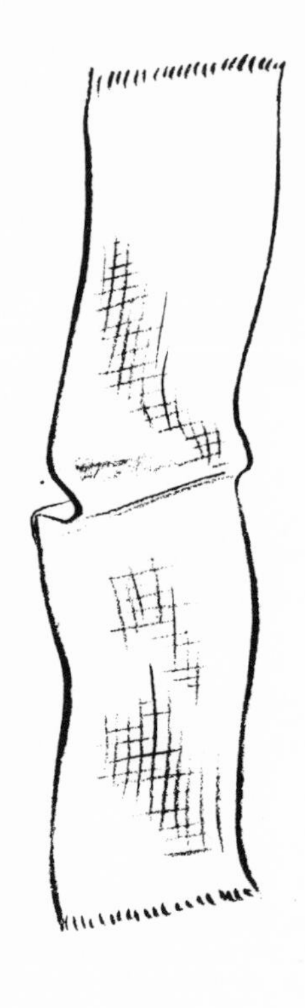

A little cloth had been made before the end of the Ice Age. Linen, felt, barkcloth, and possibly wool, were known. But as people settled down more, big looms became practical and women really began to weave. Their rectangles of cloth began to supplement hides.

Unlike skins and felts, cloth frayed when it was cut. So it wasn't cut and fitted and sewn. It was simply draped or wrapped, and tied or pinned on.

A long rectangle of linen, wrapped around the waist as a loincloth, was actually more comfortable than a loinskin in the heat of the Near East. An absorbent strip of linen around the head kept sweat out of a worker's eyes and cooled his head at the same time. So men adopted woven rectangles more and more as they settled into farming.

But they clung to skin mantles as a symbol of male dominance; for, the switch to agriculture threatened them. Women grew the field crops. Their fertility was needed to ensure a good harvest. Fertility magic was vital in building up the herds, too. Ritual re-enactment of birth, not manly deeds, now ensured the meat supply. Even the earth was a mother. Fertility was the new religion. And friendly or fierce animal spirits faded away behind gods and goddesses, the superhumans who controlled the fertile world of the stockbreeder and the planter. Now, instead of a bone disc carved with fighting mammoths, a man wore a tiny clay figurine as grotesquely fertile as the ancient little Venus statuettes.

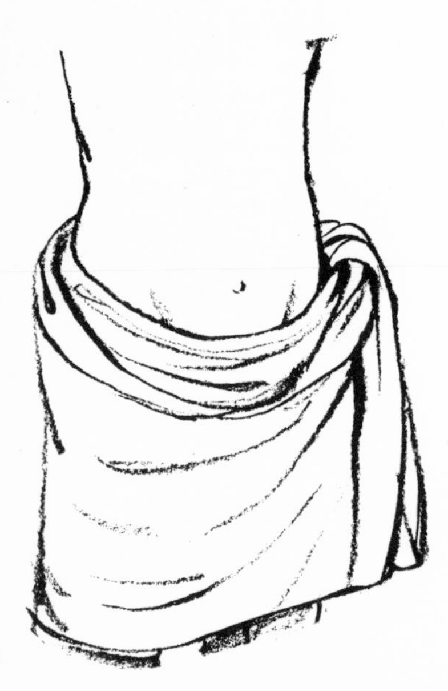

Two ways of life began to grope along, side by side, with clothing indicating the division of culture.

In the agricultural settlements, loomed linen and then loomed wool more and more replaced skins. Wrapped rectangles replaced cut-and-sewn skins.

In the camps of nomadic neighbors, felt, not linen, supplemented hides and furs. Still animal-oriented, still fearful of offending animal spirits, herders worked more closely with nature, letting the natural matting properties of wet wool dictate the stuff of their fake fur.

Then the big plow emerged in the settlements. It took a man to handle the ox that pulled it. It took a man to hold it as it tore through the soil. And as men came back into their own as the prime providers of food, people began to recognize the importance of the male in fertility. One ram or one bull could father a herd. Men were back in command.

As though reasserting male dominance, they started to wear a long, shaggy, fleece robe with sheep or goat legs that fell down along the arms, like the animal disguises of ancient rituals. And though women adopted this garment —called the *kaunakes*—for ceremonial dress, it never lost its masculine look.

People were obviously reluctant to abandon skins. For they developed a cloth replica of fleece and called it *kaunakes cloth.* They pulled tufts of sheep's wool or goat's hair through a coarse weave, in horizontal rows, to get the old familiar bulk and smell.

Evidently, as they pushed forward into unfamiliar ways, they needed to cling to old familiar ways to feel secure. Why else would the weavers have gone to so much trouble to produce a fake fleece?

Rectangles of this new, shaggy kaunakes cloth were worn as mantles before 2500 B.C. Farmers, needing to free their shoulders, soon slipped them down around their hips, originating the kaunakes *pagne*, or long loincloth. They also draped and pinned the kaunakes cloth into ceremonial mantles with capelike sleeves.

The bulky flounces of kaunakes cloth soon wrapped the hips of both sexes. But less active than men, and already caught up in the beginnings of modesty, women covered themselves more by using a longer rectangle and tossing one end up over the left shoulder. The pagne, or wrapped skirt, became the basic garment of early civilization. And significantly, at the back of the pagne was a tassel of tufts—the vestigial tail.

Perhaps kaunakes cloth and the vestigial tail got the old hunter through the painful transfer to civilization. For he slowly began to wear a thick woolen mantle, instead of a skin cloak, over his kaunakes pagne.

Where the Tigris–Euphrates poured into the Persian Gulf, the soil was rich and easy to till. The supply of water was unfailing. And since game took refuge in the lush lands and marshes, there was a surplus of food that freed some of the people to specialize in things like weaving, trading, pottery, metalworking, brick-making. Villages could grow into prosperous towns.

With a dozen towns competing for mastery in what later became known as Sumer, there was always some rousing dispute over land or water rights. And when the dispute came to a battle, the town elected its big man, or dominant male, as king to lead its fighters. The ablest man led; it was the old tribal way. And the king threw a skin across his shoulders to enhance his wild animal vigor. He asserted command with a headdress, the ancient mark of leadership.

But the king's command didn't last beyond the battle. His status didn't compare with the priest's. After all, it was the gods, not the neighbors, who caused the real catastrophes. And with more and more to lose to drought, flood and pestilence, people depended more and more on the traditional skills of the tribal magician. They paid more and more "protection" to the gods, through their priests.

Descended from a long line of witchdoctors, the priest was in touch with that other world, the spirit world. He was not just abler than other men, like the king; he was different from other men. In touch with a divine god (who could enrich or ruin life), he was separate from ordinary humans. A tall headdress stretched him up closer to his gods, but it was not enough to mark his status or enhance his function. The priest also shaved his head to clear his "receiving set" for divine emanations.

Since a town's patron god owned the real estate, the high priest conducted the town's business from the temple. He collected tribute. He ruled the town.

Human ambition being what it is, the temporary position of king and the permanent position of priest gradually merged into the priest–king. Then the dominant male was no longer just the ablest among able men. His divinity set him apart. And the old kinship between tribal leader and tribe was gone. Though the priest–king wore a pagne like other men, human comradeship was lost in the deep split that kept widening between the ruler and the ruled. Rectangular shawls began to separate him from bare-chested working men. Hampering wraps slowed his walk to a dignified pace.

The kingly headdress that covered the priestly shaved head was no longer of plumes and tusks. A tall, stiffened cone, wrapped in cloth had more relevance in a society of craftsmen, farmers, and traders.

The old hunter's display was obsolete.

4

Whether it's a stag's antlers or a vestigial tail, personal display says something. And man used it widely as a communications medium when he was setting up civilization.

He had to bring order out of a confusion of new occupations and new levels of prestige; and to a great extent he did it with clothes. He even managed to do a lot of it within the limitations of a rectangle of cloth. For the evolution of the pagne showed what could be done to make one simple shape say more and more about a man's place in society.

Everybody started with the pagne.

Then by and by a master craftsman, perhaps, set himself apart from his workmen by adding a fringe to his pagne.

By the time all the master craftsmen and head farmers and their wives had fringed pagnes, its statement was rather general. A rich merchant would feel he had more to say about himself. So, taking a longer, fringed rectangle, he extended the pagne into a shawl-like sweep over his shoulder. And his wife extended her display of modesty into a display of status.

When the town was full of extended pagnes, a town administrator asserted his extra prestige by using two rectangles. In place of an extended pagne, he tossed a separate *shawl* over his shoulder, above the wrapped skirt.

Eventually a dyed, embroidered, fringed shawl artfully draped over a fine wool pagne said many subtle things about a man's position. And at the other end of the scale, nakedness began to imply slave status.

Better dyes and finer weaves that draped more elegantly gave scope and variety to cloth. The pagne began building towards a tunic, as men draped a large piece of cloth under the right arm and pinned or knotted or sewed it over the left shoulder. Simple pins and brooches gradually went far beyond their function of holding ends of cloth together. They became a showcase for artistry, wealth, and rank.

A man with an excess of wealth and prestige let his display spill over on to his wife. She, having slaves, had time to play with the drape of the cloth, and with colors, cosmetics, and jewelry.

Ornament became very important. Its color and glitter had always delighted people. Its magic had heartened them. Its tribal significance had bound them into secure groups. But now it became vital to social communication. Gifted people began to pour their skills into ornament. And the world's first real jewelry began, using leaf, flower, and plant motifs that seem natural to a society based on planting.

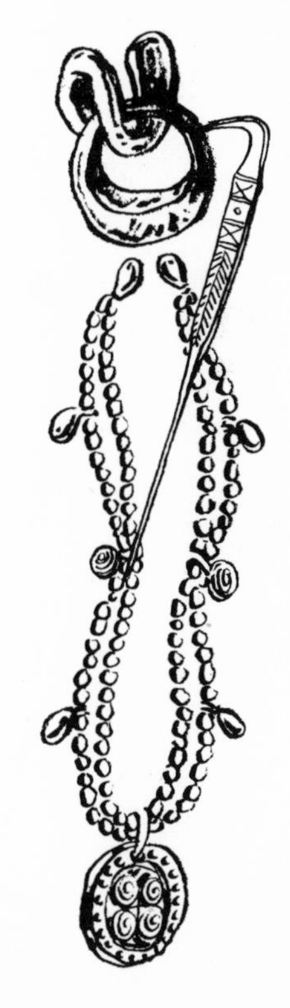

Before, ornament had related mainly to animals. Now it related to the weather and the earth and to the gods who ruled the crops. Before, gold had been no better than shiny quartz; they both shone. Now, gold's likeness to the all-important sun made it of first importance. And the moon's silver ranked just below it.

As they shifted from animal magic to the magic of the earth and sky, people began to find beauty in semiprecious stones. Gold necklaces and silver bracelets were set with polished onyx, carnelian, obsidian, agate, and the marbled deep blue of lapis lazuli.

Before, ornament had been chiefly involved with survival. It had worked for magical enhancement of power; it had held groups together. Now, more and more, it indicated personal status. A man communicated his social position through his armbands and brooches, through his wife's golden headbands or filets, her necklaces and earrings.

Gold cockleshell compacts, found in tombs and filled with red and green and black cosmetics, suggest how wealthy women spent their leisure. Diadems and other apparel found in one royal tomb tell a charming, ghastly story:

When Shub-ad, a Sumerian Queen of Ur, died nearly five thousand years ago, her ladies-in-waiting and her serving women prepared to accompany her on her mysterious journey to the after world.

Fearing the unknown, the ladies needed all the courage they could muster. So they dropped long, crimson wool robes over their heads. Red, the magical surrogate of blood, would revive them. (The robes were probably made of big rectangles sewn together to leave holes for the head and hands; golden cuff decoration suggests that they got the effect of sleeves from the loose fall of cloth over the arms.) The heavy gravitational fall of the robes enhanced the ladies' sense of stateliness, just as the long, heavy fur mantle had enhanced the old hunter's sense of proud uprightness. Reacting to their own clothes, they stood straighter.

A cascade of glittering earrings and necklaces and bracelets and rings heartened them further.

Hushed and excited, their maids adjusted their wide wigs, binding elegant chignons firmly with silver ribbons before placing the coronets. For who knew what the ladies might face out there, in the after world?

They had already dressed the dead Queen. Her lavish cape of gold, silver, and quartz beads hung from a silver collar and ended at the waist in a band of beads. Her hair ribbon was of gold; and she wore tiers of diadems to assert her rank.

The lowest diadem had a fringe of gold ring-pendants, which lay on the Queen's forehead. The middle one was a chaplet of gold beech leaves. The top one was of gold willow leaves and gold flowers inlaid with blue and white petals. And springing high above all the glittering glory, was a stylized bouquet of lapis lazuli flowers set on the gold stems of a tall comb. Gold hairpins and pendant amulets of

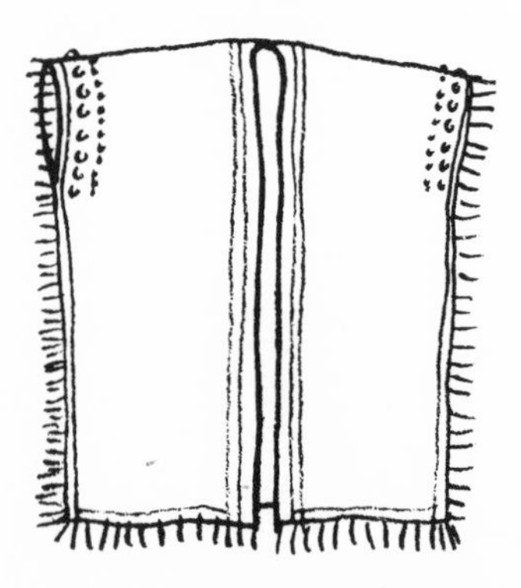

lapis lazuli completed the Queen's headdress. And crescent moon-shaped earrings fell to her shoulders to please the Moon Goddess, the patroness of Ur.

No doubt her ladies had packed her long, ceremonial kaunakes cloth robe in a chest. And looking forward to a lively after life, they had put in gaming boards, cosmetics and gold and silver drinking cups.

Trusting in gods and magic, they accompanied their Queen to her tomb. And tense with controlled apprehension, they waited in the chill outer chamber while charioteers drove oxen down the ramp behind them.

Then, stilling a wild desire to live, they drew dignity from their own splendor and drank the drug: they, the serving women, the harpist, the drivers, and the grooms. They lay down on mats, holding their silver cups. They would all make the journey together, in style.

5

The people in the towns may not have meant their symbols of power and wealth to reach far to the north. But they did.

And the steppes barbarians got the message. There was rich booty to be had in Sumer.

The origins of the tall, fair-skinned, Indo-European barbarians are elusive. But their later history can be traced through the family of languages they left behind as they moved: Greek, Italian, French, Gaelic, German, English, Russian, Sanskrit. For they are the ones who tamed the wild horse, and once they did, they were the most mobile people in the world. The horse pulled their carts across much of Europe and Asia.

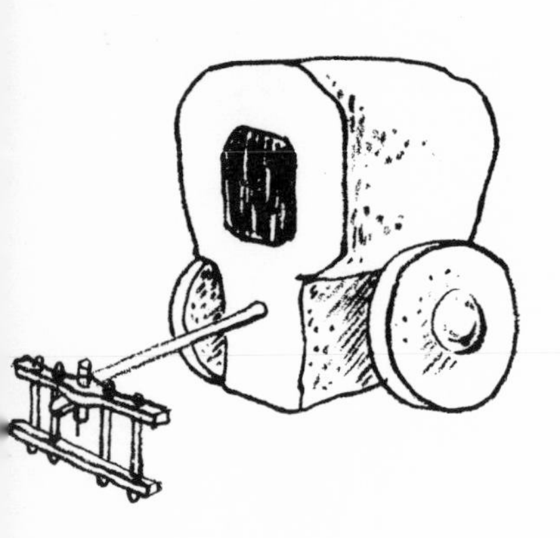

The horse, and the vastness of the area that spread before the people, made restlessness a virtue. Indo-Europeans took to nomadic herding, not to settled farming; though they raised casual patches of grain.

Their mobility affected their dress. Basically, their clothes were made to suit physical action. Indo-Europeans learned to soften leather and cut it into the clean lines of a sleeved or sleeveless belted tunic, sewn down the sides. And they wrapped hide into boots. With these went fur capes and cloaks.

Mobility meant portability. Nomads had to carry their wealth with them. When gold became valuable, their gold glittered on them, not on temples.

Their very mobility made tribes bump into one another and compete for grazing and water. Strong tribes grew dominant. Weak tribes became submissive.

Dominant tribes swept through the steppes displaying their splendor in crude gold ornament, bright appliqued felt, swaggering black fur capes, conical leather caps, bracelets, boots and animal totems.

And the weaker tribes understood. When a warlord and his band swept into a tribal encampment demanding tribute in return for protection against other warlords, the weaker tribe accepted the visible signs of dominance. And the warlords grew stronger and richer.

Being cattlemen, Indo-Europeans had endless need for space. And being accustomed to taking what they needed, dominant tribes soon mounted a push into civilized territory. Bumping south in their wagons about 2500 B.C., they took up commanding positions in the Turkish hills and in the Iranian plateau.

Bronze was a new discovery at that time. And barbarian tribes like the Hittites, in Turkey, forged bronze into battle axes; they turned the clumsy wagon into a light-spoked, two-wheeled chariot. And then they were ready to sweep down on the rich cities below.

Outlying villages felt them first as the wild, yelling barbarians came clattering out of the hills behind terrifying horses that plunged and reared and trampled people. Arrows, fire brands and battle axes completed what the horses had begun.

Sometimes the barbarians were naked and painted blue. And though the purpose of their nakedness was religious (clearing the body for better contact with helpful nature spirits), it communicated nothing to civilized people except "wild animals" and "savages."

The first aggressive response to the barbarian assault came from Sumer. After uniting all the bickering city-states of Mesopotamia, Sargon the Great mustered an army in about 2200 B.C. And he established its prestige with clothing.

Officers' gold helmets went far beyond rank markings

and head protection, they asserted the high value of men of war.

Fringe, a mark of the elite, swung from every soldier's knee-length pagne of neat wool. And tucked into the belt at the back of the pagne was a trophy tail. The soldier was a man who killed for the good of the group, like the ancient hunter. And a huge kaunakes cape protected him.

Broad bands of bronze-studded leather crossed the soldiers' chests; leather helmets protected their heads. And the armor had a function beyond protection for the wearer. It reassured frightened farmers and reminded them that these were men who faced danger for them.

Though motley compared to the glittering uniformity of later armies, this was the first specialization of costume to separate soldiers as a class. And Sargon's military dress disciplined his men so effectively that his army moved all the way to Turkey, Egypt, the Indus and perhaps even to Ethiopia.

Protected by this army, stimulated by its foreign contacts, Sumerians began to enhance still further the basic forms of their culture and their clothes.

Except for the nakedness and the loincloths that forever marked the lower classes, a war austerity in Sargon's days gave way to rich variety. Rosettes and trellises of sparkling sequins were sewn to garments. Pattern and color were woven into and embroidered on borders.

Centuries of civilization had changed response to certain colors. The old hunter's eyes had looked first at bright color and glitter. He had loved red best. The civilized man still responded to red and to other pure colors. He still gave red symbolic importance. But now he added a new dimension to it.

The richest red he could get to dye his cloth was a deep blood red called Tyrian purple. It took 240,000 molluscs from one spot on the coast of Asia Minor to make one ounce of the incredibly rare dye. The dye was taken drop by drop from tiny glands and during a delicate procedure, the sun turned the mollusc secretion into the rich color.

Tyrian purple delighted the eye. It had the ancient prestige of red. It was rare, difficult to get and very costly. So it became first the mark of the wealthy, then the emblem of royalty.

The wealth it represented was more and more tempting to the barbarians. They continued to raid, and some, wanting more than just booty, gradually settled in. Their presence, in cut-and-sewn leather, got people thinking of new possibilities for the woven rectangle. Leather techniques could be adapted to cloth to produce new forms.

The result of barbarian infiltration into civilized communities was an unfitted, short-sleeved cloth tunic—usually just two rectangles sewn together at the shoulder and side, leaving holes for the arms to come through. Later, smaller rectangles were sewn on as sleeves.

Worn by both sexes, the rectangular and T-shaped tunics began to replace the pagne and the draped, one-shoulder, pinned tunic as the basic garment under the shawl. And gradually the pagne was relegated to the lower classes.

Kaunakes, meanwhile, joined the old trophy tail as a treasured heirloom, useful only for ceremonial. On a tiny, stone cylinder seal that a merchant or an aristocrat rolled over wet clay to make a signature, about 2000 B.C., a lady and a goddess walk hand in hand. With one shoulder gracefully bared, the lady is swathed in a long, tassel-fringed shawl. The goddess is wrapped in bulky kaunakes.

Except for laborers, the lean tunic had become the thing to wear. Worn in various lengths by both sexes, it was simple, cool, and comfortable. Yet it was just long and hampering enough to say that the wearer was not available for physical labor. Of wools and linens, natural color or dyed in reds or yellows or greens and sometimes woven with stripes of color, the tunic was standard dress by the time the Babylonians succeeded the Sumerians as the dominant culture in Mesopotamia (about 2000 B.C.). It was the perfect backdrop for the embroideries, girdles, jewelry, and shawls that spoke of wealth and rank and leisure.

Controlling floods, exploring astronomy and writing laws, the Babylonian ruling class had more confidence in itself, than the Sumerians had had. People were no longer

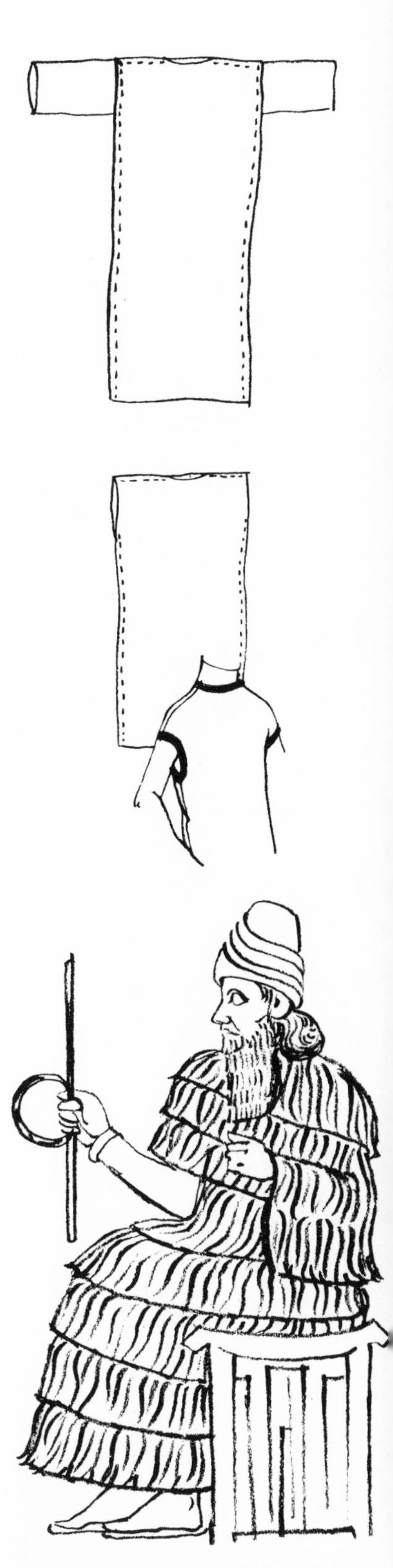

so fearful of the gods. Although the Babylonian ziggurat (temple) spiralled higher than it had in the days when it was the heart of a Sumerian temple town, it was becoming part of the king's display.

The palace was the center of power. And the king's kaunakes, or fringed, purple shawl, spiralled in as many as twelve twists around his tunic; while a turban-like tiara spiralled above that. This elaborate, constricting, spiralling construction, reserved for the king and the high priest, spoke about as eloquently as a simple rectangle could speak.

Rich merchants, scholars, and physicians feasted lavishly in apartments that shimmered with glazed tile. Reclining in sumptuously embroidered tunics, they were entertained by women who clinked from wrist to elbow with gold, lapis, and carnelian bracelets. Male wigs were curled and perfumed. Female catogans (elaborate, twisted chignons) glittered with jeweled hairpins.

Yet the barbarians were always up in the hills, ready to sweep down. And Babylon fell to them, as Sumer had. It took a tough people out of the turbulent Mesopotamian north, the Assyrians, to subdue the Babylonians and then restore Sargon's old empire. But the Assyrians themselves soon ruled a threatened empire, seething with revolts inside, erupting into wars at the outer edges. And insecurity made the Assyrians as defensive and ferocious as a watchdog.

Their military state eventually developed some of the world's first coats of armor by covering full-length, short-sleeved tunics with small iron scales. Ordinary soldiers in leather or bronze helmets were given the protection of wide leather belts, crossed shoulder straps with metal discs at the intersection, quilted stockings, and strong boots. Officers had a cuirass (a short leather shirt covered with small plates of metal) and a leather skirt with metal scales.

The Assyrians carried army regimentation and rank insignia over into civilian life. The colors that indicated status were bold: rich red, yellow, blue, green, purple. The precise width of the colored border at the hem, neck, and sleeves of a tunic, the precise width of fringe on a shawl, kept each man in his place. A short, or a long scarf-of-rank (a small, fringed shawl thrown over the shoulder or drawn through the girdle) served the same purpose as military gold braid. Gold embroidered borders on tunics and shawls were like extra gold braid for the top ranks.

At the very top of the hierarchy, the king wore a gold-embroidered, lavishly fringed, purple tunic and a tightly wrapped shawl, topped by a spiked, truncated cone of stiff felt.

The king's aide, the high priest, wore white instead of purple; he had bullock horns instead of a spike.

Assyria was a man's world.

Only the lowest class of men went barefoot, like women. Men wore curled wigs; they crimped their beards rigid. Heroic earrings and necklaces added to the general effect of male grandeur. Gold medallion bracelets and armbands focussed the eye on arms that were bronzed and muscled.

This is what they were: men fiercely defending a rich, brilliant, shaky, old civilization. Men terrified of the least breach in a wall. Even marriage was rigidly protected. Assyrian law required married women to cover their heads in public with a veil.

Although the tendency to cover up women may date back to primitive seclusion during menstruation, or to primitive marriage taboos, it seems to have been really promoted by early agricultural society.

Civilization is largely a matter of putting checks on the instincts. And perhaps, in a fertility oriented society, it was a good thing to put checks on the sexual instincts. Especially since the success of a farm could depend on the loyalty of the farm wife.

When priests strengthened the old tendency to cover up women by making it a moral virtue—something that was pleasing to the gods—women began to feel guilt and shame for any sort of nakedness. And in Assyria, they actually began to feel shame for nakedness of the head.

The fact that people accepted the idea of shame in the body, as well as the idea of the superiority of whole classes of people, is easier to understand when we consider researchers' findings about animals. For biologists tell us that the whole bearing of animals is involved in their communication of status. They tell us that among high-ranking mammals, the sense of sight is the most highly developed of the senses. It is the sense of sight they depend on for survival. And because they must depend on it, they believe what it tells them. Biologists say that high-ranking mammals seem to accept the whole bearing of dominant animals as proof of their right to dominate.

A primitive streaked with paint felt more courageous than a man without paint; so his whole bearing broadcast courage. The fall of heavy red cloth made Shub-ad's ladies feel dignified; their whole bearing conveyed dignity. Similarly, the glitter of ornament increased the arrogance of the early barbarian elite. The Babylonian king's gold-embroidered purple wool shawl made him feel, and look, luxurious and privileged. An Assyrian man in a shawl with a wide embroidered border and a two foot fringe felt superior. His whole bearing showed it. And when the man with no borders, no fringe, glanced at him, instinctively trusting his eyes, the poorer man accepted the richer as a superior class of man.

In the same way, the rich Assyrian's wife, believing that a woman's naked body was displeasing to gods and society, swathed herself from neck to heels. She drew her mantle or veil up over her head. And, responding to her own clothes, she developed a modest bearing—a more modest bearing than a poorer woman could afford. Gracefully draped, moving with dignity, eyes demure, she gave prestige to modesty.

People looked at her and instinctively felt that modesty in women was admirable. They felt shame for female nakedness.

6

Basically, early civilizations were similar. Tribes along the big rivers of Mesopotamia, India, China, and Egypt all developed agriculture, fertility cults and woven rectangles. They all created cities where people draped the rectangles into loincloths, shawls and tunics. They all designed jewelry with nature motifs. And they all used the jewelry and the draping to identify social classes.

Yet each achieved an unmistakably different effect. We have only to think of ancient India, ancient China, ancient Egypt to see that each regional group came up with a distinctive image. Each added some different, individual quality to the common factors. And this distinguishing quality seemed to derive from the region itself.

The steppes barbarians, the common threat to all those early civilizations, developed in turn an entirely different image. And their difference clearly derived from their territory.

They had the wild horse and an endless horizon. Their grassy steppes swept across the double continent of Eurasia, through a corridor between the mountains to the south and the forests to the north. Consequently the Indo-European of the south Russian steppes dressed for movement. No spiralled shawls encumbered him. His short, wrapped skin tunic freed him for action. And his winter mantle swept back as he moved, seeming to exaggerate his movement. His tree spirits and his storm gods and his

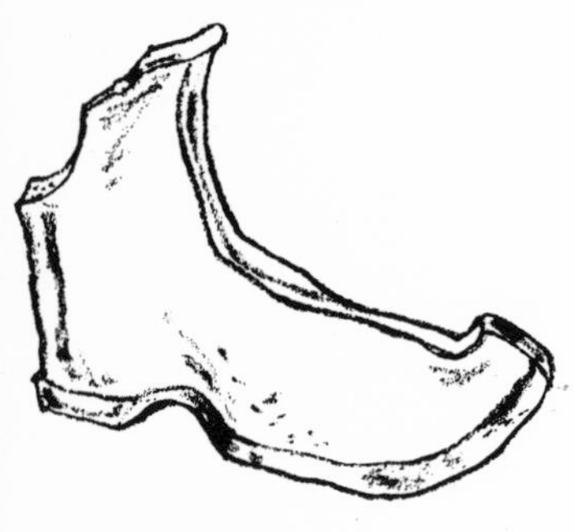

clothes identified him with his land.

In his invigorating climate, he worshipped the warming sun. Awed by its daily journey, he told stories about the sun's chariot and made the spiral the symbol of its rolling wheels. Heavy circles of glinting metal and spiralled bangles ringed his neck and wrist and hung from his ears. The spiral motif merged with animal shapes on his buckles and bracelets.

When they broke out of the steppes, pushing south beyond the mountains, they moved in among people culturally superior to themselves. And though they soon dominated this territory as well, they were sufficiently impressed by civilization to adapt to it.

In the Turkish hills, the Hittite tribes who had settled there during the early Indo-European migrations designed the two-wheeled chariot, and used iron to build themselves up into one of the three big powers: Hittites, Assyrians, Egyptians.

They also threw up crude, massive stone buildings that seemed to have erupted from the mountains. Theirs was hill country. And their steppe boots turned up at the toe for the rough trails. Their stiff conical cap sometimes flopped over at the top, as cloth gradually replaced leather; but the cap kept the protective flaps (lappets) over ears and neck for cold or battle.

As their wives began to weave more and more rectangles for them, they wrapped cloth into a straight, brief *kilt* that allowed leaping among the crags. But their kilt had the lean spareness of leather. And it was held up by a broad belt. For warmth in the hills, they tucked a short-sleeved skirt into the kilt.

Hittite kings wore the Assyrian tunic and long, wrapped shawl.

Hittite women took to civilization's long, full, concealing, sleeved tunic, belted in.

Heavy jewelry carried not only the old steppe motifs, but also the Egyptian sphynx and the Assyrian lion. For this is what the Hittites became—hill men with a barbaric tradition behind them and civilization within reaching distance in front.

When Aryan barbarians reached India about 1500 B.C., they found cities of the Harrapa culture along the Indus.

Here were the "trees that grow wool"—cotton. And the people dressed in cotton. Embroidered tunics were caught at one shoulder. Loosely wrapped loincloths were long, and often white to reflect back the rays of the burning sun. And long strips of cotton were wrapped into turbans.

Women who could afford it wore a separate shawl and loincloth. Those who couldn't, extended the loincloth up around the body, anticipating the *sari.* Rich women accented big, dark eyes with kohl and wore elaborate, fan-shaped headdresses. Their jewelry showed the same urban tastes, technical skills, plant designs and class consciousness as Mesopotamia's.

Yet the image was utterly different.

In India, a parched season was followed by torrential rains and an incredible, tropical burst of growth. And the fertility theme twined through everything like a vigorous vine.

Instead of concealing the body, gauzy, blossom colored cottons veiled women's breasts and buttocks, accentuating their roundness. Cotton cloth was twisted and tied round the hips, as a low-slung girdle, and decorated with tinkling ornament.

When the Indo-European invaders came, they crushed skulls and destroyed cities. But they could not destroy a primitive patience carried to extremes by a langorous climate; for India had a sense of timelessness that let a man sit happily for twenty-four hours drilling one hole in one bead.

The Aryans almost destroyed the Harrapa culture. But like seed blown into a hothouse, Indian culture moved from the Indus and took root along the Ganges. And there the steamy heat invigorated and ripened all the Indian sensual tendencies into a greater voluptuousness.

Life throbbed along the Ganges. With lush fruits and perfumed blossoms always within reach, even a poor man in a low caste could enrich his simple life with sunny color, perfume, religious ritual and happy sound. Indian clothing glowed with the saffrons, reds and oranges of local vegetable dyes. Flower patterns were woven into gossamer cottons, and flowers were worn fresh in the hair. Music and dancing were made gayer with the jingle of tiny bells on bracelets, anklets, and armbands. And color and sparkle and tinkle appeared on the low-slung girdles, along with pearls and carnelians, or with shells and knots of cloth. A surfeit of sensual and mystical satisfaction kept men content within their caste.

The fair-skinned Aryan barbarians couldn't change that. They could only become another caste, grafted on to the top of the vine. They could only take to cool, draped cotton too.

Aryan dress survived in the rugged hill country to the north. There, where it suited the climate better, the sleeved tunic worked its way slowly into Indian dress.

China was different. China was three kinds of territory: the northern and mountainous frontiers, the tropical south and the vigorous, temperate, fertile river valleys.

The cold north wore skins and furs. The tropical south tended to nakedness and loinskins. And in the great, agricultural regions, hemp cloth was wrapped around the loins or belted on in long, wrapped skirts or made into simple tunics.

The elite had silk robes. For here the mulberry tree grew and silkworms flourished. And thousands of years before Christ, the Chinese were unwinding the long, strong threads from the silk worm's cocoon. They were patiently devising looms that would let them capture the shine that was in silk.

They started with the simplest weaves, crisscrossing threads at right angles in the basic tabby weave. But the resulting cloth had little shine. Paint or dye or embroidery made it look richer, but it still didn't have a great deal of luster.

Then, with the discovery that threads raised up from the background caught the light differently, the Chinese found the secret of displaying silk's natural beauty. They had developed the brocade weave. A raised pattern of threads let the silk itself paint a pattern in light. With every movement, it created a living, shifting beauty, like the sheen of irridescent feathers. Eventually the weavers even gave high luster to the plain background by raising the threads into tight diagonal lines—the twill weave. This was the basis of satin, which fell in simple, glossy folds.

Silk was unique among the fabrics of the world. It scattered light the way feathers did, giving it the same lively sheen. For display of civilized refinement, silk far outranked wool and cotton, especially since it took color so well and could be woven into heavy grandeur or into fluttering delicacy. It lured warlords towards the courts and cities, but helped tame them once they had put on the robes. And as Chinese culture contrasted more and more with the roughness of their neighbors', the Chinese may have seen silk as a special gift from nature to a superior people. Other cultures had been given only tough hides and lifeless cotton, linen, and wool.

Certainly they treated silk like a sacred trust. They gave it royal protection and developed it patiently. And they wove it into the very fabric of Chinese society, using its luster and richness as a restraining and refining force in a turbulent country.

Yet design motifs suggest that China's agricultural society didn't move completely away from the animal magic of the old hunter. Threatened by barbarians, China's survival called for spirited symbols like the tiger and the dragon. Chinese farmers wore tiger amulets; since tigers ate the black pigs who ravaged the crops, the tiger was a friend. The blue or green dragon, the red bird, the white tiger and the black tortoise each represented one of the four seasons. The dragon (*lung*) symbolized thunder and lightning; but since storms brought needed rains, the dragon meant good luck and happiness.

The slowness with which complex looms were developed kept fads and impulse out of silk; it let the weaves and patterns evolve slowly with the culture. And the nature of weaving—which kept threads to horizontals and verticals—tended to abstract plant and animal patterns and make them fall into orderly repeats. Writhing tigers and dragons that might have distracted the eye were restrained

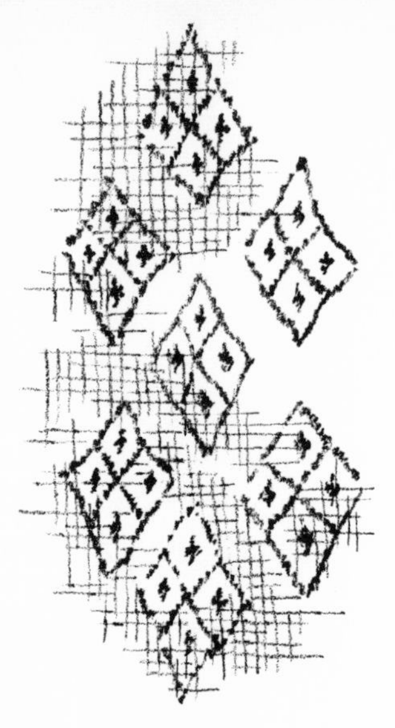

by firm, geometric lines. Their liveliness was contained as they became simply shapes that let the eye flow evenly over the silk, enjoying the changes in luster.

One of the earliest woven patterns was a crisscrossing of diagonal lines, the *lozenge*. The Chinese were using it in complicated ways by 1500 B.C. By the time of Christ they were filling the diamonds created by the lines with colors and images that had held magic for the early farmer: yellow, red, blue, tiger, cloud, phoenix and dragon. As China's society elaborated, the colors and the symbols fell into an order of value. The two highest, yellow and the dragon, became the marks of royalty and were restricted to royal use.

Because eventually everyone understood and respected the significance of each bird, flower, or animal in every shade of yellow, blue and red, patterned silks became a potent social force in China, marking status, refining barbarians, motivating ambitious men, and supporting the divine emperor. In fact, people began to value silks almost more for their meaning than for their beauty.

Steppe barbarians wanted to get at China and her silk. Indo-Europeans reached the Chinese frontier about 1300 B.C. But northern Chinese warlords stopped them, and then used barbarian-style chariots and bronze armor in their own attacks on Chinese cities to the south.

Aristocrats in any society would have fought for silk. But there was a formidable stretch of desert, mountains, and steppe between the Near East and the Far East. So silk stayed a legendary cloth until the oasis-by-oasis wagon road of the barbarians became the fabulous Silk Road shortly before the time of Christ. And the Chinese stayed an isolated, legendary people.

The Egyptians had a different kind of elegance.

Egypt was a land of sunshine and clear color: sand, blue sky and green along the river. Palms grew tall and straight, like marsh reeds and papyrus stems. The air was dry, the light intense. Outlines were clear. Contrasts were sharp. And the eye lingered on the birds and flowers along the river.

Flax grew along the river; so the people wore linen—white to reflect the sun, or light blue or green because linen did not take rich, deep dyes. And the Egyptian passion for cleanliness kept white linen white.

Men wore the *shenti*, a cool linen loincloth that wrapped the hips and passed between the legs, with the end falling in a tab at front.

Straight as a shaft of limestone, the *kalasiris* of the women fell from bare breasts to bare ankles. The kalasiris was a rectangle of linen hanging from shoulder straps or from a jeweled collar. And in a kalasiris, even a peasant girl with a basket of ducks on her head had a look of proud directness.

Egyptian ladies wore fresh flowers in their small, dark wigs, and sometimes their kalasiris shimmered with a pattern of feather tips or with strings of tiny beads caught up along the weave in a way that duplicated feather tips. An occasional kalasiris may have been made of a network of feathers.

Their jewelry revealed a great refinement of taste. *Faience*, an opaque glass glaze, added rich blues and greens to gold necklaces. And *cloisonné*, an arrangement of semiprecious stones or faience in gold wires, gave a brilliant mosaic quality to stylized designs of birds and papyrus blossoms.

The unfailing sun and the unfailing Nile insured good crops. The Nile's delta was fertile; its upper reaches were a source of gold, ivory, ostrich feathers, gems, wild animal skins, and slaves. Mediterranean and Red Sea ships laid jewels and perfumes and cedars and jars of olive oil on Egypt's wharves. With the resources of Nubia, Ethiopia, and fabled Punt (Somaliland), accessible to her, Egypt had little need to reach out in other directions. And as though expressing contentment with the way things were, the kalasiris stayed in style for fifteen centuries.

Pyramids, the Pharoah, the shenti and the kalasiris were the image of Egypt.

Egypt saw the sun as radiations, not as spirals like the barbarians. And as Son of the Sun, Pharoah, the divine ruler of Egypt, wore a wide, gold festal collar that radi-

ated out, richly inset with lapis lazuli and faience. The royal shenti too had a radiating quality. Skillfully stiffened and ray-pleated, it spread like a sunburst of linen in front.

Pharoah's headdress symbolized the union of the two lands of the Nile, north and south. A towering white mitre, fitted into a red crown with cobra, made him move slowly and regally. When the crown was put away, a royal kerchief —a square of stiffened, striped linen—covered his shaved head and framed his face and false beard.

The hunter heritage, as well as the nearness of an Africa teeming with wildlife, was marked by the lion tail fastened to the royal shenti. And also by the full leopardskin thrown across the priests' shoulders.

The more popular, luxurious image of ancient Egypt was actually a corruption of the original response of the people to their land.

Foreigners filtered in from the Near East and from Negro Africa. And just after 1700 B.C., the Hyksos invaded and dominated Egypt for a hundred years. Who the Hyksos were is uncertain. But a princess's diadem (fronted by a stylized stag's head and ringed by four octofoil blossoms and four gazelle heads) suggests an Asiatic, possibly Middle Eastern origin. At any rate, the Hyksos opened the gates to sheep and to wandering peoples all of whom the Egyptians called scornfully, "Asiatics."

Refined Egyptian sensibilities were affronted by gaudy stripes and embroideries, and by red and blue and yellow fringes. The wool from the newly-introduced sheep took dyes richly, as linen did not; but to the Egyptians it was itchy, unclean, animal, "Asiatic."

Egypt finally spat the intruders out like a bad fig. In vicious raids, she chased her conquerors out to Asia Minor, Nubia and Crete, and took some of their territories under loose control. But the experience had shocked her. It had cracked the pure, confident shape of fifteen centuries. And the old kalasiris collapsed, fissuring into pleats.

Egyptian barons surged with a new ambition—empire. They could no more help decrying the limitations of the old borders than their wives could help decrying the limitations of the old kalasiris.

But Pharoah's daughter Hatshepsut felt a divine call to restore Egypt to its old self. Shouldering aside first her husband and then his heir, she declared her own divinity. She was Pharoah. Putting on the double crown, she went to work: restoring temples, sponsoring industry, encouraging isolationism and erecting monuments to the glory of Queen Hatshepsut. And Egypt prospered.

The frustrated heir urged a military campaign to firm up the loose empire. But she fitted out a fabulous expedition to get myrrh trees for her temple at the foot of the cliffs near Thebes.

He may have poisoned her. Succeeding her as Thutmoses III, he smashed her statues and chiselled out her name to obliterate her. Then he made Egypt a real empire.

This was a new Egypt. Before Thutmoses, soldiers had been protected by a quilted shirt and by the magic of feathers. Now they had helmets and coats of mail (gold and bronze scales on heavy cloth). And they made Egypt the world's greatest power.

As her boundaries blurred and extended, so did the lines of the old kalasiris. It covered the body more, in the Asian way. Worn by both sexes, the new kalasiris was still based on a rectangle. But now it was wide and finely woven and skillfully ray-pleated. Sometimes worn in several layers, the new kalasiris was wrapped and knotted in a restless variety of ways. Sometimes it was pulled in at the waist by an outer loincloth or girdle, giving it the effect of short sleeves at first over one shoulder and later over two. And the clean, open nakedness of bare breasts gave way to the seductiveness of breasts veiled by sheer linen. For the partially concealed body is always more sexually stimulating than frank nudity.

The goddesses got the old kalasiris. A wall painting shows a later queen, Nefret-iry, hand in hand with a goddess. Nefret-iry wears the new kalasiris, pleated and sashed below her veiled breasts. The goddess wears the old kalasiris.

As time went by, Egyptian eyes became more glamorous with black line and blue shadow. Lips and nails got redder. Very wide collars blazed with gold and jewels. Wools gave

variety and color to the wardrobe. Wigs widened into frizz, or into masses of tiny black braids perfumed with cones of melted fat.

Egypt tried to revive the old classic purity of dress in the 5th and 6th centuries B.C. But she couldn't bring back the old confidence. She was eventually conquered by every major Mediterranean power, and her dress took on more and more alien traits.

Basically, the early civilizations were similar. Yet each regional group achieved an unmistakably different visual image, a different style.

And the differences seemed to come out of the territory itself.

7

Geography was only part of it. Harmony with the hills and adaptation to climate and vegetation were by no means all there was to the development of distinctive regional dress.

Three neighbors who shared the hills, blue waters, warmth, and olive groves of the Eastern Mediterranean came up with three kinds of dress, even though they were all traders as well as neighbors.

Semitic traders had a heritage stretching back to the Arabian desert.

The deserts of Arabia could not support many sheep. Pastoral nomads had to wander north into lusher lands. So over the centuries, Semitic tribes gradually drifted out of deserts in their sheepskins. They wandered through Mesopotamia while the Sumerians, Babylonians and Assyrians were building their cities. And in these countries, the nomads discovered that a large rectangle of woolen cloth gave better protection against the heat and cold than skins.

Trading was a natural sideline for these people as they moved on from town to town, bartering raw wool for cloth. And trading developed from a sideline into a way of life as the towns' need for clothing and ornament increased.

At first magical and traditional ornament were about

the only things any people needed from outside. But as some people began to rely on clothes to sort themselves out into social order, luxury textiles, fringes, dyes, jewels, precious metals, and embroideries became necessities. Civilization needed finer fabrics. It needed more delicately wrought jewelry.

Civilization needed bronze for helmets as well as for jewelry. And century by century, more and more Semitic wanderers abandoned their flocks to concentrate on moving luxury and war goods. Trading became a way of life. Areas at the crossroads of trade routes became their homes. Farms and cities grew up around them.

Many Semitic tribes settled in the Levant, along the eastern coast of the Mediterranean. And among these, the Syrians, the Phoenicians and later the Hebrews became the dominant traders.

In those days of small, fragile ships, donkey caravans and lurking hillmen, trading was a highly adventurous business. And traders had stimulating contacts with foreign peoples and places. They absorbed the color and sumptuousness of the luxury goods they handled. They discovered new kinds of dress and new needs for dress in the many places they went.

Tramping in the hills to get metals, they discovered the warmth and comfort of long sleeves. Bartering in hot southern bazaars, they found coolness in a loosened Assyrian tunic. And in a full length, long-sleeved, loose robe, they found the dignity they felt appropriate to men who were important to all the civilizations. The rich colors, bold patterns, and stately fall of cloth in the robe they adopted announced immediately to strangers that here was a man of business, not of battle.

The molluscs that were the source of Tyrian purple grew in Phoenician waters. Secure and wealthy in their monopoly on this precious dye, Phoenician sea traders wore purple robes as a protective identification in strange lands, and as a showcase for the cloths and rich dye they dealt in.

Syrian traders advertised their linen and wool in a striking manner. They sewed red and blue braid along the seams and edges of their long-sleeved white robes and white shawls. Then they spiralled the shawls over the robes, creating a dramatic pattern of bold diagonal stripes over a base of vertical streaks of color.

The Levant's seaports were dominated by the Phoenicians and the Syrians, so the Hebrews built great caravan centers. Their traders' dress was influenced by the same desert traditions that made Palestinian shepherds cling to sheepskins and plain, coarse wool.

Hebrew traders brought brilliant colors into their wools. But they wore them like the old wrapped skin skirt or like the old sheepskin tunic caught up on one shoulder. And instead of popular leaf and flower patterns, their cloth had eye-catching stripes, zigzags and spots, designs with animal origins. Their bright rectangles of wool announced them as donkey caravan traders.

The Levant was the crossroads of the known world, the battleground between Egypt and Mesopotamia and the Indo-Europeans in the Turkish hills. Its traders were bumped and jostled and overrun. But not even the bloodiest Assyrian, Hittite, or Egyptian conqueror cut the trade routes. All of them needed things.

The Levantines could not avoid turmoil. But they made themselves so essential that nobody would ever completely destroy them. They managed to survive; yet rubbing their bruises and resettling their rich but gaudy robes about them, the merchant princes of the Levant must have looked enviously out across the sparkling waters towards Crete. Nobody could jostle Cretans out there on their island.

Levantine sea traders and Cretan sea traders operated in the same, small eastern end of the Mediterranean. They met the same people in the same ports, handled similar merchandise, enjoyed much the same climate. Yet Levantine dress was very different from Cretan dress.

The Levantines were committed to being indispensible and accomodating. Their dress spoke of trade while it flattered the best customers with subtle imitation. Cretan survival was based on isolation by the sea. Though near the customers, Crete itself was free from disruption. And the dress of the Cretans expressed independence and the mood of the sea.

Crete's earliest settlers must have been strongly influenced by the sea that surrounded them and by adventurers from Egypt who came as early as 3,000 B.C.

Egypt was not aggressive. Stimulated, but not dominated by this powerful land to the south, Cretans had long, sunlit ages to evolve a culture and a dress as natural to the Aegean as its birds. A swell of influence from Egypt, or from Mesopotamia, could roll in, move and change as fluidly as the octopus that became a popular art motif. Life and dress could flow easily from one stage to the next.

The original hunters' and herders' wives probably wore the skin bell skirts shown in cave paintings. But when the Cretans switched from skin to cloth, they didn't drape rectangles like everyone else. They apparently let the stiffness of the old hide garment dictate an architectural shape for the cloth skirt. And they ended up with a flounced, bell-shaped skirt.

Similarly, their bodice probably started as a half-circle of leather with its ends laced together under the breasts and its curve rising behind the neck. A tunic from the Near East may have suggested sleeves when the bodice changed from skin to cloth. But here again the Cretans preferred the shape of their old skin garment. Their cloth bodice had short sleeves and was laced below bare breasts.

Together, the flounced skirt and laced-in, short-sleeved bodice gave Cretan women an hourglass figure that was unique in a world where civilized women were all draping themselves in rectangles. It set the Cretans apart, as the sea set their home apart.

Isolation freed Cretans from constant warfare. Olive groves gave them a basic food; and seafood and sea trade freed them from drudgery in the soil. Perhaps the resulting leisure to observe dolphins and sea birds refined their sense of sight. For they caught the essence of a fish, a bird, a man, a woman. And they gradually glorified the characteristic forms of both sexes in dress.

The *cache-sexe* of Crete (a smooth, double apron cinched in tightly at the waist) emphasized a man's healthy expanse of chest above it.

The skintight, open fronted bodice framed a woman's bare breasts. And the flounced skirt swelled her hips out below a tiny waist.

It is possible that the bared breasts were part of a fertility cult. But fertility was not an obsession in Crete. Their little fertility figurines look more like charming companions than like symbols of motherhood.

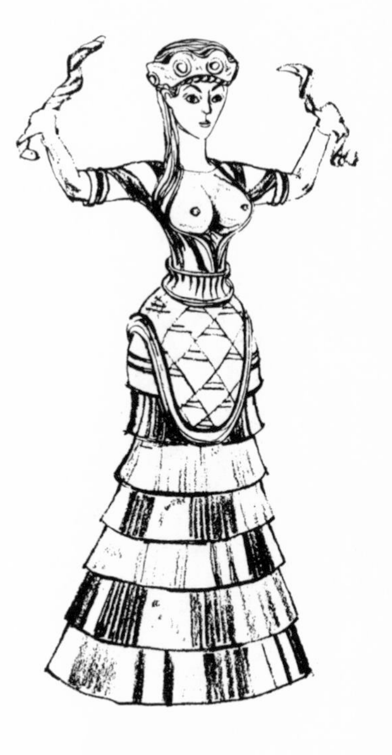

Seamen's women had to be capable. And Cretan ladies could leap into a chariot and gallop down to the docks, dagger at waist. Their cloth patterns featured large, bright checks or waves. Tiers of flounces moved with the dash of a flamenco dancer's skirt. An apron-like overskirt dipped at front and back in the lines of the masculine cache-sexe. High-piled hair was a seaweed tangle of curls entwined with pearls. Bracelets tinkled and glistened on bare forearms and ankles. Though bold and free, the Cretan woman was very feminine.

Earthquakes were the main threat to survival. And the divine bull, the *earth shaker*, was the focus of brilliant ritual in the courtyards of temple-palaces. Religious performers kept themselves agile so they could confront the danger of a bull's horns. Naked, or clothed in brief shorts, young men and women caught the horns of a charging bull and somersaulted lightly over him; while men watched and women gasped and gossiped.

From approximately the 18th to the 15th century B.C., Cretan sea traders dominated the Aegean. Even the semi-barbaric Mycenaean traders from the Greek mainland paid tribute to Crete.

The dress of these very close neighbors and fellow traders was different again from Cretan dress and from Levantine dress. And again their dress seemed to express their particular slant on life.

The fair-skinned ancestors of the Mycenaeans reached the Greek peninsula about 2,000 B.C. Though they quickly dominated the native farmers and herders, they were outclassed by the Cretans. To the south of them, the island of Crete was a flourishing center of the civilization so despised and yet so admired by the beef-eating, beer-

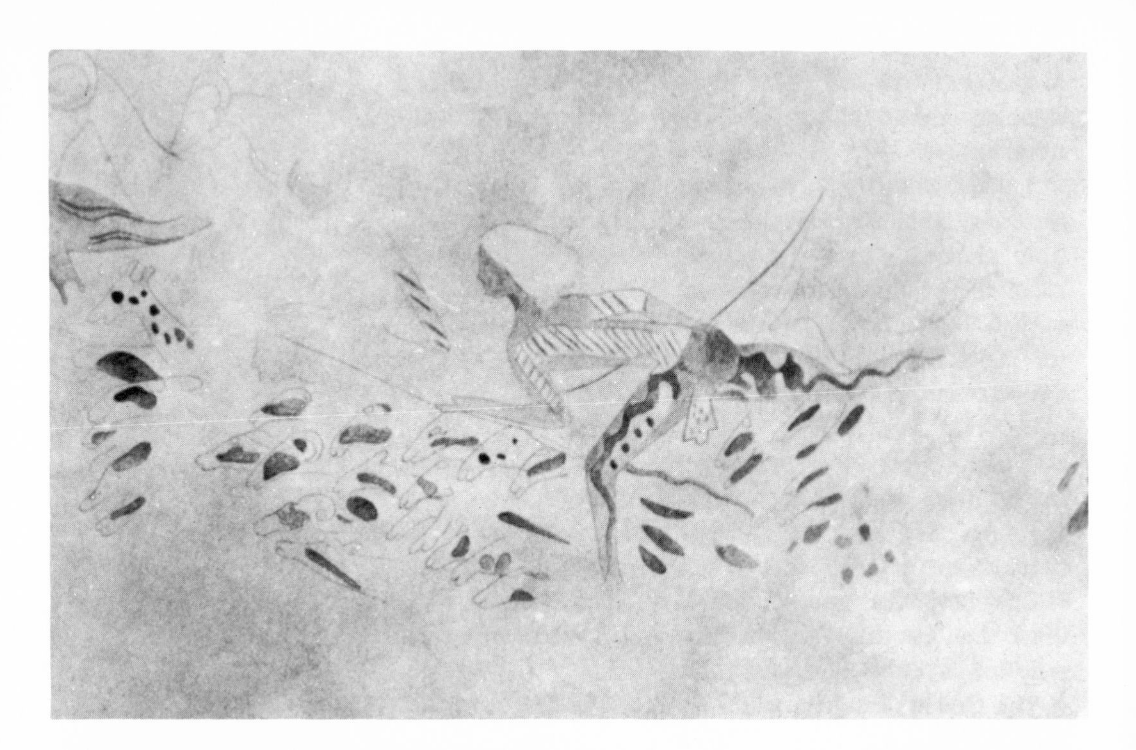

These frescoes from caves in the Sahara show how occupations, from earliest times, helped dictate what men and women wore. The hunter needs freedom to run, and he needs paint for magical protection. The squatting and child-caring chores of his wife led to the more hampering skin skirts that were often worn by stone-age women.

The earliest Sumerian farmer hovered between old and new ways of life, drawing security from shaggy tiers of kaunakes cloth, which tried to duplicate fleece. As he settled into farming and civilization, he wanted the more expressive rectangles of cloth, and kaunakes were relegated to the goddesses for ceremonial clothing. Above, a goddess in kaunakes leads a worshipper in fringed cloth shawl. Left, a man in kaunakes pagne.

This radical change in dress paralleled Egypt's shift from a civilization that was self-contained for thousands of years along the Nile, to a sophisticated world power, absorbing other people's styles. The lean kalasiris, in style for 15 centuries, was handed over to the goddesses, while ladies wrapped themselves in restless arrangements of sheer linen, huge jewelled collars and wigs. Here, the goddess Isis in classic kalasiris leads Nefret-iry (19th Dynasty) wearing the new style.

Both Romans and Greeks draped great rectangles of cloth on their bodies. But Greek draperies fell in vertical shafts of cloth. Girdling and more draping pulled the cloth in against the body, exploring the form underneath, and dividing the body into graceful proportions. The Romans built their rectangles up into layers of tunics and massive shawls. The Greek woman is in a 4th century chiton. In the Roman frieze of Emperor Augustus' family, even children are burdened with the weighty toga.

This gold torque necklace says much about the Scythians: their commitment to the horse, their love of bold gold ornament and the perfection of their riding coats and trousers. The Assyrian warriors kept tunic skirts, quilted leg wraps, and often dismounted to fight. The Persians were the most successful at fusing the needs of the old civilizations with the horseman's functional needs. But this Sassanian silver plate (4th century A.D.) shows a gradual loss of Persian efficiency in fluttering silk and jewels.

Byzantium encrusted the simple old Roman tunics and chlamys cloaks with jewels and embroidery. In this 6th century mosaic Empress Theodora's gold and pearl diadem glows like a halo. Even the angel, in the simple clavii-striped tunic and pallium seems to reach for heavenly glory.

Charlemagne promoted Roman scholarship but was too active to be weighted with Byzantine jewels. He set a dynamic example of Germanness in his own dress: short tunics and cloaks, trousers held with crossed thongs, and a few jewels in his sword hilt and crown to set him above the farmers. Barbarian energy pulsates in this Carolingian carving of the Virgin. Wielding her cross and wearing a Roman soldier's shoulder lappets, she must have been a convincing symbol to a still wild and militant Europe.

Though in the 12th century both men and women had taken on the long, layered tunics associated with the church, worldliness was creeping into dress. Fitted tunics showed the shape of the torso; sleeves were taking on an unfunctional flare, and decorated bands were lavished on hems and cuffs.

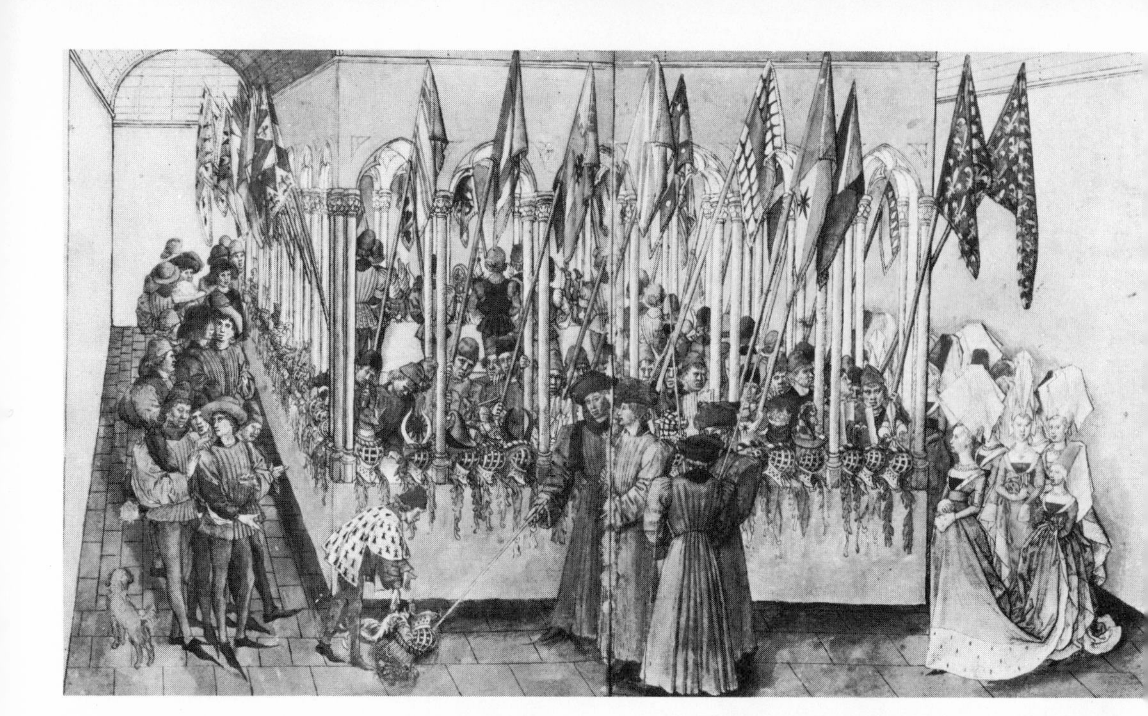

Unsure of its future, 14th and 15th century Europe escaped into fantasy and ritual, clinging to and exaggerating the old feudal forms: knights' wars became tournaments, veils grew into towering hennins. Banners and helmets mixed with the fashionable houppelandes and tight hose in one of clothing's most extravagant periods. Even in Italy's full-blown Renaissance, parti-colored hose (a vestige of heraldry) persists in the elegant wedding procession shown here.

The long presence of the Moslem Moors in Christian Spain sharpened her pious, aristocratic tendencies. Backed by New World gold and pride of empire, Spanish dress hardened into a straight-backed style of high ruffs, farthingale skirts, and doublets and bodices stiff as cuirasses. Dark colors emphasized the formality of the clothes.

The exquisite nature patterns that cover every surface and express Persia's artistic vitality are evident in this 16th century garden. Below, Shah Jahan, a 17th century Mughal emperor, combines sensuous Indian jewels with silks and sheer cottons worked into horsemen's trousers and caftans in the continuing steppes tradition of riding, hunting and warring.

In simple villages today, Indian women liven the draped sari with glowing color, sparkling ornament, flowers and perfumes as they have for 4000 years. Both 10th century Indian sculpture and the early 20th century English painting show the sensual combination of ornament and draped cloth that gives Indian dress an almost universal appeal.

8

Ancient dress seems to say that the group was always more important than the individual. And some thinkers suggest two reasons for this clinging together in groups.

One reason comes out of prehistory. Ages of quite desperate mutual dependence in the hunting society developed an instinct for making individuals firmly and visibly part of a group.

The other reason comes out of infancy. Human beings are so helpless for so long that they never really gain self-confidence. They feel secure only as part of a group.

Yet everyone has always wanted to be a little different, to be a little special.

For early people this was not easy. To be different was to, perhaps, be noticed by the gods. It could result in disaster.

The Greeks seem to have been the first people really to challenge the power of the gods. They seem to have found a little human self-confidence in the idea that there might be natural laws—not whims—controlling their crops and their lives. And Greek dress began to encourage individual self expression.

The ancient Greeks were a composite of two groups: Doric and Ionic.

The Dorians were the first to find a little independence; though their independence was physical rather than intellectual. It wasn't the gods they challenged—just the aristocrats.

After the fall of Crete, Mycenaean rule of the eastern Mediterranean brought disaster. Mycenaean piracy ruined the sea trade. And Mycenaean raids were only part of a general wave of piracy caused by another barbarian group that had started to push down from the steppes.

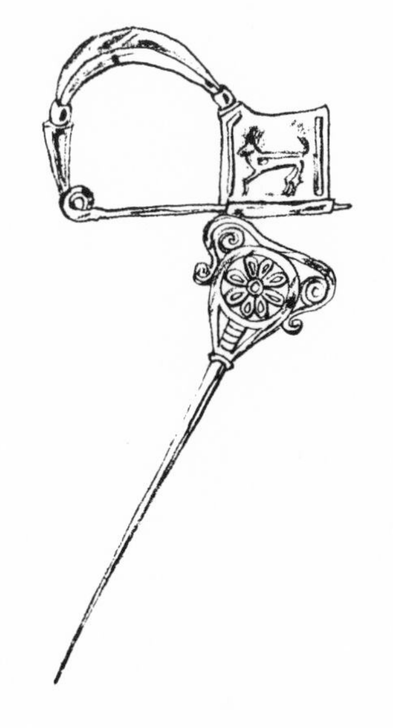

This latest surge brought the Dorians down into the Greek peninsula. Armed with iron, the Dorian was a new breed of barbarian.

Mycenaean nobles had ruled by force of bronze weapons, which only they could afford to own. But iron was cheap, and with it a common man could split skulls as efficiently as his lord could. He didn't need his lord's protection. And that fact upset the whole social order in Greece. It weakened warlords and strengthened the common man.

The Mycenaeans had been in trouble long before the Dorians arrived about 1200 B.C. Raiding and being raided, they had still sought an aristocratic image with luxuries from Egypt and Asia Minor; while at the same time, they were running out of food. When the Dorians arrived, the Mycenaeans had little left but their battered pride.

Rather than go down before commoners armed with crude iron, many aristocratic Mycenaeans moved over to a trading outpost on the coast of Asia Minor. They took jewels with them and gold cups, heroic but obsolete bronze weapons and memories of their great days as Lords of the Mediterranean. Since their headquarters were in Ionia, Mycenaeans began to be known as Ionians. Grouping into tight little city-states, they framed laws to bring order and to protect themselves from the Middle Eastern despotism that surrounded them.

However, one group of Mycenaeans stood fast in and around Athens in Greece. This provided the crude Dorian conquerors with a nagging, humiliating center of superior culture, aristocratic contempt and frayed remnants of rich dress.

The Dorian stuck to the simple dress of the militant shepherd. He came in sheepskins and rough wool garments held with thorns, dagger pins or *fibulae*. The fibula was

the big, practical safety pin of Europe's barbarians. Basically a clasp to secure heavy wool mantles and tunics, it was a mark of simple, early dress.

The Dorian's basic garments were the *himation* and the *exomis.* The himation was a big, woolen rectangle that served him as wrap by day and blanket by night. Slung under his right arm and caught at his left shoulder, the early himation could be thrown off quickly to let him work or fight naked or in his exomis. The exomis was the simplest of tunics—a short rectangle folded around him, pinned on one shoulder, girdled, bloused a little and left open down one side.

His wife's dress too was a rectangle, a rather wide one, folded around her and pinned over both shoulders with dagger pins. After a while, possibly in imitation of Mycenaean tunics and Cretan cinched waists, the gown became narrower and was pulled in with a very wide belt.

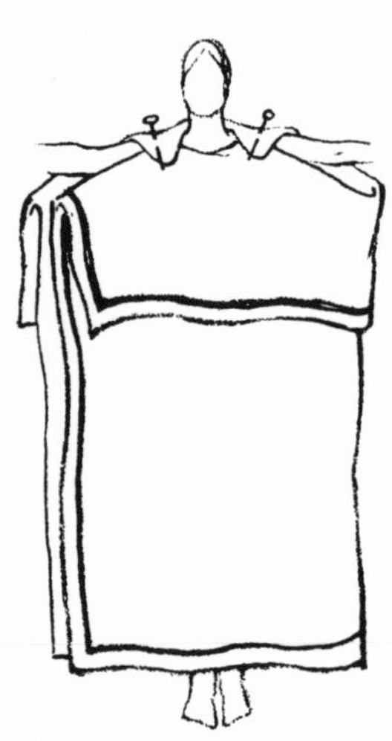

Later, the rectangle was made long enough to allow for an overhang at the top which could be pulled up over the head. And then it was called the *peplos.* Full length, slim, following the body's shape, and open down one side, the peplos expressed pride of body. For the Dorians were dedicated to physical perfection. Deformed infants were allowed to die.

In weaving and decorating his cloth the Dorian rejected the soft, curving lines of Mediterranean decoration. He squared off the sensuous wave pattern, pushing it into the short, straight lines of the *Greek Key* or *meander.* And this classical Greek pattern, embroidered down the front or woven in horizontal bands, broke the straight shaft of a woman's red, yellow, or black wool peplos.

The Doric woman's duty was to produce hardy, fighting sons. As a girl she ran naked or in a boy's exomis, and she ran competitively with the boys. Her adult column of wool seemed as disciplined and simple and strong as she had to be. In it, she stood out, sculpted like the hills and trees of Greece.

Life was rough in Doric Greece. Men had to fight for what there was; there was never enough for everybody. And under Dorian influence, every little pocket of people disciplined itself into a fighting unit.

The Dorians adopted Mycenaean armor. Leather or bronze *greaves* protected the Dorian warrior's legs from knee to ankle. A simple breastplate of leather, or of metal plates sewn to cloth, was strapped over his chest. And a crested leather helmet covered his head. Though he had a round shield, he wore the *aegis*—the old trophyskin—on his shoulder, to protect his body.

The Dorians developed a cult of militant austerity. And the cult was strongest in Sparta. Athens, however, cultivated her ties with the Ionic city-states.

Over in Ionia, life became more and more different from the austerity of Doric Greece. Centuries of stimulating contacts around busy docks and gossipy bazaars had their effect. Ionian dress absorbed the rich purples and golds, the graceful floral motifs of Asia.

As they became prosperous traders and agriculturalists, men and women took to the Phoenician robe, or *chiton.* At that time, the chiton was simply the long-sleeved, free hanging robe that suggested wealth and leisure throughout the Near East.

Yet they clung fiercely to their own Mycenaean identity. Cherishing their past in legends, they gradually turned piratical ancestors into heroic adventurers like Ulysses. And the stories gave them a strong emotional tie with the old homeland of Greece.

As the years passed, the Dorian Greeks also began to change. But the common man still had iron and the spirit that went with it. He didn't have to cower before a lord with a horse. For under Spartan discipline, a group of foot soldiers formed a military machine—the Greek phalanx—that could stop men with horses. Massed behind a bristling wall of shields and spears, they could hold fast against anything.

Aware of his worth, the individual *hoplite* in the phalanx was a real citizen, with a voice in the assembly, and slowly he began taking power away from traditional kings and nobles. Over a brief, skin-protecting exomis, he wore a waist-to-shoulder armor of bronze or leather plates, a hard fringe of leather lappets to protect his thighs, bronze greaves, and a bronze helmet. His helmet went far beyond its function of protecting the head. Its great horsehair crest swept back like a clipped mane. And his round shield was emblazoned with an animal design that was half way between primitive totemism and medieval heraldry. A short, warrior's cloak—the dashing *chlamys*—gave him warmth and distinction. Pinned over one shoulder, the cloak was boldly patterned and was cut roughly like a semicircle.

Military life began early. A boy moved into the barracks at the age of seven. And from the age of twelve, he had to survive any conditions, any weather, in the one small oblong cloak he was issued.

Dorians, like Ionians, had been stirred by stories of aristocratic warrior heroes out of the Greek past. And after 800 B.C., some tried to revive the aristocratic tradition with rich tunics and status markings in dress. But the phalanx was a blow to the revival. The worth of the hoplite made class markings in dress look pretentious. Young lords soon stopped wearing embroidered tunics; they dropped bands of purple and red embellishment from their cloaks. Simplicity swept Greek clothing. Men returned to the simple himation—the one, practical garment of shepherds and workmen. And the women's simple, useful peplos spread even to Athens.

Over the years the woman's basic woolen rectangle had acquired an allover, geometric pattern and colored bands. But it was still a blanket when the pins were pulled out.

Athenian women sewed their peplos up the side. For female nakedness was considered disgraceful in Athens, where constant contact with the Ionians brought in Oriental concepts of modesty.

Completely different from Sparta, Athens was encouraging sea trade and becoming a sea power. Olive oil and wine were her basic trade items; banks of rowers kept her ships moving. And her dependence on farmers and rowers forced her to keep extending her basis for citizenship—though never as far as to slaves and women.

A deep awareness of the vital importance of the ordinary

man to Greek strength kept the simple, useful blanket the core of Greek dress for a long time.

Yet over in Ionia, the other Greeks were developing a rival dress. Free and prosperous in their law-abiding little city-states, the Ionians had time to wonder and to think. Events like a predicted, and explained, eclipse of the sun suggested to them that men might not be as subject to the whims of the gods as they had formerly believed. Indeed, there might be laws for the universe, just as there were laws for the city.

Making the gods a little less terrifying made man a little bolder. And the Ionians stepped out from under the concealing Oriental robe. Their chiton, worn by both men and women, became two huge rectangles of finely-woven, body-revealing linen, sometimes two or three times as wide as the body, and often pleated in the Egyptian way. The tops were pinned together with tiny safety pins or little hinged brooches, or were stitched together along the arms from wrist to wrist, leaving spaces for the head and hands. Girdling and blousing created the effect of loose, elbow-length sleeves. Great variety of arrangement was possible and eventually the Ionic chiton brought new grace and rhythm to movement. It made the viewer aware that an individual was inside.

The chiton symbolized leisured, artistic, intellectual life. Which may be why it was resisted in sternly disciplined Greece. Yet it did infiltrate Athens, where the old blood tie persisted. And the obstinate Dorians built up a legend to account for its success against the peplos.

Herodotus, the Greek historian, recorded the legend:

Athens had a dispute with the offshore island of Aegina over some treasured statues. And she sent an armed force over to get them. But the islanders slaughtered the Athenians. Only one man escaped to tell of the disaster. And in a fit of fury and humiliation, the Athenian widows stabbed him to death with their peplos pins. In punishment, they were forbidden to wear the Doric peplos. In the future, they had to wear the Ionic chiton, which was held with tiny brooches or stitches instead of lethal dagger pins.

Athens and Sparta were at war, in fact or in planning, most of the time. The feeling of hostility was so high it was necessary to declare a truce of the gods every four years to let competitors in the Olympic Games pass through one another's cities without being killed.

Nothing brought the two cities together until they were faced with a common enemy. Then it was stand together, or fall to the Persian invaders.

The two styles of Greek dress that stood opposed to the lavish dress of the Persians in 480 B.C., represented two incompatible attitudes.

A shaft of heavy wool—the Doric peplos, the Doric exomis—expressed primitive strength, simplicity, discipline and a commitment to the vigorous, toughening, outdoor action of the old country life.

Light and flowing, charming and graceful, the Ionic chiton expressed sophistication, a lively freedom to explore ideas and a commitment to urban life and enjoyment of the senses.

But both showed an awareness of the body. Both showed a spirit of independence. Both gave confidence to the individual they revealed rather than concealed.

9

Everyone knows about the glory that was Greece. But who has ever heard of the glory that was Scythia? Yet the modern, restless Western spirit, and basic Western dress, took shape there in the steppes.

The dash and color of the booted European folk dancer started there. The original cowboy lassoed steppe cattle from a fancy saddle. And men in tailored coats and trousers outrode covered wagons there over twenty-five hundred years ago, while their wives bumped along in ankle length dresses with tight, sleeved bodices.

Scythians were part of the recurring movement of Indo-Europeans. While the Dorians were drifting towards Greece, the Scythians were still roaming the vast steppes. Somewhere between China and the Danube, they were taming horses, hitching them to wagons, and discovering the limitations of the wagon. Soon they were leaping onto their horses' backs and tearing off after cattle, discovering the usefulness, as well as the excitement of freer, faster movement.

Once horseback riding started, it was taken up by every nomad on the steppe. But only the Scythians seemed to achieve a total adaptation to riding. As they gradually moved west over a period of several centuries, they evolved horsemanship and riding clothes into breath-taking efficiency and beauty. The man and his horse became one great, wild, glittering unit of energy. And the family followed in

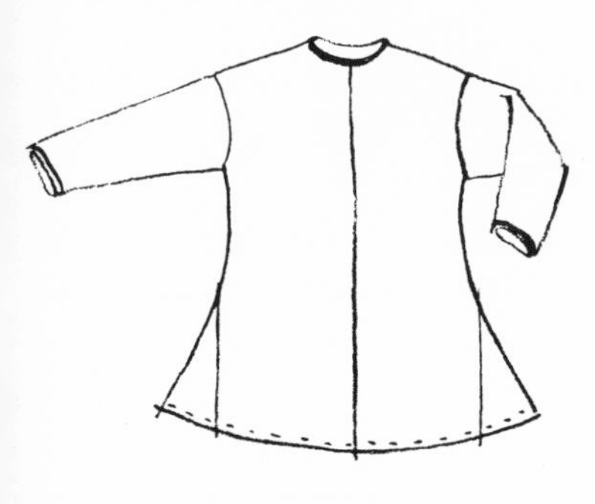

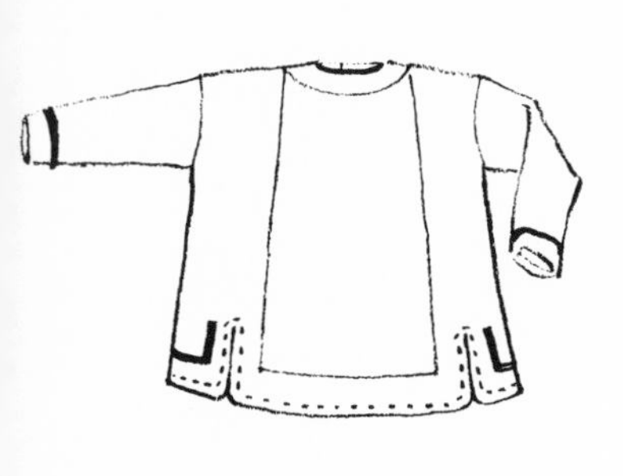

a felt-covered wagon, living on the move.

The mounted herder-hunter-fighter was always competing with his kind for more grass. He needed clothes that would protect him from blows and branches without hindering his action. What he wanted was a close fit, one just loose enough for movement. And a close fit demanded supple leather and expert tailoring. Scythian women must have reeked from working leather. But they gradually learned to achieve a superb softness that let them turn crude leg wrappings into fitted riding pants, which tucked into boots.

The Scythian woman fitted in sleeves to eliminate the underarm bulk of the old tunic. She tapered the skin shirt at the waist and inserted triangular pieces to give it the needed flare over the hips. The rider's pointed leather hood, tied under his chin, covered his ears. And for extra protection there was a wrapped, belted coat made with vents at the side to let it fit over the saddle. For this coat there might also be a winter lining of sable or wolf, with the fur showing at the rolled-back collar and lapels.

Scythian women didn't ride or wear pants. Perhaps they didn't have time. For, like everything else in the Scythian world, they served the horseman. And as the horseman's pride grew, his display demanded still more skill and artistry. Ornamental stitching and applique in rich cherry red—the ancient color of blood and life and fire—began to enhance and express, perhaps, the aliveness and vitality he felt.

Instead of weaving, Scythian women made felts, both thick and fine, and dyed them. Their felt-on-felt or felt-on-leather applique was so delicate, intricate and lavish that it looked like allover embroidery when it appeared on sleeves, tunics, coats and saddle cushions.

The utter unity of the man and his horse is shown by the fact that the mount was as splendidly turned out as the man. Other members of the family, the covered wagon that carried their goods and the felt tent they lived in were also richly worked. But the horseman and his horse were the focus of Scythian artistry and Scythian life.

When they burst out of the steppes as part of a great

barbarian movement in the 8th century B.C., Scythian horsemen terrified civilized towns the way chariot invaders had terrified them centuries earlier. But to this invasion was added the horror of scalp locks, scalp cloaks and drinking mugs made from human skulls.

Some of the earlier barbarian invaders, like the Hittites, had become settled and powerful. Others, like the Medes and Persians off to the east of Mesopotamia, were still hovering between barbarism and civilization. All were still physically tough and still breeding horses. All were developing some riding skills.

The Medes and the Persians took one look at the mounted Scythians and determined to be horsemen. Tired of coping with the near desert conditions of the Iranian plateau, they saw cavalry as ideal for conquest. For they had conquest in mind, not just spirited roving like the Scythians'.

While the Persians started acquiring skills and tactics and armor for extensive mounted war against civilized armies, the Scythians went off to help the Medes and the Babylonians topple the Assyrians.

Scythians sat lithe and trim in the saddle. Fitted leather tunic, pants, boots and caps gave them flexibility and a capacity for agility and speed while charging, wheeling and shooting arrows back over their shoulder.

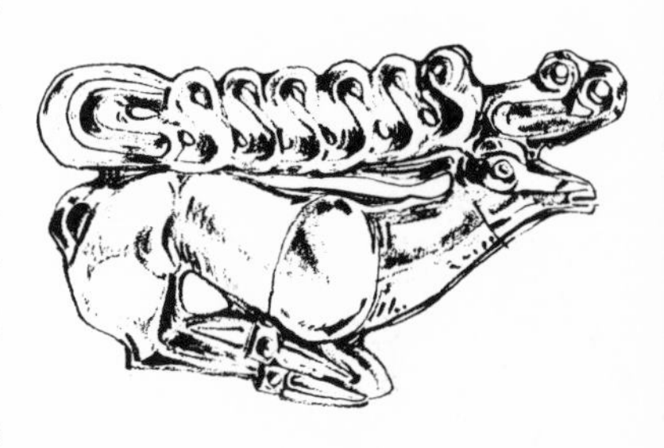

The Assyrians had taken to riding too, but a rigid commitment to old ideas and old rank markings sent them into cavalry battle with an encumbering fringed scarf emerging from below chest armor and heavy metal plates. They had padded leggings, but no trousers. And each dismounted to shoot his arrows while a groom held his horse.

After their completely predictable victory, the Scythians had no interest beyond booty. They rolled on towards the Black Sea, where they headquartered as wealthy stockbreeders, grain growers, traders and raiders.

They began to decorate themselves with gold. Single earrings, neck torques and massive belt buckles were added to the embossed discs of gold and bronze sewn to clothes and attached to horse caparisons. A Scythian genius for animal design gave a wild beauty to stags, lions and swans, tensely confined within the shape of a belt buckle or a bridle ornament.

They built towns. But their towns did not lure men in away from animals. The towns simply served the mounted rover. And in the towns, Greek craftsmen joined Scythian saddlers and jewelers in producing magnificently decorated portable gear.

Similarly, Scythian farming settlements first raised grain for the horses. What was left over was sold to the hungry Greeks.

The Scythian man and mount became more and more splendid as gold, felt applique, and ornamental stitching increased. Fur and fine leather were dyed for working into patterns on boots and saddles. Saddle leather was deeply tooled. Saddle cushions and tasseled saddle blanklets were brilliantly colored with cherry red, dark blue, black and white. Ivory handled riding crops were laced with gold. Yet everything was designed for hard and constant use.

The splendor spilled over onto the tent and the wagon and the family. Part of the horseman's display was his wife, gay with rings, bracelets, earrings and necklaces. Her long tunic with close-fitting sleeves was even more ornately decorated than his short one. An embroidered felt stocking has been found stitched to a leather sole; and even the sole is magnificently tooled.

But under all the gold and cherry red was the functioning, disciplined efficiency of a tribe that coped with nature by being as ruthless as nature. Scythians were freer than civilized men. With no big cities, they were less vulnerable to attack. They carried their wealth; and their utter mobility let them melt away with it.

Though some were more or less settled around the Black Sea, the Scythians were always mobile and restless. They carried their clothes and color and dynamic art into the Balkans. And from there the clothes and the color and the art drifted even farther west with the centuries, influencing the Celts and Vikings and Germanic peoples who built Europe.

While the Scythians were still riding on towards the

Black Sea after toppling the Assyrians, the Persians were getting ready to conquer the Middle East. Planning to do more than raid and run like the Scythians, they developed cavalry tactics. And they created a light, flexible, fine scale armor to go over their riding clothes. They designed a sword belt secured between the legs.

In the middle of the 6th century B.C. they were ready. They rode out of Iran and into much of the Mediterranean world. They took the Near East, subdued Greek colonies along the coast of Asia Minor and thrust the boundaries of the Persian Empire out to the Nile, the Volga and the Indus. It was the biggest and most sudden empire the world had ever seen. And it gave the world its first good look at a real *coat*, with seams that made it fit, with set-in sleeves and a collar. Eventually called a *caftan*, the Persian coat was the direct ancestor of the coat we think of as a distinctive mark of the West.

One of the Persian Empire's earliest rulers was Darius. Just a generation out of the hills, King Darius was lord over the wonders of Babylon, the pyramids along the Nile, the traders of the Levant. And he must have felt a bursting need to express the extent and richness of his territory, to live up to the dignity of ruling so much.

He selected from the resources of his empire with a purposeful eye. In building his capital city of Persepolis, he integrated the columns of the ancient civilizations into a Persian column that towered with lotus and scrolls and lions and winged bulls. And to his clothes he added Egyptian and Assyrian and Indian elements to indicate clearly that he was a horseman ruling much of the known world.

His dress was based on riding clothes in the same way his empire was based on cavalry. But cloth, not skins, suited his civilized status. In fact, only silk could express his unprecedented power, for he controlled the Chinese silk coming into the northeast border of his empire. The silk of China, the jewels of India, the embroideries of the Near East flowed into the royal garments. Yet silks and jewels and embroideries were only the surface embellishment, like the tooling on saddle leather.

Darius wore gold embroidered, crimson, Chinese silk

trousers tucked into riding boots with the turned-up toes of Asia Minor. A fitted, brocaded tunic with set-in sleeves and a flare over the hips was covered at Court by a flowing robe, the richly colored Median *kandys*—two huge rectangles sewn at the top, belted in, and falling in capelike folds over the arms. From Assyria he took a fluted crown. For battle he took the *Phrygian Cap,* the conical cap of the steppes that had been softened in Asia Minor. But to this cap he added the fullness of a turban, making it an impressive headdress. Like his capital city, Darius' dress was bizarre, yet splendid and uniquely Persian.

A commitment to riding kept the basic form of Persian men's dress virtually unchanged for two thousand years. This, and the old tradition of decorating everything, made their fabrics the focus of Persian expression. Persian textiles were a museum for the plant and flower patterns of the agricultural civilizations and for the animals, hunts, horses and battle scenes of the barbarians. Persians were always the first to use the advanced weaving techniques that slowly filtered out of China. With a great sense of design, they wove and embroidered silk so beautifully that their textiles influenced clothing right through the Crusades.

Persian women didn't fare as well as Persian design. They exchanged useful, boisterous, warm tribal life for the refined boredom of city courtyards. Many may have ridden and worn pants before; and some in the mountains still did. Behind the walls, many had great power in the household, and considerable freedom; they influenced their husbands. But once in the cities, Near Eastern concepts of modesty threw veils over many of these spirited women. And as their husbands acquired more and more wives as a display of wealth, upper class Persian women moved towards harem life.

In tribal villages and encampments, aristocratic women had set the standards for exquisite craftsmanship in decoration. Now they sometimes became part of the decoration, treasured like rare gems.

Though they probably had more freedom than Westerners imagine, its limitation is revealed in the fact that women were rarely portrayed in art. And women had to cover their faces in public. Denied more deeply rewarding outlets, many poured their energies into cosmetics, perfumes, jewels, sensuous textiles, submissive manners and competition for one man's favors. Since they gradually disappeared from sight, not too much is known about their clothing. But when a woman does appear in art, her coat and tunic are cut much like those of a man, though hers is always long.

The Persians, though they had conquered much of the known world, were not unchallenged masters of all they could see. The Ionian city-states along the coast of Asia Minor were pockets of rebellion in a remarkably submissive, orderly, well run empire. They challenged the idea that life depended on the whims of a god or a king, that a king could lop off a hand the way a storm could lop off a branch.

As far as the Persians were concerned, this had to be stopped. Darius decided to crush all the Greeks. But he died before he could muster his forces.

His son Xerxes seemed to lack his father's drive; he was nervous about the Greek campaign. And he was further frightened by signs that the gods were against it. But he finally gathered the greatest armed force the world had ever seen and marched it to the Mediterranean. He reviewed his troops from a white marble throne placed on a hill above the sea near the Hellespont.

Mustered from all over the empire, the Persian army and fleet were a motley assortment of races and tongues, primitives and sophisticates, warpaints and silks, camels and horses and foot soldiers, transport wagons and oared ships.

Herodotus reported the event. He told of wooly haired black troops, "Ethiopians," who had come from the south of Egypt in paint, amulets, and animal pelts. The red paint on half their body and the white chalk on the other half spoke of their primitive trust in magic. They were moving into an iron war with stone-tipped arrows and antelope horn-point spears.

Libyans from west of Egypt were in long oxhide tunics caught at one shoulder and painted in animal stripes and spots. Though they obviously domesticated cattle, they also obviously still depended on wild animal magic.

Skin cloaks dressed both Caspians from the northwest edge of empire and Pactyans from the eastern frontier. Apparently the more remote people were from the cities and capitals, the less stimulated they were to change from their old way of living and dressing.

Swinging their lassoes skillfully, the Scythians had the best developed riding clothes in the army. In their skin tunics, trousers, boots, and pointed caps, they depended on speed and maneuverability for protection, with a little help from the animal spirits honored in their decoration.

Horsemen from the north and east were obviously in transit between Scythian and Persian ways of life. Oxhide, cloth and some Persian armor marked stages in the transition.

The Arabian camel corps came loping along in the *zeira*, a great, girdled cloak of hide or wool. The Arab, like the camel, had adapted to the desert. His zeira allowed free movement of air while giving him protection from sun and cold. The harsh demands of the desert allowed him little time or energy for embellishing his dress.

Troops from the Indus were in "cotton dresses." This may have been an early form of the *jamah*, the full-skirted dress of North India, which combined barbarian sleeves with Indian drapery.

Egyptians and Assyrians wore helmets and breastplates over cloth tunics that were still just a step beyond rectangles. The old cultures were tired now and defensive. Apparently the more civilized people were, the more they relied on metal and the less they relied on magic.

Three life styles could be seen in the units from Asia Minor. Those living nearest Mesopotamia were most heavily armed. Those from along the coast showed Greek influence in greaves, breastplates and lappets over a short chiton; they also had crested helmets, and the aegis skin on their shoulder. Those from the north tended to the better fit, longer sleeves, and skin boots of the steppes. They showed less dependence on armor.

The Persians were the ultimate fusion of function and

embellishment. Herodotus, in *The Persian Wars,* recorded their magnificence:

"The Persians, who wore on their heads the soft hat called the tiara, and about their bodies, tunics with sleeves, of divers colors, having iron scales upon them like the scales of a fish. Their legs were protected by trousers . . .

"Of all the troops the Persians were adorned with the greatest magnificence, and they were likewise the most valiant. Besides their arms, they glittered all over with gold, vast quantities of which they wore about their persons."

Vast quantities of gold were encumberingly heavy, as were iron scales. Sumptuous blue, purple, crimson, and yellow kandys robes covered the battle dress of the elite Persian troops. They were even perfumed for war. They were followed by concubines in litters. And it all seemed a long way from the early mounted rover, who had loved his freedom.

And in the end, it was those who were still free, and who were willing to fight to be so, who won. The Greeks stopped the Persians.

10

What would happen if, while a child was still fresh and creative and uninhibited, we gave him one or two big rectangles of cloth, some safety pins, a length of cord, and invited him to dress himself? He would probably copy things he had seen other people wear. He would undoubtedly pin and tie the cloth at some natural places. But he would also do some imaginative things that expressed how he felt. No matter how regally he wrapped himself up, though, or how swaggeringly he draped himself, he would keep free enough to run. And watching him, we might come as close as we can come to understanding what Greek dress was.

We see Greek dress at its most expressive in sculptures from the Golden Age which followed the Greek victory over the Persians. For in their search for the ideal, godlike form, Greek sculptors put clothing to work for them. In the way they let drapery play over the bodies of the gods in the pediments of the Parthenon, they revealed mood, personality and character. In fact, the expressive poses and arrangement of dress have proved as useful as faces and symbols in identifying crumbling figures.

The Greeks didn't hesitate to use clothes as a social tool. But in addition, they used clothes to glorify the body. Dorians had a passion for a healthy body. The Cretans had added to Greek thought a pleasure in the beauty of the human form. The Ionians were fascinated with proportion and harmony. Put together, these ideas made the Greeks begin to think that the human body was the most perfect creation in nature. Even before the Persian wars, their clothing was increasingly devoted to letting the body express itself.

Then the stunning victory of a few Greeks over the massed might of Persia in 480 B.C. raised interest in a search for the godlike body. For the Greeks believed they had been touched by the gods or they could not have won the victory. Their self-confidence soared.

The old, democratic, and purely Greek peplos, himation and exomis became symbols of Greek strength, though the peplos had become wider, bringing Doric and Ionic dress closer together. Displaying the body, and depending utterly on the individual body for shape, these garments managed to express group solidarity without denying the individual his chance to express himself through girdling and arrangement of folds.

Temples and festivals sprang up everywhere to honor the gods and the Greek heritage of heroes. Sculptors idealized a model's body to make it a god's. And people, inspired by the idealized body, as well as by the idealized feats of their heroes, reached towards godliness.

This reach towards godliness led sculptors to the great art of the Golden Age. It led clothing to a peak of dignity. Weighted corners gave the peplos and himation long, gravitational folds; they turned a weak flutter into a strong swing of cloth. Girdles shifted with each individual's search for perfect proportion. And above, the neck was left uncluttered by hair or jewels. A man's hair was cut short. A woman's was pulled back from her forehead and extended behind her head; its great waved masses were firmly controlled by a filet wrapped three times around. The whole bearing of the Greek was affected by the dignity of dress and head.

Sparta's army and Athens' navy had won the victory. And for a few years in the 5th century B.C., the city-state seemed a perfect form of society. A surge of confidence in Greek institutions let people submerge their independence in the glory of their city-state. A man could best realize

his own potential, they reasoned, by pouring his talents and energies into his city-state.

But the city-states were as fiercely independent as the people. The glory of one meant the humiliation of another. And as a sea power, Athens was supreme. Even Sparta paid her for naval protection; for the greatest threat was from the sea.

Funds from a joint war chest built the Parthenon to house a forty foot gold and ivory statue of Athens' patron goddess, Athena. Athena's gown was a peplos, not a chiton. But it was not the heavy peplos with an overhang falling to the waist. It was the fuller and softer postwar peplos; belted in, its overhang fell to the hips.

It was a superb example of the expressiveness of Greek dress. The total effect was like the graceful strength of a fluted column. Yet the girdle pulled the cloth in against the body, softening impersonal majesty into womanliness; for Athena was goddess of the home as well as goddess of war and wisdom. A jutting knee thrust out in the flutings of the skirt, showing the power behind the serenity of the gown. And Athena's warrior role was further shown by the aegis on her shoulders, the old protective trophy-skin that was now the vestigial symbol of the warrior. Her dress said clearly what she was.

A smaller, older statue of Athena demonstrated the importance of clothes to Greek culture. Every fourth year the women of Athens put a new cloth peplos on the statue that had come through the war with them. The presentation of this peplos became the greatest of all the festivals of Athens—the *Panathenaic Festival.* It was one of the few occasions when Athenian matrons could appear in public.

Athens' position as a trading and sea power had brought so many foreigners flooding in that she had begun to limit her citizenship. And her citizen bloodline was more and more protected by the strict seclusion and covering of Athenian women, a practice that heightened the Asian concept of modesty that had been creeping into Athens.

Citizens' wives were closely guarded. But there were other, freer women in Athens—the *heterae.* These outsiders could be the educated companions that wives could not be. Witty and seductive, they ran lively salons in gauzy chitons tied with gold girdles. But they could not marry a citizen. And they could not join in the Panathenaic Procession to the old statue of Athena.

For women as limited as wives were, the dressing of Athena must have been a great emotional outlet. Athena was the patroness of the home and of the domestic arts. And since her gown was the star of the greatest festival of the greatest city in Greece, women asserted their own worth in the creation of the gown as gloriously as they could. Its workmanship was a public display of their best skills.

Citizens' wives and daughters wove the great rectangle of wool. They embroidered it with scenes from the battle of the gods and titans. Then they spread it like a sail on the mast and yardarm of a ship-on-wheels. All the splendor and pomp of Athens escorted the peplos to the Acropolis.

With all the beauty of weave, color, embroidery, and drape, Athena's peplos expressed the ambivalence of the Greeks. It covered the body modestly; yet it could express the body better than nakedness. Its vertical lines had restraint and dignity; but its loose folds let action and emotion come through. Its serenity was defeated by its battle scene. It was Doric, yet Ionic.

Yet, in spite of the surge of Greek pride in that which was inherantly Greek, the Ionic chiton had been infiltrating since the 6th century B.C. The big pins had been giving way to the small brooches and stitched seams of Middle Eastern dress. And in spite of the post war surge of enthusiasm for the old garments, in Athens a fine linen chiton gradually became a basic garment for both sexes, though athletes, fighters, and laborers often stayed naked. The chiton was a less positive, a less stately garment than the peplos.

Sensitive to the mood of the times the chiton expressed, sculptors eventually stopped idealizing men and women. Their heavily muscled warriors gave way to effeminate, boyish, almost sexless figures. Though the sculptures were still beautiful, it was clear that the Greek dream of godliness was fading.

As men got the feel of personal ambition and political power, as they began to watch sports instead of participate in them, their himation—their outer wrap—grew in size. Its arrangement became all important in communicating status. There were dozens of loose, elegant ways to drape it. There were elaborate fibulae to pin it. A skillfully arranged himation over a long chiton gave a man a leisurely, aristocratic bearing that showed a swing away from austere classlessness and from pride in a vigorous body.

All over Greece, oriental purples competed with the old, bold, clear colors. The Egyptian lotus, Mesopotamian palmette, and Cretan wave patterns varied the strong, straight Greek Key.

The chiton eventually almost eliminated the peplos. Where the peplos was still worn, it continued to widen and to soften in texture. And a constant fluctuation of girdling and blousing on both peplos and chiton made them deeply expressive garments. But more and more they expressed the self, and not the reach towards godliness.

More and more the old Doric ideals were concentrated in Sparta, along with a bitterness toward all things Athenian. And in 404 B.C., Persia financed Sparta's crushing of Athens.

Success and contact with Persia swiftly changed Sparta's old one-garment approach to clothing. Men in flowing chitons and elaborate himations were soon importing elegant, sleeved gowns from Asia Minor for their wives. They were joking about the old Spartan code of honor. Foreign mercenaries were hired to do the fighting.

The Golden Age was really over.

Following the usual pattern, tough men from the north were getting ready to take over the softened city-states. Along Greece's northeast frontier, the Macedonians were growing strong in skirmishes with the barbarians. And when they developed a combination of the Greek phalanx flanked by a light cavalry, they were unbeatable.

The Macedonian cavalry didn't wear pants. Trousers were spreading, but not to Greece. Persia, still holding a big empire, was spreading them eastward. In fact, the richly embellished Persian tunic and trousers were becoming the symbol of cultural prestige from Egypt to north India.

Though the Greeks had been riding for centuries, they had not chosen to adopt "barbarian britches"; for they considered the barbarians a little less than human. Too, Mediterranean heat and Greek pride of body had combined to keep horsemen naked or in light drapery. The old exomis was riding dress.

Macedonian cavalrymen dressed like foot soldiers. Because they lived in a cooler climate, Macedonians had long sleeves on their tunics. But over them went the breastplate and lappets, the greaves and crested helmet of the hoplite. The cavalryman's cloak was a flashy, striped version of the old Greek military chlamys.

When the Macedonians conquered Greece, they thought of themselves as Greeks. The Macedonian Court promoted Athenian arts and graces. Chitons and lutes and Hellenic festivals kept the young nobles around King Philip happy. Prince Alexander, a pupil of Aristotle's, was caught up by Homer's Heroes. And when he succeeded to the throne, he dedicated himself to a glorious Hellenizing of the world.

Alexander of Macedon led all the Greeks off on an incredible twelve year conquest of the entire Persian Empire. Subjects from the Nile to the Indus had to prostrate themselves before their Greek God-King Alexander. And in a frenzied misinterpretation of the Greek spirit, he put on the kandys and began to impose Hellenism like an Oriental despot.

But Alexander the Great died of a fever at the age of thirty-three. And his generals split his empire into three parts: Macedonia (Greece), Egypt and Syria (Western Asia). Three powerful rivals built their empires within the framework of an Hellenic world. And with captured wealth to finance all three, the civilized world went into one of its dressier ages.

Educated and skilled Greeks flowed out of the homeland into all the best jobs in new cities like Antioch and Alexandria. Ambitious foreign subjects took up the Greek chiton and the Greek language as fast as they could. Greek literature and art, science and philosophy flourished

everywhere. (Even in far off India the first sculptures of Buddha showed him in Greek drapery.) A common Greek culture linked the upper classes around the eastern Mediterranean. Similar dress and manners made shifts from city to city easy for a new cosmopolitan set.

Wealthy, sophisticated women enjoyed chitons that had shifted from buoyant experimentalism to expression of refinement and taste. Gowns became foils for embroideries and jewels.

Working the peplos out of their dress, women gradually got rid of the overhang. Girdling moved up towards the bust for a more elegant line. Cords crisscrossed the breasts, pulling the chiton in under the arms to give the effect of real sleeves. Cutting-and-sewing and neckbands moved it even closer to the Eastern gown. Gray-blue, violet, and rose replaced clear, bright colors.

When merchants in chitons began to use the himation to indicate position and power, it had come a long way from the simple wrap that could be thrown on or off in an instant. Complication and grace of drape boasted of a distaste for sweat and action. The simple, direct, active man had evolved into a more complicated individual who was part of a large cosmopolitan society, not just of a city-state.

In Greece itself there was growing disillusionment. The gods had been relegated to cold, impersonal state pageantry. And the city-state, which had once demanded all of a citizen's energies, was no longer a place to look for satisfaction.

Though poor, Athens was still the center of thought. And her philosophers gave their poverty dignity by returning to the dress that they felt had expressed simpler, more honorable values. The old shepherd's himation, thrown over nakedness, became the symbol of the unworldliness of the scholar. Moving among the fine linen chitons and himations of the rich and worldly, it became an effective reverse status symbol.

Forty foot Athena still symbolized the Greek of the Golden Age; but that Age had passed. By 300 B.C., the dynamics of dress had moved her peplos to the top and bottom of the social scale. It had become the garment of goddesses, an honored part of the Greek heritage. And it had become the dress of servants. A lady in a chiton was waited on by a maid in a peplos.

A group of little terra cotta figurines from Tanagra show clearly what the Greek woman had become. Made for the Mediterranean trade several centuries after the Persian wars, the statuettes are charming studies of fashionable women doing the things women did. They seem happy in a weblike wrapping of chitons and himations. Their movement is relaxed and natural, but the weight of drapery on their heads and shoulders takes away freedom and majesty.

For, as the himation began to fall over the head, and to hold the body in, the Greek rectangles moved from the expression of an active mind and body to a more Oriental expression of leisured gentility and modesty and restraint.

11

Imitation is the sincerest form of flattery.

Small boys wear cowboy hats not because they like hats, but because they like cowboys. They want to identify with the man in the saddle.

Exactly the same principle was at work all around the eastern end of the Mediterranean over two thousand years ago. Upper class men and women in all the cities were putting on Greek chitons and Greek himations because they wanted to identify with Greek art, Greek literature, Greek philosophy and science. And perhaps a lingering faith in contagious magic was involved in the imitation.

Greek horsemen did not adopt barbarian britches, not because britches were impractical but because they were barbarian. The Greeks had no wish to identify with a rowdy people who couldn't even speak a civilized tongue. They had no wish, either, to identify with the trouser-wearing enemy they had beaten.

Alexander the Great does seem to have adopted trousers for his cavalry's northern campaign. Trousers were warm. And, however reluctantly, Hellenic cavalrymen could only admire the horsemanship pants represented at that time.

What Scythian pants represented was hugely admired all along the steppe. Every man in that restless, shifting world was eager for riding and roping, shooting arrows at a full gallop, living vigorously and excitingly. Trousers eventually spread to the Atlantic and to China.

The early, belted tunic and trousers represented a vast and vital world. But it was a world that didn't leave written documents and impressive monuments, as Egypt and Greece and Persia did. It was a world whose best art was hidden in chiefs' graves all along the steppes.

The Scythians themselves disappeared from history. But with coat and pants now almost the symbol of Western man, the history of dress has to give the tunic and trouser men their due.

Although historically the Persians may seem to us to be the most successful trouser wearers, they were just the most visible fringe of a vast body of Iranian horseman who rode from the Tigris–Euphrates to northwest India, from the Persian Gulf to the Ural Mountains.

Alexander's armies marched through this country and established Greek garrison cities. But there was little in Greek culture to attract the horsemen. Instead they, and especially the Parthian tribes, started breeding heavier horses. They began making better, more flexible armor.

Their neighbors to the east were the wild Huns of Mongolia, a hunting, food-gathering people who lived in caves and wrapped themselves in rough wool. The Huns were very much impressed by the Iranian cavalry and saw in horsemanship a means of getting at the booty in wealthy Chinese cities. They had harassed the cities on foot for centuries with little success. But in a little more than a hundred years—sometime during the 5th and 4th centuries B.C.—they changed themselves into fierce, highly skilled, mounted raiders in belted skin tunics, trousers, and boots. The unusual shift from wool back to skins indicated values quite opposite to the values civilizations were cherishing. And in their new dress, the Huns' harassment of the Chinese frontier was so successful that it drove the Chinese to trousers.

Jao was a Chinese state bordering on Mongolia. During the frontier war of 325–298 B.C., the King of Jao ordered his troops to dress and fight like the Huns. The result was such an improvement in his fighting power that he held off the Huns and then dominated much of China.

Stopped on the east, the Huns pulled back to build a

Mongolian empire that gradually spread westward and later terrified Europe.

Jao's army had switched from foot to horse, from short sword to bow and arrow; it had switched from slippers and a loose robe over a long tunic to boots and britches. From the time of this shift, China was able to control barbarian raids on her steppe borders. From that time on, also, Chinese wore trousers.

Tunic and trousers evidently adapted well to the Chinese climate. In fact, there may well have been skin leg wrappings in the coldest regions even before the Huns came. But the gradual spread of trousers during the next thousand years made the Chinese the most universal wearers of tunic and trousers in the world. For both sexes adopted them. Although loose robes continued to dominate in Court circles, trousers became a standard garment for most Chinese and ceased to be, there at least, purely a symbol of barbarism.

As a civilized island in a barbaric sea, China was proud of her cultural accomplishments. Cavalry might keep conquerors out. But China's real defence was her ability to seduce conquerors with silken luxuries and the scholarly delights of her courts and cities.

In China the ideal was refinement and learning combined with public service. Elegant scholars ruled the empire. And in spite of the widespread use of trousers, the loose-sleeved, flowing, embroidered, wrapped silk robe of the sedentary, scholarly bureaucrat became the symbol of success in China. Since even a poor boy could work his way up the ladder to the silk robe through government examinations, every clever country boy dreamed of one. Every ambitious northern warlord wanted one. The silk robe spoke of blossoming walled courtyards, silks and porcelains, elegant manners and scholarship, all of which made the Chinese superior to anyone else on earth.

China did not place high value on trade, physical labor, or skill at arms. Only refinement and scholarship and decorous behaviour lifted men above the rest of mankind. And these were what the silk robe represented.

The history of China became a long repetition of the

same pattern. The fierce feudal warlord would ride south in trousers and conquer the Courts of China; and trousers would spread. But the warlord and his family would quickly lay the trousers aside; they would hurry to put on silk robes and become decorous, scholarly gentlemen. Then another fierce feudal warlord would ride south in trousers and conquer China. He too would lay aside his trousers and put on the silk robe. And so on, again and again throughout China's turbulent history. The Imperial Court perpetuated the prestige of silk robes; the northern warlord demanded a healthy respect for trousers.

As for outside invaders, diplomacy was more China's way than fighting. She began paying Hun chiefs to stay away. She sent them the silks and jewels and metals they needed for their personal display. For even the Huns wanted a touch of what China had.

Using diplomacy, as well as arms, China managed to acquire the string of oases along the eastern end of the ancient silk route between the Far East and the Near East. This gave security to caravans as far west as the Jaxartes River, north of India.

Though officially contemptuous of trade, Chinese gentlemen and Court ladies liked the gold, gems, luxury cottons and pearls they got in exchange for China's silks. And more and more people were wanting silk. Ambitious people in the West were desperate for it. It alone said the things they wanted to say about themselves. But the western end of the route ran through territory that was controlled by Iranian horsemen and infested by wilder barbarians out of the north.

The Iranian Parthians along this route had bred a heavy warhorse. They had also perfected body armor of metal plates sewn to leather or cloth. A rider and his horse were almost completely encased in metal scales for combat. Even the horse's legs were protected. And once the old conical leather helmet was banded with metal, the armored Parthian looked very much like a Crusader who had arrived on the scene well over a thousand years too soon. These Parthians soon dominated the other Iranians and forged them into a loose empire. Then it was possible to police and tax the western end of the silk route from China.

About a century before Christ, the Parthian king and the Chinese Han Emperor opened the *Silk Road* with much pomp and glitter. Caravans were protected all the way and taxed for the protection. A controlled quantity of silk travelled under Chinese escort to the edge of the Parthian Empire. There the Chinese handed the caravans over to a Parthian mounted escort. And the Parthians saw the silk through to the Mediterranean.

In this way China was linked up with India and with the whole Hellenistic world beyond. Purple was added to her traditional yellows, reds, and blues, though it did not replace yellow as the Imperial color.

Cottons began to flow east in return for the silks that flowed west. Over the centuries, India had learned how to weave cottons so gossamer that they were called "woven air." Timeless patience produced textiles wonderfully patterned with birds and flowers, or interwoven with gold wire or inset with gems to cool the skin.

Along the Silk Road, way stations became exotic little trading cities, remote yet in touch with the luxuries and the gossip of all the known world. And as rugged Parthian nobles grew rich taxing the silks and jewels and slaves that flowed along the Road, some discarded their old pointed caps for domed tiaras embroidered in pearls.

To the north, there was also a constant movement to the west. The big, basic drift along the steppes was always westward towards better weather and better grass and more civilized behavior. The first barbarians had moved out from South Russia. But more and more the barbarian movements started deep in the central Asian steppes. From there, one wild group after another moved out against Europe. In the 4th century A.D. the Huns arrived; in the 12th century, the Mongols of Ghenghis Khan. And different peoples were thrown against one another, changing life styles, changing dress.

Imitation of barbaric dress has given us more than coats and pants. It has given us plaids (tartans). Plaids came from the Celts who migrated west as part of an early Indo-European movement. From about 1500 B.C. to 300 B.C., they were the power north of the Alps, from eastern Europe to Spain. They spread a cattleman's culture across Europe, one that clung to traditions of a chariot aristocracy, and to a love of music, story and ornament.

Their basic garments—like the garments of the primitive farmers they ruled—were the short tunic and cloak. But Celtic tunics, derived from skins, were fitted to the body. Linen or wool tunics were often dyed saffron yellow. Celtic cloaks were big, rectangular blankets woven from clear red and green and blue and yellow wools into the bold checks and stripes that eventually became tartans. This big, patterned rectangle was called the *plaid*.

Celts flung their plaids around them and pinned them on their right shoulder with heroic-sized bronze or gold fibulae, the ornamental safety pins that replaced thorns and dagger pins in holding heavy mantles and tunics together.

Celtic women wore a simple, sleeved tunic tucked into a large, gathered, belted skirt of homespun; or they wore a long rectangular tunic—sometimes sleeved—pulled into gathers at the waist by a belt. Their belted waist and long gathered skirt marked the beginning of the familiar silhouette of the western woman.

Celts carried their wealth with them in gold, silver, and bronze bracelets, anklets, belt buckles, and fibulae. Chiefs and aristocrats of both sexes marked high rank with a heavy, ornamented twist of gold wires bent into an open circle, or torque, that fitted around the neck.

Ancient spiral, tendril, and lattice designs on torques, fibulae, and buckles were given a new vitality when Celtic tribes picked up Scythian art in south Russia. The Celts also learned horsemanship and borrowed trousers from the Scythians; and they carried both westward when some of their tribes shifted into Gaul (France).

Celtic trousers were distinctive. Celts were basically forest men, and their pride in their own culture made them cut their riding pants out of their own bright patterned cloth as well as out of skins. It made them ride

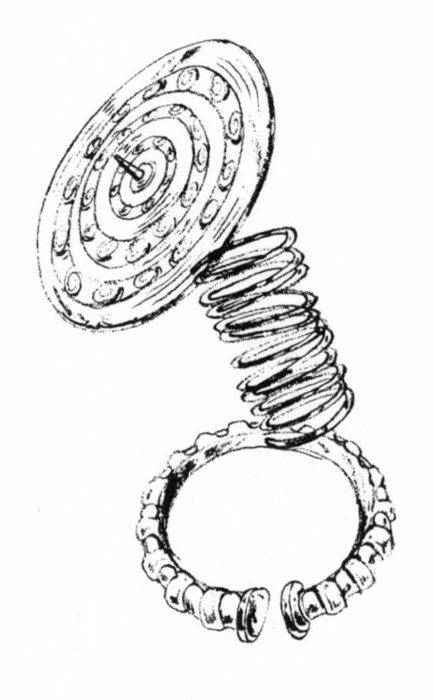

off from south Russia not in a Scythian-like wrapped coat, but in the boldly checked, rectangular cloak pinned on their right shoulder by a heroic-sized fibula.

The Celts spread trousers across Europe, but not to the British Isles. For although there were Celts there, they belonged to tribes who had a fierce pride in their pure Celtic heritage. These Celtic tribes had migrated to Britain much earlier, and had taken with them chariots, bronze battle-axes, Druids, bards, naked blue-painted warriors and the Celtic spiral. And they stayed in saffron tunics and big plaids.

Nearly two thouasnd years later, there were Celts still resisting trousers in the British Isles. Fantastically good Irish horsemen preferred to leap from a galloping horse in a saffron tunic. In fact, the wild dignity of the Irish Celts was not really destroyed until English kings humiliated Irish kings by forcing them into trousers and silk robes in the 14th century.

Celts in the Highlands of Scotland developed identifying clan tartans for their plaids, and the precision of the pattern was guaranteed by carefully marked measuring sticks. In the 16th century, Highlanders started wrapping their identifying clan blankets around their bodies to create the Highland kilt. This belted-on, all purpose, action garment was short. And the large end of the plaid left over when the body had been wrapped was pulled up over the shoulders from the back, and pinned on by the ancient fibula.

There are Celts still wearing the kilt instead of trousers, though now mainly for ceremonial. And it's still a matter of retaining their own identity, or of not wanting to identify with someone else.

12

While the Celts of Britain were successfully resisting the trouser, another group far to the southeast was not tempted to use it at all.

The Romans wanted to imitate the Greeks, not the barbarians. The Romans seem to have started as Indo-European barbarians drifting into Italy about 2,000 B.C., probably in skins, rough wools, and magical ornaments. They made the usual transition from hunter-herder to settled farmer, from sheepskin tunic to cloth rectangles and wrapped pagnes. Big rectangles doubled as wraps and blankets. And old skin cloaks grew into the hooded, bell-shaped stormcapes that Europe's climate seemed to inspire.

They can't have changed deeply, though, as they became farmers and townsmen. For a chaplet of oak leaves crowned the earliest kings of Rome. And oak leaves were the symbol of the barbarian god of thunder and sky and oak. (Because the oak was so frequently struck by lightning, it seemed to be the link between earth and sky.)

They weren't confronted with their own backwardness until civilized people from the East began moving into the western Mediterranean after 900 B.C. First the Etruscans settled north of Rome; then the Phoenicians started trading out of their colony at Carthage on the north coast of Africa. And finally, land hungry Greeks began to colonize southern Italy and Sicily.

The arrival of the Etruscans must have shocked the

Romans into a realization of their own crudeness. Turned up toes and narrow embroidered tunics suggest that the Etruscans were refugees from Asia Minor. Their advanced techniques in farming, building, engineering, metalwork, and warfare let them quickly dominate the rather primitive farmers of Latium. Before long there were Etruscan kings in Rome. And the original Romans were learning Etruscan skills as forced labor.

Like any people who have lost confidence in their own ways, the Romans copied the newcomers. Latin women began covering their heads with shawls and veils like the Etruscan women. And since Etruscans wore handsome, curved wraps, the Romans began cutting the hem of their rectangular wrap until it evolved into the semicircular *toga*. Imitating the superior Easterners, Romans put colored stripes—*clavii*—down the front of their tunics and wove colored borders into their togas.

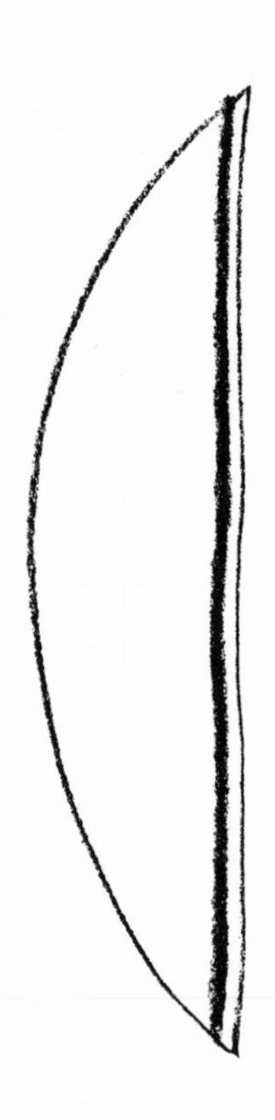

But the sturdy independence of the small farmer kept the Romans clinging stubbornly to many old ways. Instead of abandoning their pagne, or wrapped skirt, they shrank it gradually down into a loincloth, which both sexes used as underwear. The toga, which early became their basic outer wrap, kept an all purpose bigness and simplicity that made it different from the multicolored, smaller Etruscan wrap.

Then Greek ships began coming up the Italian coast. And even the Etruscans were awed. They began switching to sandals and chitons and the latest Greek armor.

Romans began to give their tunics and wraps the draped fullness of Hellenic dress; they caught the folds up with brooches. And they began to wear sandals. But they kept learning practical things from their Etruscan masters.

By 509 B.C., they had built up enough skill and self-confidence to throw the Etruscan kings out of Rome and organize a republic.

At first Rome was a very small and vulnerable republic. Barbarians and Etruscans threatened it from the north. Greeks, Carthaginians and rival Latins pressed up from the south.

Rome's survival depended on Romans standing together.

And they bound themselves into a visible unity by adopting the plain, useful toga as their symbol. The wearing of the toga was restricted to voters and their families. Worn over the loincloth and the *tunica* (the girdled, rectangular tunic), the toga was a big semicircle of undyed wool. One end was draped over the left shoulder. The other was passed across the back, under the right arm, and was then flung over the left arm or shoulder. Since it was unpinned, the toga could be wrapped around the arm for protection in a fight or it could cover the head in bad weather. And when a man went into battle, he girdled it around his waist to free his arms.

Though not a citizen, a woman also wore a toga over her tunica and loincloth.

Strong, centrally organized Rome slowly became a power. Within a century, all the Latin neighbors had been drawn into the republic.

Then the barbarians struck. Celtic Gauls came thundering down, yelling and brandishing battle axes. Naked, blue-painted bodies, horned helmets, shaggy moustaches and glittering torques were parts of their terrifying image. The Gauls were after booty, and Rome paid them off. Then, shocked and humiliated, the nation organized its defenses.

Security seemed to lie in expansion. And the toga became an even more widely used, more potent symbol calling forth the loyalty of all who wore it, and teaching loyalty even in childhood. All free born boys were given the purple-bordered toga of the highest official. This *toga praetexta* identified them with the men who ran Rome. At puberty they were stripped of their rank. They were given the birthright of every Roman, the plain *toga virilis,* the mark of full citizenship. Only relentless devotion to duty could put them back into the purple.

The chain of command in Rome was clearly marked by the precise width of the purple border on official togas, and by the widths of the three purple clavii running down the front of the tunic from the shoulder to the hem.

Knights wore narrow clavii. They were the new class of wealthy men who provided Rome's cavalry. Members of the elite cavalry were allowed an extra distinction—a small scarlet-striped toga in addition to their big toga.

There was nothing personal, nothing individual about the Roman's dress. If he wore a plain, undyed toga, he was a citizen. If he had a purple border, he was an official. If he wore a small, scarlet-striped toga, he was an elite cavalryman. If he had a black toga, he was a mourner. And if his toga was chalked to signify purity of devotion to the state, he was a candidate for public office.

Length, width and arrangement of the toga followed strict rules to indicate the more subtle distinctions of status.

Rome had become the dominant power in Italy and Sicily by 240 B.C. By that time she was challenging Carthage for supremacy in the western Mediterranean. She was keeping the Gauls in their place. And she was receiving envoys from a great power like Egypt.

As Rome got bigger, the toga, too, got bigger and more complicated. By the time Rome was enjoying power and prestige, the toga was seven feet wide and three times the length of the wearer. Its drape expressed what Rome had become, a Mediterranean power.

But the Mediterranean world had been conditioned by Greek thought to give highest prestige to cultural refinement. But the Roman hadn't produced great art and literature and music and philosophy and science.

The Roman was sensitive to his cultural lag. Increasingly in command of, yet culturally inferior to, the Hellenic world, he borrowed Greek styles, Greek art and Greek teachers. He Hellenized himself to make his dominance more acceptable.

Women abandoned the toga for the *palla*, which was a Greek himation under another name. They adopted the *stola* as the mark of the Roman matron, and the stola was basically a chiton.

The stola was so like the Hellenistic gown then in use that it gave the Roman matron the confidence she needed for her new position in the Mediterranean world. Two large rectangles of fine wool were sewn up the sides and pinned or sewn along the top, leaving holes for the head and arms. When the stola was girdled, the top fell over the shoulders with the effect of loosely-draped sleeves.

But the stola did not make the Roman matron Greek. On a Greek woman, the drape and movement of the rectangles explored and expressed the grace of the naked body underneath.

On a Roman woman, the rectangles were a third layer, building the body up into a substantial, dignified pillar. The effect was solid rather than fluid. For what people are always seems to come through; and the Romans were builders.

The Roman woman's foundation layer was the vestigial loincloth and a soft leather band that controlled her breasts. The second layer was her *tunica intima*, the original, simple, rectangular tunic, which still served as housedress and nightdress. Her third layer was the stola, girdled and bloused under her breasts and again around her hips.

Even the girdling expressed the difference between Greek and Roman attitudes. The Greek girdle shifted constantly with the search for the ideal proportions. It tried this; it tried that. The Roman girdles stayed in one position for six centuries, controlling the length of the gown to make it precisely appropriate to its wearer's station in life. Extra prestige was indicated by adding a long train to the stola. For adding on rather than creating seemed to be the Roman way.

Yet the fullness of the stola did give the Roman matron the curving folds and the fluted fall of Greek drapery. And with the palla draped over head and shoulders for her fourth layer, she was Hellenistic.

But on the day before she got her stola, her wedding day, the Roman girl was ancient barbarian as well as Hellenistic. The Roman bride draped a fine saffron yellow palla around her shoulders, over an ancient form of tunica. She slipped on sandals dyed yellow to match. And when she had arranged a flame colored veil on her hair so that it fell partly over her face, she crowned herself with a wreath of myrtle and orange blossoms.

The wreath of flowers spoke of fertility; for flowers

The toga rises and falls with Rome. The toga brought Romans together, motivated them to greatness, let them display their power. When it got too big and elaborate, it gave frustrated men something to fight. As it shrank to a stiff brocaded vestige, it became a reassuring symbol of the past to a dying empire.

This small 5th century B.C. Etruscan wrap probably inspired the toga.

In 100 B.C., the toga is the simple, multi-purpose wrap of the Roman citizen.

By the early empire, the toga is an unwieldy mass of drapery.

The toga shrinks to a ceremonial strip of heavily embroidered silk in 6th century Byzantium.

were part of the fertility of springtime. But the palla and the veil restrained joy in fertility by covering her flesh modestly.

The big toga, the substantial stola, the modest palla: They were the image of classical Rome. It was the image of the Romans who would conquer the entire Mediterranean world and keep it mainly at peace for the first two centuries of the Christian era. And it looked as solid and enduring as a Roman triumphal arch.

Yet the Roman in the days of conquest did not wear his uniform with the same pride he once had. By the 2nd century B.C., the toga had become increasingly uncomfortable and unsatisfying. And so had Roman life.

The early Roman family had been a loyal, vigorous, hard working unit proud to wear the toga that stood for staunch unity. The state, too, had been a loyal, vigorous, hard working unit. Every citizen had found pride and satisfaction in his contribution.

But wealth and power were changing everything. Family ties were loosening. A professional army was making war a perpetual institution rather than an occasional, exciting civic duty. And the toga, now expressing Rome's expanding glory, was becoming so big and so complicated that only a man with servants could get it on. Only a sedentary official could afford the time it took to go somewhere with the slow, stately pace the toga imposed on its wearer. It was, according to Tertullian, "not a garment, but a burden." And the average Roman citizen gave up trying to cope with it. He just kept it to be buried in. Gradually he took to simpler wraps like the *pallium* (the Greek himation) and the *paenula,* a big, hooded, circular stormcloak.

Roman women seemed to lose their old sense of worth. They were no longer the center of a warm, rousing, pioneer family. They had no part in the state. And they had no emotional outlet in religion; for religious festivals were run with the efficiency of military campaigns.

As if to compensate, wealthy matrons filled up empty hours with baths, perfumes, cosmetics, and hair styles.

They swathed themselves in rich Eastern yellows and subtle Oriental violets and blues and pinks. They valued any bits of Chinese silk cloth they could get their hands on, unravelled it, and rewove it with their wool or else made it into decorative bands, embroideries and fringes. They piled gold and rubies and emeralds on earrings and girdles.

During one of Rome's last wars with Carthage, men hit out at women's extravagances with a law restricting the wearing of gold and too many colors. But the women protested so publicly and so violently that the men repealed it with comments about women and their harmless little indulgences.

The passion of the protest should have warned men that something deep was involved here. And in fact, the things that made the women fight so desperately for their bits of silk were the things that were undermining Rome even before she became an empire: boredom, a sense of futility, and a lack of outlet for the emotions. The women were not the only ones unfulfilled. Rome was a man's world. But many of the men were shut out, too. Their toga was an impressive mockery. And they wouldn't wear it.

Intellectual Romans scorned what the toga stood for. Seeking the ascetic dignity of Greek philosophers, they threw a pallium over nakedness.

Even the army had its problems. Rome had subdued the Celtic tribes in Gaul. There were Gallic troops in the armies that were holding back Germanic barbarians all along the Rhine and the Danube. Gallic wools were coming into Rome. And Romans loved the bright red and green and yellow and blue Celtic checks and stripes. They loved the thick durability of Gallic wools.

Soldiers on garrison duty in the north were wearing the *saggum*, a red, rectangular Gallic cloak that had originally been pinned with a thorn. Some had even started wearing knee-length trousers; though trousers represented a crudity and a barbaric wildness that made civilized Romans shudder.

The soldiers were probably wearing the saggums and

the trousers to keep warm. But a man will stand a lot of physical discomfort where pride is involved. And in his imitation of others' dress, he has often revealed an otherwise well-concealed lack of pride in what he was.

13

Whether a man communicates by text or by dress, his message has to be given in symbols.

Words are just symbols. The word *mink* is not a mink; it's just the symbol for the little animal. Similarly a crown isn't a king or a kingdom; it's just the symbol.

Before the age of mass media and mass literacy, people depended heavily on the symbolism of dress to keep society in order. A fringe or a purple border spoke of status. A veil on a woman's head said she was both married and modest.

The effectiveness of the symbol depended on the sender and the receiver putting the same meaning on the symbol. White meant death in China. Black meant death in the West. Purple was an international symbol. By the time of the Roman Empire, blood red Tyrian purple meant high rank from Persia to Spain. Its exciting color, costliness, intensity and unfading quality made it a natural symbol for personal power. People scarcely saw it as a color. They looked. Saw purple. And stepped aside.

In early Rome, the toga stood for active citizenship. The width of the purple border on the toga signalled the amount of authority the wearer had. And those symbols had kept order.

In the last century of the Republic, symbols changed and blurred. Citizens didn't wear their togas. They used purple freely, enjoying it as a color for gowns and a background for jewels.

When Rome became an Empire shortly before the birth of Christ, Emperor Augustus tried to bring back the old order by restoring the symbols. He ordered citizens to start wearing their togas. He restricted the use of Tyrian purple to himself and his high officials.

Roman emperors managed centuries of political stability by an increasing centralization of power in the hands of the emperor, generals, governors—not in democracy. And the growth of despotism was clearly displayed in dress.

A chaplet of real leaves had crowned the consuls of the early Republic. Their undyed, useful, democratic toga had had a simple purple border.

In the early days of the Empire, the leaves became gold. The purple bordered toga was bigger.

Half a century later, Nero's *corona radiata* had gold points radiating out from his head like sunbeams. And there was probably silk woven into his completely purple, gold embroidered toga.

Aurelian dropped the toga, in the third century. He wore a radiant diadem with a pure silk purple and gold tunic.

And later in that century, Diocletian's imperial diadem was a broad band of gold set with pearls. His purple and gold tunic was silk, and frankly Persian. His blue and gold silk court robe was fashioned like a Persian kandys and embroidered with pearls and jewels. His nails were gilded, his hair sparkled with gold dust. The Roman Emperor had become a sun god.

As the emperor became more and more, the ordinary citizen naturally became less and less. He paid staggering taxes to support the army and the civil service. And when he finally collapsed under them, the tax base was broadened. People in the Roman provinces were given citizenship and tax assessments.

The old aristocrats made desperate efforts to shore up their privileged position. Romans had been the elite. And to assert this prestige when Roman citizenship became common, they assumed more and more silks and jewels and purple.

Tyrian purple was restricted by law. But they found other purple-giving molluscs. To express subtleties of social position, they diluted purples to get violets and mauves and pinks. They concocted artificial dyes.

Roman matrons began fluttering with silk scarves and fringes and fans and sunshades. And in addition to their sensuous enjoyment of textures, perfumes, glitter and color, wealthy Romans were gorging themselves emotionally on bloody spectacles, and physically on exotic foods like boiled ostrich and Jericho dates.

The poor could afford only the bloody spectacles. More and more small farmers were losing their little farms to patrician landowners, and were drifting rootlessly in the cities. Many were finding hope and emotional satisfaction in Christianity.

Because they were misunderstood and sometimes persecuted, the Christians banded together the way the earliest Roman citizens had banded together. And like those earlier Romans, they adopted similar clothing to hold themselves together and give them courage.

Christ had been born in a Roman province. And He was believed to have worn the *collobium*, the workingman's single garment, a girdled, rectangular tunic. So the earlier Christians adopted the collobium. And they enlarged its symbolism by sewing two broad purple clavii down the front. Clavii had started as rank stripes on Roman tunics, but over the centuries they had moved down the social ladder. Now they were often used to decorate the livery of servants. So Christians felt they were right for the servants of the Lord.

Christ, it was thought, had also worn the pallium. This common, rectangular wrap had been given further connotations of asceticism and unworldliness by the philosophers who had worn it as a protest against decadence.

The third garment the early Christians adopted was the paenula, the old hooded stormcloak. Now closed up the front, the huge, circular paenula swathed the body, eliminating sex and the flesh, and making all men and women equal before God and man.

In little groups all over the Empire, Christians gathered

in these simple, unadorned garments of the poor to mark their commitment to a communal life of humble service to God.

When Romans began to weave the rectangular collobium into a T-tunic with wide sleeves, it was called the *dalmatic*. It proved to be even more useful than the paenula. Long, loose and ungirdled, with increasingly wide, flaring sleeves, the dalmatic eliminated class and sex.

Later, when Christianity had been accepted as a preferred religion, some converts from the upper classes moved out of their extravagant clothing into the simple, symbolic garments. Or ladies sewed purple clavii down the front of their long-sleeved stola. Against the lavish silks and jewels of the later Roman Empire, early Christian dress was a powerful symbol, challenging the Empire's values.

In later centuries, when all these garments had gone out of common use, the Church retained them in priestly vestments. Versions of the collobium, dalmatic, pallium, paenula and clavii were incorporated into clerical dress.

Since the clergy so often had to take Christianity to people who couldn't read words, the Church depended heavily on other symbols. Biblical characters, and ethical traits ranging from pride to humility were identified by clothing and colors. In pictures, Mary was always wrapped in a blue or purple palla. Christ was in blue and gold before the Resurrection, in purple and gold after. A pallium of kaunakes spoke of the humble asceticism of a disciple.

By the end of the third century, three forces were shaping the Roman world: Christian, German, Persian.

Christianity was victorious in battles with paganism all over the Empire. Vigorous German barbarians were battering at the Roman frontier all along the Rhine and the Danube. And at the same time German horseman were joining the Gauls in the Roman cavalry, and even gaining power in the Roman army.

Constantly reinvigorated by horsemen from her eastern frontier, Persia had armored and trained cavalry, using the heavy horse, so effectively that she had revived as a power.

During her time of domination by Greece and Rome, she had concentrated on putting her rich heritage of pattern to work in textiles, especially in broad, decorative silk bands that were coveted everywhere around the Mediterranean. Her revival in the 3rd century gave her control of parts of the Silk Road, which resulted in access not only to silks but to jewels as well, and gave Persian dress a new sumptuousness that soon passed on to Rome, especially eastern Rome.

At the end of the 3rd century, the Roman Empire split in two. Co-emperors had headquarters in northern Italy and in northern Greece, near the military fronts on the Rhine and on the Danube.

The split had already occurred in dress. The West, apart from its ruling class, had been moving towards poorer, simpler, more Germanic and Gallic dress. The East had been adding Oriental embellishment to Greco-Roman dress. Western Christians had been stressing simple moral values in humble, undyed garments. Eastern Christians had tended to mystical ecstacy in tunics increasingly enriched with purple, gold and jewels to suggest the glory of God and the radiance of Heaven. The West was now the poorer part of the Empire. The East controlled the rich trading cities with their exotic bazaars.

Early in the 4th century, the Emperor Constantine built the city of Constantinople, in the old Greek colony of Byzantium at the northeastern end of the Mediterranean, the very crossroads of Europe and Asia. And he made Christianity the state religion.

Constantinople was New Rome, complete with seven hills. Its officials were imported from Rome. Its citizens called themselves Romans. But Byzantium was leaving the Greco-Roman world behind.

Greece and Rome had been concerned with men. Greek dress had expressed the beauty and physical power of man. Roman dress had expressed his practical power. And marble sculpture and Roman portraiture had been ideal for showing man as he was.

But Christianity was trying instead both in art and dress to show the mystical relationship between God and

man. Mosaic replaced statuary; fused with color and gold leaf, bits of glass became haloes and rays of heavenly light. In mosaics, faces took on a wide-eyed, other-worldly intensity. Jewelled silks were given a new authority by the new state religion. The Emperor's relationship with a greater, universal God was indicated by his dazzling gold and silks and jewels. Such radiance was confined to the Court and the Church. And its contrast with ordinary tunics and cloaks heightened the effect of Heavenly splendor.

Court dress in the new era was based on late Roman forms, which were really old Hellenic forms altered by Christian, barbarian and Persian influence. Dalmatic, clavii, layered tunics, pallium and palla, paenula and chlamys were all a part of the magnificence of Byzantium. But in Byzantium, the basic forms of Roman dress were heavily and brilliantly encrusted with Christian symbolism.

The circular chlamys replaced the toga as the outer wrap. Originally the short cloak of an active man, it now fell to the ground, covering the body in Christian rejection of the flesh. It kept the old, slung-on simplicity; but the fibula that held it on the shoulder also supported three jewelled pendants, which represented the Holy Trinity.

Copts, a Christian sect in Egypt, found a compromise between the simple symbolism of clavii and the beauty of Persian bands. They cut up the long, severe clavii, and into the shorter strips they wove richly colored traditional motifs. The Copts used the same technique on small circles and squares called *roundels* and *tablions*. These bold patches were sewn on to cloaks and tunics, turning the garments into mosaics of color and pattern. The old classical simplicity of Greco-Roman drapery was gone.

The increasingly heavy silk needed to support the weight of Byzantine decoration was ensured when silk worms were smuggled out of China in the 6th century. Almost immediately the already flourishing Byzantine silk industry became a major industry.

The heavy silks of Byzantium achieved the Christian purpose of hiding flesh and sex. But they did it at the expense of humility and equality before God. More and more the Emperor of the Eastern Romans was an Oriental despot. By the 8th century his tunic had become a Persian tunic. His sandals had turned into jewelled, purple, silk, Persian *buskins*, or closed boots.

The Empress of the Romans wore a heavy silk stola encrusted with gold and jewels. Streams of gems cascaded over the shoulders of her long, gold-embroidered purple chlamys cloak. Her fibulae was a massive cluster of jewels with a trinity of sparkling pendants. Marble-sized pearls glistened in her hair and in her crown.

But things were splendid only for the Emperor and his court. Early in the 4th century every Roman was frozen to his place and his job, making him a serf instead of a free man. By the end of the century, men were no longer required even to own a toga. And the toga when it was worn had been folded into accordian pleats (which were sewn or pinned together). This eventually narrowed into a long, wide, thick band, and gradually the pleats were removed; the remaining band was the stiff, jewelled *toga palmata*, which hung around the body much as the original toga had been draped.

14

The sensual appeal of silks may have been a vital factor in drawing Christian Byzantium into the Eastern orbit, away from the West.

The Chinese silks that began to come down the Silk Road long before, under the vigorous Han Dynasty, were breathtakingly beautiful. And though their symbolism might be lost on alien peoples, their gleaming beauty captivated everyone. Any culture that could, began to weave its own silks to meet the insatiable demand.

The people who undertook silk weaving most eagerly, and who were most sensitive to the nature of silk, were the Persians. During their eclipse by Greece and Rome, they had added Western art motifs to their own collection. And they had kept up their own tradition of filling the surface of things with pattern. They had developed a rich range of reds and purples, deep blue, yellows, dark green, buff.

While Europe went into the homespun wool of the post-Roman period, Persia continued to pour much of her best creative effort into the production of gorgeous silks. The knee-length, long-sleeved, slim-cut, silk Persian tunic was an influence on dress throughout the Middle East.

Like the Chinese, the Persians had shown an early sensitivity to silk. They had been doing delicate gold embroidery on silk since the 6th century B.C. And they had turned Scythian-style appliqued edgings and seam trimmings into decorative silk bands that were sewn around the neck, upper sleeve, hem, wrist, and down the center of the gowns of all of the Middle Eastern and Byzantine people who could afford them. Bands of pattern and color along the edges of tunics and shawls seemed a natural way of decorating clothes. It was as if bracelets, necklaces and girdles had been transferred to the dress itself.

When the Persians threw out the Iranian horsemen, and regained power in the 3rd century, they captured some expert Byzantine silk weavers. Building on the patterned weaves of China—brocade, damask, twill—the Persians brought the old idea of allover, repeated pattern to a new beauty.

The characteristic Persian motif was the roundel, a circle filled with a central, stylized Tree of Life flanked by paired, nature forms like eagles, flowers, peacocks or winged lions. The roundel itself was surrounded by small rosettes or stars. The whole design was repeated endlessly over the fabric. The symmetry of the paired forms, the ordered repeat of the design, kept the eye following the shifting sheen of the silk instead of stopping to explore it.

As silk became more and more available to all classes in Persia, increasingly extravagant designs had to be created to let the elite mark their special position. More and more gold thread was woven in.

The rich used silk so lavishly that the lines of their tunic and trousers softened into folds. A silver plaque shows a Persian king hunting lions with a fluttering silk sash flying out behind him. His draped trousers were ruffled at the seams and were so fully cut that they had to be caught up at the crotch by joining the bottom of the back and front of his tunic together, to let him ride his horse. The tunic itself was so full that it had to be held in to his chest for riding with crisscrossed straps.

Such loss of efficiency may have been a symptom of the weakness that let Persia fall to Islamic troops in the 7th century.

To Mohammed, the merchant founder of Islam, the luxurious nature of silk was corrupting. In fact, he had

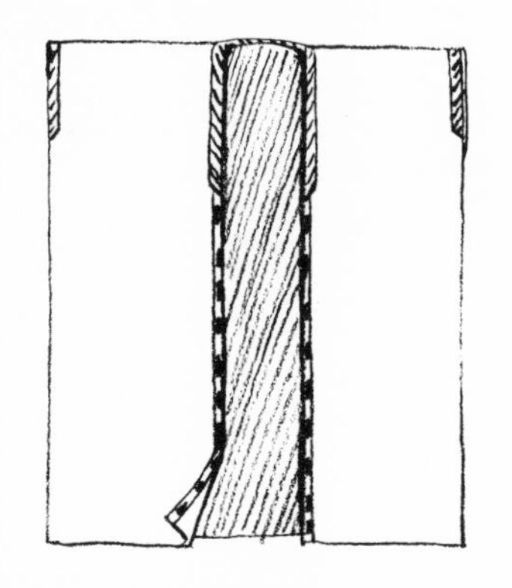

come to believe that all luxuries were corrupting. So he wore a black turban and the starkly functional robes of Arabian desert nomads: a wide wool tunic and an open-fronted robe derived from the earliest rectangular and T-shaped garments of the Near East. He did sometimes wear green; and a green turban became the mark of a pilgrim who had been to Mecca.

The outer robe of the Bedouin army that spread his teachings was the forerunner of the Arabian *aba*, the huge robe that still wraps Arab kings and sheiks. Made of two rectangles sewn together at the shoulders and the sides with space left for the arms, and slit down the front, the aba is a very ancient garment. Its survival shows that a layering of loose garments is still good for the desert's extremes of heat and cold.

Such robes effectively concealed Mohammed's body and those of his followers. For, undoubtedly influenced by Middle Eastern traditions of modesty and morality, Mohammed taught that nakedness, like luxury, was corrupting.

He and his Bedouin followers rode out of the Arabian desert to bring a corrupt world into submission to God's (Allah's) will. And since to die in the Holy War was to go straight into paradise, nothing could stand against the fierce ecstacy of the Moslem warriors. Their loose garments streamed out in the wind as men and horses and camels and flashing scimitars became an incredible force that swept triumphantly through Persia. Later they also moved across Asia and Africa and up into Europe.

Silk was forbidden to the followers of Mohammed. But as the center of Islam shifted from Mecca to Baghdad, as the starkness of the desert mixed with the richness of Persian culture, silk slipped in, mixed at first with linen so that silk was not quite silk.

Islam is the Arabic word for submission to the overwhelming power of God. It means dissolving man into the harmony of the universe, shrinking his importance before the importance of Allah. The human figure was banned from Islamic art.

Although Persian art sometimes depicted horsemen,

Persian design had always stressed plant and animal forms. And the ordered, allover patterning of Persian silks, Persian rugs and Persian walls expressed the blending of everything into the harmony of the whole. Going on and on and on, repetitive pattern broke up solid surfaces, blending the mass of a man or the mass of a gate into the space around it. Just as the buff color of local bricks and the blue glaze of Persian tiles blended walls and domes into the sand and the sky and hills behind them.

Persia and Islam were right for each other. And suddenly the ancient Persian art of decoration took on a new depth of purpose, a new spiritual vitality. A curving line linked abstracted stems and leaves and blossoms into an endless arabesque that covered a box or a brocaded robe with equal unimportance. Patterning gave to a palace wall and to riding pants the equal value all men and all things would have on the Day of Judgment. So all things were patterned.

Arabic script from the Koran, the sacred book of Islam, began to be woven and embroidered into Persian bands. The abstract shapes and strong strokes of the script lent themselves perfectly to silk, giving endless play to its luster without ever dominating it. And the Koran gave an aura of divinity to the silks of ceremonial robes. The script was so perfect for silk designs that poems, proverbs and names were woven into bands to decorate nonreligious clothing.

The Arab Moslems who swept across Africa into Spain clung to Arabian dress, but they carried silk weavers with them to insure silk for their ceremonial robes. (The linen they wove in with their silk, in obedience to the old law, gave Spanish silks a body that had much to do with the elegance of Spanish costume of the 15th and 16th centuries. And the broad patterned bands on upper arms and sleeves—the distinctive decorations of early European medieval dress—were largely local replicas of the beautiful Islamic-Persian upper arm bands.)

But the Moslems carried more than silk weaving across Africa. Since trousers were practical for men who rode horses and camels, Moslem Arabs gradually adopted them and introduced them in the lands they conquered. But their

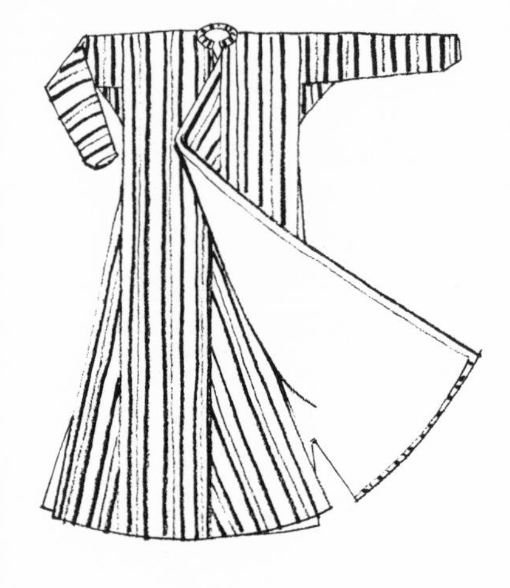

pants were sacklike and secondary. Flowing cloth that hid the limbs always dominated the look of the Arab.

Influenced too by the Persian horseman's knee-length, narrow, sleeved coat and tunic, Arabs narrowed some of their outer robes and developed a leaner, long-sleeved coat closed with a sash. The coat could vary in length, looseness, and weight of cloth, according to climate and local tradition; but the basic garment, the practical, dignified, body-covering *caftan*, was eventually worn throughout the vast Islamic world that stretched from China to Morocco. Caftan became a generic name for a wide range of sleeved, open fronted coats of the Islamic and Oriental worlds. But the Arab usually continued to cover his caftan with an aba.

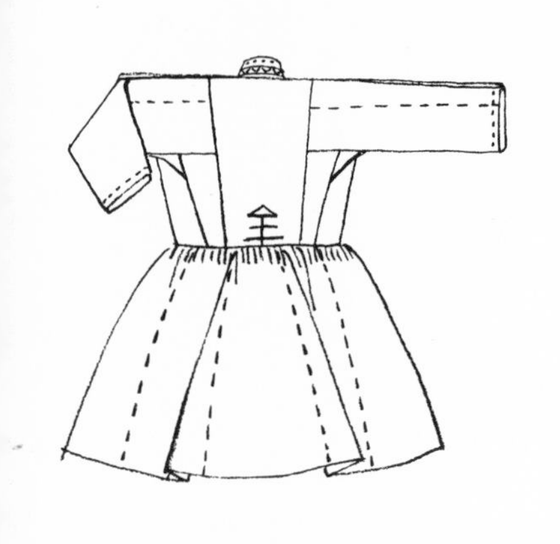

Covering the body was a basic fact of Islam, for women as well as men. The veiling and secluding of women had been developing steadily in the Middle East, since modesty was a social custom that protected the home. Islam's strict laws of modesty now turned many women into moving mounds of robes and veils, with eye slits so that they could see where they were going. At puberty, most of them went into *purdah*—complete seclusion behind walls and curtains and veils. And the higher the class, the more total the seclusion was apt to be.

Many women were highly educated and influential. But it seemed as if the overall patterning of the Persian silks that made up the harem women's long belted tunics, caftans and veils helped to dissolve their individuality into the general, richly-patterned surfaces of the rest of a man's prized possessions.

As Islam's trade and wealth grew, the turban became increasingly the mark of the Islamic male.

A turban was a natural response to a burning sun. Cloth head-wrappings had always been a part of Middle Eastern dress. Their function was to absorb sweat and insulate the head.

Mohammed had used the turban as a symbol, too, as a symbol for a young religion. And when Persia adopted Islam, the men of Persia began to develop the turban. Basically a composite of the domed hat of Persia and the desert head wrap, it became an embroidered, jewelled wrapping of exotic silks around a lofty cone. Its color, style of wrap, and ornament all spoke of wealth and rank and family. But it always left the forehead bare to touch the ground when the wearer prostrated himself in submission to Allah.

The turban eventually went far beyond its functions of protection and religious symbolism. Its size and splendor increased as Islamic countries became more and more powerful, building up towards the rotund gorgeousness of the turbans worn by late 16th century Turkish sultans, which had dozens of yards of silk in them.

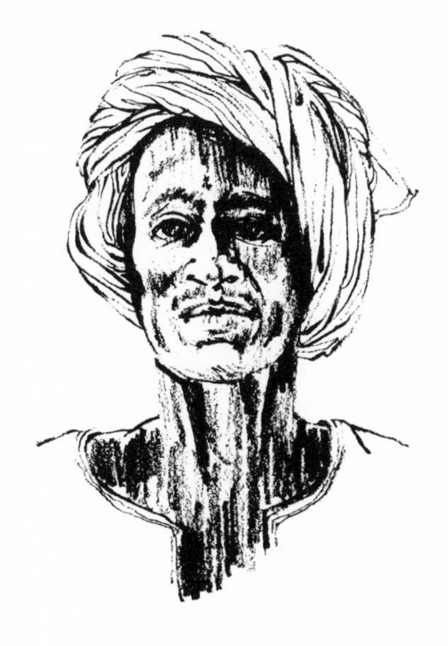

Turban, caftan, trousers, layers of robes and tunics, Arabic script, decorative bands, and over it all the rich, patterned silks of Persia: This was the image of Islam.

The earliest Moslems had been vigorous Arab horsemen. And a succession of fierce mounted warrior tribes kept revitalizing Islam: first the Berbers of north Africa, then groups like the Turks and the Mongols who followed the Huns out of the central Asian steppes.

Moslem horsemen took silk back to China's doorstep early in the 8th century. Though China was still impervious China, only the Persian silk style got through the guarded frontier. The fact that an alien silk could influence the Chinese style was a sign that China's wall of cultural superiority had a few cracks.

Yet China still looked intact. She still seemed to be holding her precarious balance between the crude strength of her northern warlords and the intellectual style of her Court. Under the T'ang Dynasty, Chinese culture reached full maturity. It was a peak of luxury that as usual lured in another northern warlord.

But although China was vulnerable to changes from within, it was well defended from foreign military invasion. The Moslems were stopped at the frontier by warriors who had picked up heavy cavalry techniques from Iran. Chinese knights were encrusted like armadillos in hardened leather and metal scales. Gold breastplates were worn above flaring leather skirts.

Yet, in spite of military power and the constant invasions of men in trousers, the core of flowing robes was never

destroyed; and elegant silk robes had a psychological effect on the brash warlords who put them on. Charming rituals and ceremonial etiquette restrained them gently while they absorbed the culture they needed to fit themselves into the delightful life of the Chinese Court. At the beginning of each new dynasty, robes tended to be fitted, fur-lined, and slim sleeved. But dress always went back to loose, flowing lines and dripping sleeves.

While common men and women struggled in hemp and wool (and increasingly in cotton) tunics and trousers outside the palace courtyards in Ch'ang-an, dainty T'ang ladies in pink and celadon green fluttered through the gardens in ribbons and serrated silk scarves. Their white, powdered faces had a porcelain fragility. Their lean wrapped outer robe, widely sashed under the breasts, was made of delicate fabrics. Side slits in long tunics had little to do with the original riding slits of the coat they were descended from; now they merely added to the general flutter of scarves, ribbons, tripping hems and dripping pendant sleeves that hid tiny hands. Precarious teacup-like headdresses added to the look of unreality and to the general air of physical uselessness.

Eventually uselessness was carried to dangerous extremes. Ladies' feet were bound and deformed into futile little stumps, called the golden lotus.

But under all the flutter of the T'ang ladies, the clothing shapes were simple and traditional. Layers of simply cut, sleeved, wrapped, broadly-belted or sashed, high-necked, long robes traced back to the layering habits of the cold north. For tradition was one of the strengths of China. Confucius, who wore layered and fur-lined robes, had said that to strip a man of his clothes was to strip him of his whole code of behavior.

The Chinese are small people; the men who climbed the bureaucratic ladder and ran China had a short build. And racial pride seems to call for an intensifying of inherent qualities. The Chinese found dignity in width, not height. Their headdress was usually a low cap; and they widened their appearances with loose robes, wide sleeves, seated posture and an excess of bowing. Since layering of clothes added more width, the more layers, the more dignity. And because all his tunics and robes were long, the Chinese gentleman could strip off layer after layer in the summer without real loss of dignity. Winter or summer, he could extend what he was into broad, lustrous bulk.

It was during the T'ang Dynasty that the dragon robe began to develop. This was the long-sleeved, outer, silk robe worn ceremonially over several other tunics and coats. Basically a wide-sleeved, full length, unfitted coat, it was worn by the emperor and the royal family, and was occasionally awarded to others as a mark of special favor, usually for service. Its most important feature was its dragon design, the Imperial mark and the symbol of good luck and happiness.

The T'angs knew the nature of silk and brought it to its peak. They made it the ultimate expression of what China was—a brilliant and subtle balance of contrasting elements. T'ang silks combined bold yellows, greens, oranges and peacock blue with gently muted tints of buff, purple and deep red. They integrated dragons and tigers with vines, rosettes and lotus blossoms.

The Chinese could even use foreign motifs without losing the integrity of their own designs. Greek, Persians, and Indian motifs were fed into fabric. Persian roundels and paired figures and the Persian system of repeats helped pull contrasting designs together into a cloth of great beauty.

Used abroad as ceremonial gift robes—Robes of Honor—T'ang dragon silks spoke to the world of China. And they were elegant ambassadors, expressing China's ancient conviction that polite negotiation was always preferable to war.

The warriors of Islam probed into India, too, from the north. But India resisted outside influence as strongly as China did. While conquerors came and went, Indian men continued to wrap cotton into turbans, shawls, and *dhotis*—the loincloths pulled loosely between the legs. Women kept wrapping the long *paridhana* skirt and the airy *dupatta* shawl around them; and if they couldn't afford both, they extended their wrapped skirt up around their body into an

early form of *sari.* Hips were slung with a *kamorband,* a girdle of twisted cloth and ornament. Sandals sometimes protected the feet.

A fitted, short-sleeved bodice and simple, sleeved shirt had worked their way slowly into Indian dress after the Aryans invaded from the north. Then, as the Aryans settled in as the highest caste, a covering for the torso had gradually become a requirement for upper class women.

Alexander the Great had marched into the north of India with Greek drapery; and Greeks had hovered at the frontiers for several centuries. Classical folds had dressed the first sculptures of Buddha, and sculptors had shown Indian women with chitons and Greek hair styles. But probably only a few ruling families had adopted Hellenistic dress. A little veiling of women began as Islam crept slowly into India from the 7th century on.

But there was no reason for the basic Indian dress to change. With one of the most fertile lands of earth for a garden, even poor people along the Ganges had fruits and flowers and cotton always within reach. The Hindu religion marked every stage of their life with emotionally satisfying ritual. Their cottons glowed with the gay colors of native dyes or were sun bleached and scrubbed white. Their jewelry tinkled with tiny bells. Their lively sexuality was still expressed in low-slung girdles that placed ornament over the genitals. Skin was perfumed. Hair was bright with flowers. And naturally fine features were enhanced with black eye salve, red lip dye, black and vermilion beauty and religious marks and by jewels set into forehead and nose.

The upper classes had even more ways of enriching the simple, basic forms of clothing as more and more jewels, silks, peacock feathers and gold thread became available for shawls, girdles, bodices and turbans. Cottons sparkled with real diamonds—like dew on cobwebs. Girdles were weighted with ropes of real pearls; they glittered with rubies, sapphires and emeralds.

Ancient and persistent reports say three garments were required for proper modesty: loincloth, shirt or bodice and shawl. Yet the overwhelming effect of Indian sculpture and painting is not of clothed bodies. It is of voluptuous nakedness and elaborate ornament.

In Indian sculpture, the loincloth is usually there—a sheer, wispy suggestion of cloth clustered at the front into a fall of pleats, the way it is pleated today in the sari. Sometimes a wisp of shoulder scarf or fitted bodice can be detected. But the eye is always caught by a heavy, knotted, low slung girdle and almost bare breasts. Obviously the Indian woman's deep sense of modesty and proper behavior was not dependent on hiding her sex appeal.

Whether it was Persia or China or India, the East fed the mind and the emotions and delighted the senses. It lured the West. For in the West, most people's minds and emotions and senses were not being satisfied. It especially lured the people of Byzantium, where Christian culture lacked deep, strong roots.

15

While eastern Rome was being drawn into the Oriental world, western Rome was falling apart under the onslaught of masses of barbarians.

These invaders were largely Teutonic and Germanic tribes who had come south from the Baltic region several centuries before Christ. Stopped at the Rhine by the Roman Legions, they had spread eastward across Europe, north of the Rhine and the Danube.

In their old northwestern home, these Germanic people had not had horses. As hunters, herders, and fishermen in a cold land, they had dressed to conserve heat. Fur vests and leather and wool tunics had covered a linen undershirt. Legs and feet had sometimes been wrapped in skins. Women had worn long, warm skirts and sleeved blouses under heavy wool shawls. And the most aristocratic wrap had been a long, sweeping *rheno,* a fur cloak magnificently banded with contrasting furs.

But in the centuries they ranged along the northern frontier of the Roman Empire, their dress had changed.

Near the Black Sea, Germanic Goth tribes discovered the Scythian horseman and Scythian art. Compressed into buckle and brooch shapes, Scythian images of stags and lions and wolves had the explosive quality of cornered beasts. And the Germans, frustrated by Roman walls, adopted the Scythian art style for their own buckles and fibulae.

They had picked up trousers too. But they had styled theirs to suit men roaming the cold forests on foot, for only their nobles could afford horses. German pants were cut from sturdy cloth and were cross-wrapped below the knee with strips of cloth. Later the pants acquired belt loops and even fitted feet.

German weaving became more and more skilled until there were checks, stripes, and herringbones. And some Germans adopted the Gallic soldier's red saggum cloak, and Gallic hooded cloaks.

Then the Huns came out of Turkestan with yells, scarred faces, flashing earrings, shaggy goatskin trousers and long, belted coats of felt or leather.

The Germans were almost as horrified as the Romans by the new hordes' grotesquely scarred faces and by the garments of field mouse skins that were worn until they fell apart. The first wave of Huns went all the way to northern Greece and northern Italy. And though the raiders always raced back to camp with booty instead of moving in as conquerors, eighty years of Hun attacks proved to be the last straw for a tottering Roman Empire.

At first some Germans huddled inside the walls with the demoralized Romans. Then a Gothic chief, Alaric, sacked Rome and carried off 4,500 silk robes. No doubt dressing his nobles up like rich Romans enhanced Alaric's prestige. With this success, Germans grew more aggressive, attacking Huns as well as Romans.

Finally the Huns left. Too specialized to change their ways, they simply vanished back into the steppes when their greatest leader, Attila, died in 453.

When the Huns left, the Germans moved out to replace the Romans as the rulers of the West. Tribes like the Goths, Franks, Burgundians, Angles, Saxons and Vandals dominated Europe and then swept across north Africa.

The West the Germans took over had been drained and abandoned by the East. And without Rome's support, local authorities had lost power. Except for the clergy stranded in the provincial towns, visible figures of authority had disappeared.

Rome's marks of authority had been many and refined.

German marks of authority—gold neck torques and sweeping fur cloaks—were bold but few. Barbaric kings sometimes took the tarnished title of *Patrician of the Romans* and put on Byzantine regalia to build up their authority in the eyes of tribesmen, rivals, and subject peoples. And there may have been some wistful identification with the civilized Romans in the widespread adoption of Byzantine court dress by German chiefs. But the West was poor, and even the powerful found life hard, though probably not unsatisfying.

The centuries that followed have been called Europe's Dark Ages. But clothing suggests that these were hopeful, constructive years with a lusty pioneer quality. Gothic Queen Arnegonde's 6th century court dress was a colorful mix of barbaric and Byzantine dress: black leather boots, Germanic, cross-thonged, woolen hose and a short woolen tunic under a Byzantine tunic of indigo-violet satin. A boldly ornamented baldric (sword belt), slung over her shoulder and across her chest, glittered through the front opening of her belted, Byzantine red silk outer robe.

Her jewelry was bold, yet delicately worked. Earrings were of gold filagree. Circular pins were red and gold cloisonné. Gold threads had been worked into a pattern of rosettes for the magnificent banding of her red silk sleeves; but the rosettes were like rolling chariot wheels. And although she wore a Christian veil, it's unlikely that she felt shame in an uncovered head. For the Germans were by no means widely or deeply Christian.

Christians were obsessed with the evils of the flesh. Building on the need of early societies to protect the fidelity of the farm wife, and on the stern old Semitic laws about covering the body, the early Christians had turned the natural, animal function of sex—a prime necessity in the survival of the species—into the sin of sins. Any lingering pride in fertility was lost in shame. Sex became guilt-ridden. "You are the Devil's gateway," preachers thundered at women. Hating the body, which tempted them to sin, they covered it with long robes.

The Queen was probably only officially a Christian. But she was a pioneer. Her baldric and cross-wrapped hose suggest that she felt herself part of the rousing, comradely effort to build a new Europe out of good land and German energy.

Everyday clothing showed little class, age or sex distinction. Simple farm clothes lacked the glitter, dash and excitement of steppe dress, and the luxury of the dress of Mediterranean cities. They also lacked the bold color of Celtic dress; expensive dyes were used only for best clothes, which may have been bright red, green, or blue. But hitched-up homespun in natural grays and browns expressed the spirit that cleared the forests and planted the fields, preparing the way for Gothic cathedrals and the Renaissance.

In parts of what is now France and Germany, the rugged Franks set the pace in long-sleeved, girdled tunics: knee length for men, long for women. Underneath were undertunics, usually of linen. Sleeves were tight enough not to get caught in things. Necks were high for warmth. And many tunics had a useful hood folded down into a *cowl* around the neck, in the Gallic way.

Men wore cross-wrapped trousers below their girdled-up *gonelle* tunic. Women wore hose, cutting them on the bias from woolen cloth to get stretch. Men sometimes wore hose, too, pulled part way up over their trouser legs.

Clothes were durable and very precious. With limited resources, display had to be concentrated in small objects; and ornamental girdles and sword belts took on a value out of all proportion to their actual value. Tunics were lovingly decorated with bright patterned bands handwoven on tiny looms in the Byzantine or Persian style. Fashions didn't change fast, for women couldn't afford obsolescence in clothes as hard won as theirs. Made to last a lifetime, they were spun, woven and stitched at home from local wool. They may have reeked of stable, smoke, damp mustiness and sweat, but they were treasured, cleaned with ashes and carefully stored in chests when not in use.

The churchmen from Rome wore the long Christian tunics. But their influence on the Germans was at first too superficial to have much effect on the pagan attitude towards the body, and on the need for short, functional farm clothes.

But then Christianity was re-introduced to the Germans by people more like themselves. In the 6th century, Celtic monks arrived from Ireland in short tunics cut from plaids or from saffron cloth vividly decorated with Celtic cross-hatch and spiral designs. Their close fitting capes were brilliant patchworks of appliqued squares. Their Christian Cross had the old, dynamic, pagan spiral at its center. And their teachings had a barbaric vitality that touched the German spirit.

Next, Anglo-Saxon monks came from Britain. Although they came in the long Roman tunics, they had been strongly influenced by the Irish monks. Full of a dynamic faith, they rolled up their sleeves, hitched up their rough homespun tunics, and made their little monasteries models of self-sufficiency. They were a striking contrast to Rome's and Constantinople's churchmen who dazzled ordinary people with their symbolic purple and gold and red and blue silks. In the end it was the simple monks who won Europe over by practical example, not by awe.

By assuming the homespun simplicity of the farmer and his family, and by working as the peasant worked, the monks gave an aura of dignity to hard work and to humble clothes. And this tended to separate the West still further from the East. For the approval given to work eventually let an industrial middle class rise up between peasant and aristocracy.

Respect for the monks made people more willing to believe the Christian teaching about the evils of the flesh. And since the monks' long-skirted tunics and hooded cloaks piously hid the body, all body-concealing garments began to take on a new meaning. Women's long tunics held an aura of Christian virtue. Popular old hooded cloaks took on a new moral significance.

Actually the average German male could not admire a man who didn't fight or raise a family to keep the farm going. But Christianity had always given hope to the least privileged; and women began to flock to the Church. They started to swath their heads and shoulders for modesty more than for warmth; they began to hide their bodies under the big poncho-like *chasuble* cape the Church had evolved from the old paenula storm cloak.

As women became more and more involved in the teachings of the church, the wrapping built up towards the 13th century look of piety, when a woman's head was completely swathed in bandage-like scarves and veils.

16

As women were flocking to the Church in woolen or homespun, their men were attracted to the new men of action, the medieval knights.

When Rome stopped collecting taxes in gold in the 4th century, it was a sign of the general breakdown of central authority. Taking payment in produce (such as beef, which could not be shipped to Rome) meant a decentralization of the economy. And provinces like Gaul begun to turn back in on themselves. Rural self sufficiency became the main fact of life.

Many Germans in the Roman army had been paid in land. And as the Germans took over the government, western Europe was broken up more and more into agricultural communities and monasteries, with no central control or protection. Each unit produced what it needed. And as farming improvements made these units more productive and valuable, the people living in them became more vulnerable to attack.

Soon the traditional elite of dominant males or nobles—in this case the landowners—became the defenders of the land. The only Europeans able to rise out of the fields, workshops and kitchens were the noblemen, who poured their energies into horsemanship and skill at arms. They began to get heavy horses from the East. They experimented with light, flexible armor, linking metal rings into a mesh of *ring mail* or *chain mail* instead of sewing discs to their tunics. (*Mail* may actually have been invented by the Celts.) They turned the old conical leather cap into a steel helmet.

Protecting the workers, chasing off the cattle rustlers, clearing bandits out of the surrounding forests, fighting each other and sometimes the Church in land grabs, the knights began to dominate the land.

Events in the 8th century spurred the development of knighthood. The Islamic faith was moving into Europe. Carried at first by fanatical Bedouin horsemen, it had swept first through the Middle East and north Africa and then began to thrust up into Europe by way of Spain. And when it moved on up into France, it threw Europe into panic.

Centuries of living with the dark forests of the northwest had developed an imaginative intensity in the Germanic people. They saw monsters among the trees, demons in every storm. And their rural isolation in Europe heightened their superstitions. Knowing nothing at all about Moslems, they thought Moslems were the forces of evil in the forms of men.

Islam became a cause for both knights and churchmen. It was as Christian knights that a group of fighting men stopped the Moslems south of Paris, at Tours in 732 A.D.

As knights go, these were a motley lot. Only the wealthiest wore shirts of mail. Some had metal helmets; though most wound their own dyed red braids around their heads for protection. Most laced a leather vest—sometimes scaled with metal—over their customary girdled cloth tunic. They wore their usual cross-wrapped trousers, with cross wraps that had been dyed red for battle.

The knights' victory gave them self-confidence. The new stirrup let them put the power of the horse into their lances. Their new role as Defenders of the Faith, as well as protectors of the people, encouraged them to refine their chain mail, although not always their manner or their Christian virtues.

Paid in land for their efforts against Islam, the knights gathered more knights around them. As some grew land-rich and powerful, they began to mark their rank and might with dress, as the Church did. Gold, jewels, silks and furs lifted baron and bishop out of the homespun mass. And mail armor gave special distinction to the men who defended increasingly self-sufficient demesnes.

The developing Feudal estates were turned more and more in on themselves by Islam's control of the Mediterranean, which cut Europe off from much civilized contact. Only a trickle of silk got in through the port of Venice, now a little western outpost of Byzantium, and through Europe's back door to the East, the Danube. But the scarcity of silk stimulated Europe to improve its own woolen cloth, which already had a reputation for good, durable weaves and for a beautiful range of bright, vegetable dyes. Big, advanced Eastern looms began to appear in Flanders, quietly shifting weaving from cottage to factories, and keeping trade alive during centuries of feudalism.

People were working farms. They were building rough castles. Yet the spirit of Europe was still restless. Knights roved from estate to estate. Artistic energies went into the old traditional decoration of functional, portable things. Carving was lavished on clothes chests, not on buildings.

People still wore their wealth. Gold or silver was still turned into earrings, bracelets, fibulae, buckles and horse trappings.

But there was a difference. Before, metal ornaments had looked as if they had been designed by men thinking in wood or thinking in crude iron. Huge fibulae still clasped mantles, and their shapes still came out of barbarian tradition—spiralling rosettes, dagger-like T-shapes, birds, animals. But now the metalwork was sophisticated. Jewels and semiprecious stones and enamels were laid into gold cloisons as if they were tiny models for the later stained glass windows.

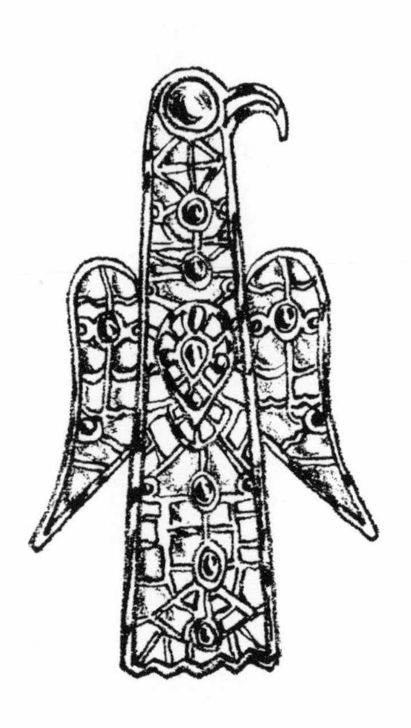

Slung low on the hips like a sword belt, in the military mode of the age, men's and women's cloth or leather girdles were embroidered and often set with precious metals, amber, carnelian, paste gems and rock crystal. Cloth circlets for the head were interwoven with gold and embellished with anything from precious stones to bits of polished glass. Women worked endlessly on the weaving of brilliant decorative bands to give color and dash to tunics and cloaks.

In the boisterous jumble of classes and ages and sexes in the great halls of castles, chaos might have occurred if nobles had not been able to create a feeling of authority around themselves. Though dressed basically like the servants, their bits of silk and magnificent furs marked them off just enough to make peasants keep their distance, and to give everybody a reassuring sense of social order. Bishops' silks had the same effect, making the elaborate hierarchy of the Church clearly visible.

In the insecurity of forests and small holdings, the sight of a mailed knight on his big horse made people feel protected. The knight was the outward, visible expression of a social system that was new to Europe, though old in the Iranian world. It was a system based on the power of strong men on horses, and it put the perfecting of mail above scholarship.

When Charlemagne came into power in 771, he wanted to combine the education, refinement and Christianity of Rome with the dynamic energy of the Germanic people. Together, he thought, they could make an empire that would be stronger and more humanly satisfying than the empire that had failed.

Charlemagne was king of the rugged Frankish tribes who had settled between Paris and the Rhine. At the age of eleven, he had commanded the escort when the Pope visited the Franks. The boy may have been deeply impressed by the Pope's glittering cloth-of-gold and shimmering silks. For when he came to power, he used clothes as bluntly and as enthusiastically as he used his sword. After he and his knights had extended Frankish rule over most of Europe, he was crowned Emperor of the West by the Pope. And for the occasion he put on Byzantine regalia to show his support of Roman civilization and Christianity.

His tunica on that day had gold-edged sleeves and was covered by a dalmatic and by several other garments, including a brocaded silk robe patterned with elephants and

a cloth-of-gold robe set with rubies. His scarlet leather shoes were brilliant with gold embroidery and emeralds. His gold crown was magnificently ornamented with jewels and enamel plaques.

But he wore this Byzantine regalia only twice in his life. Suspicious of softening luxuries, Charlemagne wore a simple Frankish tunic on normal days. His hair stayed long. And he cross-wrapped his trousers like any hunter or peasant. His favorite wraps were fitted coats of otter and marten fur. This is what he was: a tough, northern outdoorsman.

Charlemagne's clothes persistently showed his pride in his Germanness and in his vigorous body. And when he sent a state gift to the Islamic Caliph of Baghdad, he had the integrity to send the best symbol of what he was—a cloak of good Frisian wool, in scarlet and blue. And he was not intimidated by the gorgeous silk robes and elephants he received in return.

To convince his nobles of the foolishness of exotic silks and cloaks of pheasantskins and peacock feathers, he led a preening group of courtiers on a hunt through thickets and thorns and water. When their tattered elegance was shrinking by the fire, he simply shook out his own intact sheepskin.

He held his authority by setting himself apart with subtle touches: silk hem bands on tunics, a jewelled sword hilt, and a gold diadem on feast days.

He was dedicated to education and brought Church scholars from England for the court school. And he kept the scholars and students in long robes. He made his daughters visible symbols of civilized refinement, pampering them like dolls in his castles and smothering them in silks and jewels, even when they were out hunting. But barbaric tradition dominated.

Children had no chance to get soft. Boys and girls were dressed and treated like adults. A youth of sixteen could command an army or run an estate. At the ages of four and two, his own sons took their places as kings of the subkingdoms of Italy and Aquitaine. Tiny Louis of Aquitaine was carried to Orléans in a cradle. Then he was buckled into a miniature suit of armor and mounted on his horse. A two-year-old man rode into his kingdom.

One clothing item spoke of deep change in the Germanic spirit at this time, however. The fibula began to disappear. For centuries it had pinned on the uncomplicated clothes of restless, active men. Now laces and seams began to suggest men with more time to dress. The Germans were settling down.

But the old tribal spirit was still there. And after Charlemagne's death, rivalries flared up. Feudalism promoted strong lords and weak kings. Each lord had as many knights as he could support, and though all lords and knights owed homage to the king, they seldom paid it with more than lip service. Vassalage, an arrangement by which lords gave underlings land and protection in return for military service, created more knights; it established a hierarchy with social ranks ranging from squire to king.

This feudal Europe was still in a state of development when a challenge from the North almost destroyed it. Desperate for a more hospitable land than their own gloomy, dark regions, Norsemen (of the same barbarian stock as the German tribes) seized land, pillaged the coasts and captured people for the slave trade with Islam. They came from what is now Scandinavia in long ships with brilliant shields, red-striped sails and fierce dragons on their prows. A blood red mantle whipped back to expose the Norsemen's shaggy bearskin vest. And though he had a metal helmet and chain mail, it was his vigor and abandon that terrified people.

As a result feudal walls got thicker. Castles were made stronger with stone. And a poor man found it increasingly easy to choose to be a serf, who was protected by a noble and his knights, rather than a free man, who might be grabbed by the terrifying Vikings and sold to the even more terrifying Moslems.

The Norsemen were finally contented with a gift of land in Normandy. And their intermarriage with families in France and Germany soon led them to adopt Feudal ways. Norman knights became the best in Europe.

Further east, on the Dneiper River, Viking Swedes intermarried with Slavs and became known as *Rus*. Turning easily from piracy to a thriving trade with Islam, they exchanged slaves, fur and amber for the brocaded silks and the food-preserving spices so desperately wanted in Europe. Russia was trading while most of Europe was farming. They also traded with Byzantium and were converted to Christianity. This molded infant Russia in a Byzantine image, setting it further apart from the rest of Europe.

One by one, all the enemies of Christendom were contained or converted. The land was becoming safe. And peasants began to carry bits of surplus wool and linen into the little towns that were growing up outside old village or castle walls. Escaped serfs risked the dangers of unescorted travel to carry tradegoods. Old trade routes began to come alive again with French wools, Baltic furs and amber, wonderful brocaded silks and leathers from Islamic Spain and airy silks from the Middle East and the Orient. Wool from Flanders was now so beautifully made that Italians craved it almost as much as silk. And by the 10th century, lively fairs were bringing goods from everywhere together in the plains of France.

But with a settling Europe, the knights were running out of work. Trained only for fighting, educated only for battle, the knight was as dangerously over-specialized as the Hun had been, or the Scythian.

There were too many knights. There were too many baron's sons, and not enough land for them. Norman barons solved their problem in 1066 by conquering England. From there, they ranged as far afield as Sicily where they discovered a precious Islamic silk weaving industry. The old roving Viking spirit found a new outlet—sea trade. A spirited exchange of goods along the northwest coast of Europe was soon launched.

But landlocked barons had no place to expand except to each other's lands, and Church lands. The Church did what it could to protect its lands. It found work for the knights by offering indulgences to any who would ride off to Spain to help the Christians there throw out the Moslems. Then, at the end of the 11th century, Byzantium called for help. Islam was becoming too strong. And the

Pope issued a ringing call to a Crusade against the Moslems, who were threatening Constantinople and attacking Christian pilgrims in the Holy Land.

The knights were delighted. The Crusade not only gave them something to do, it sanctified their whole way of life; it squared their Christian conscience with their job of fighting and killing. It also offered them adventure in the fabulous East.

The call to a Holy War heightened the emotional excitement Europeans were beginning to find in the Church. By the mid-twelfth century, they were starting to build Gothic churches that seemed to soar up into infinity the way the Celtic spiral had spun out into space. Candlelight in the vast, shadowy interiors had the feel of heartening fires in a gloomy forest. Carved saints were dressed like themselves. And churchbells were scaring away the old, old pagan demons.

The Crusaders rode off in a wave of religious enthusiasm. Their symbol was a red cross of sanctified fabric, sewn to their tunic. And in the intensity of the time, their Cross seemed full of magic. Men believed that if they died wearing the Cross, they would gallop straight into paradise.

Because the Palestine sun turned their polished armor into a blinding glare, the knights protected their eyes by covering their coat-of-mail with a *surcoat*—a sleeveless, open-sided tunic. And they wore the Cross on the surcoat.

Chain-mail leggings, mittens, and hood had been added to the knee-length *hauberk*—the mail tunic split at front and back to allow riding. The body was sheathed from head to toe. And this metal skin had the flexibility and the living, moving, glinting quality of a salmon's body. It was a display of pride in a whole system, in a whole set of values.

But while the knight was glorifying the body in his new steel skin, others were trying to conceal the body. For as the first Gothic cathedrals went up, the hems of tunics were falling to the ankles all over Christendom. Even the surcoats that carried the knights' heraldic devices were dropping to the ankles.

Over the centuries, long dress had become more and more visible as monks, women, students, church officials

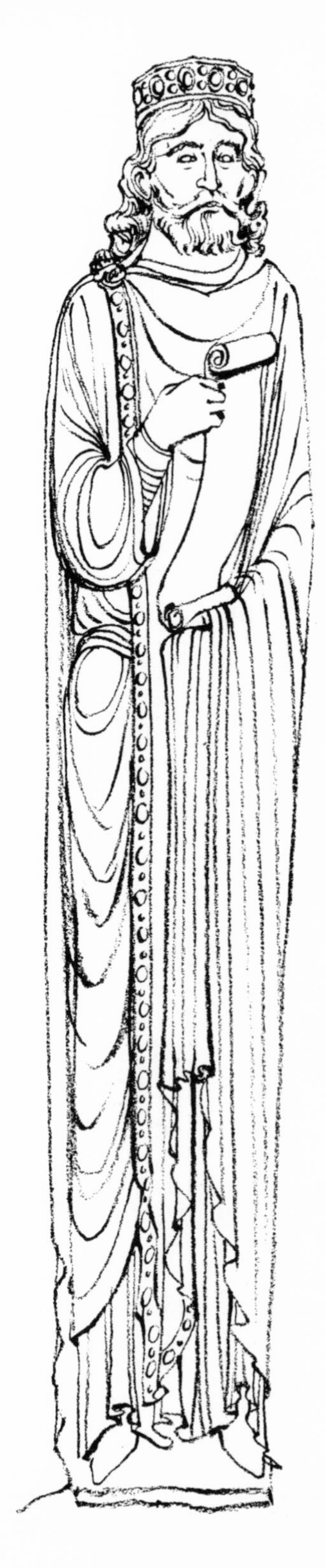

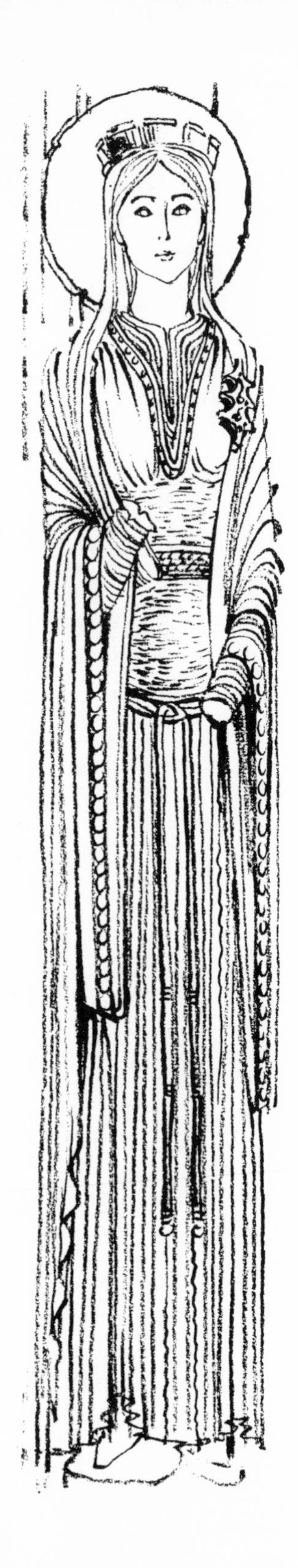

and nobles in ceremonial dress spread it over Europe. Cold weather and draughty castles made it practical. And by the middle of the 12th century, even the short working tunic of Frankish men gave way to an ankle-length tunic, putting everybody of both sexes into the body-concealing skirts of medieval Christianity.

Yet the body was not really concealed. This can be seen in the human figures that were carved into the portals of Gothic churches and that stood as saints at the altars.

At first glance, the carved kings and queens and saints seem to be in the standard, long, tight-sleeved undertunic and the loose-sleeved, dalmatic-like, outer tunic. But the wide sleeves of the women's outer tunics, or *bliauts*, drip extravagantly down to the floor. And instead of hiding the body under fully-bloused or free-falling lines, their tunic bodices are pulled in tightly across the chest; they are shaped by shirring, gathering, tucks and back-lacings to make the outline of the body and breasts very clear. Decorative girdles call attention to the abdomen. And soft fabrics—perhaps the airy silks brought back from the Crusades—let the folds fall in a gentle, feminine way.

In the 9th and 10th centuries, women had begun to flare and lavishly band the sleeves of their outer tunic in an exaggeration of the current Byzantine style. By the 11th century, the tunics of both sexes were narrowing through the chest. And a basic change had occurred; though it was almost hidden under the elaborate girdles of the day. The top was being sewn to the skirt. With that, skirts could begin to flare out with gores and gathers; tops could fit snugly. This bliaut tunic seemed a natural development for a northern people with a tradition of cut-and-sew and fit. And by revolutionizing the tunic that had never really moved far from the rectangle, the bliaut became the basis of the characteristic silhouette of Western women—fitted bodice and full skirt.

The decline of the fibula after Charlemagne's time had seemed to symbolize the fading of the old nomadic spirit. Perhaps the old barbarian identification with animals had been fading too. For in the same years, human figures had begun to replace plant and animal forms in decoration.

Monks had begun to enliven illuminated manuscripts with people; the figures were emotional and dynamic. Then sculptors had used human figures to decorate church portals, altars and apses.

In the second half of the 12th century, even the dropped hems couldn't suppress the body. And by 1200 A.D., says medieval scholar Thomas P. F. Hoving, in his introduction to *The Year 1200, Volume I,* "for practically the first time since ancient Greek and Roman times, draperies curl and caress the bodies underneath, and limbs are proudly and successfully shown as organic entities."

In the sculptures of the Cloisters' collection of Medieval Art in New York City, a 12th century portal sculpture of a submissive Vigin holding a sticklike infant Jesus in her lap, is pressed into a tall Gothic throne. She has still not broken free of church decoration. But her tunics (originally lively red and green) are molded to her body; and the outer bliaut has long, dripping sleeves.

But the Church had been thundering against worldliness and dress excesses since before the Crusades. And after plagues, Crusading disasters and great social upheaval, people seemed ready to hide themselves again. In the 13th century, loose, heavy, symbolic robes concealed the body. Hair is hidden under *wimples* and *gorgets.*

The wave of recession did not last long, however. A statue of a 14th century Madonna cuddles a baby Jesus in a red tunic on her hip. She stands completely clear of the church woodwork. And a huge, gold brocade shawl sweeps at an angle across her body, showing a new status symbol—a fur lining. Her outer garment is still simple. But the cloth is soft enough and girdled high and firmly enough to reveal her body. And the outer sleeve is fluttering and impractical again. The throat and hair are visible; in fact, a surprising amount of flesh shows at the neck and shoulders.

By this time the nobles, as well as the church, were trying to control excesses in dress. In a move to contain the rising merchant class, nobles were making laws that restricted the wearing of rich cloth and certain furs and colors to the aristocracy. But the bourgeoisie of the towns could often afford to dress better than the castle families,

The body emerges as Europe moves from the Middle Ages to the Renaissance. A group of French church sculptures clearly shows the body underneath the long gowns that had kept it shrouded since the beginning of the Christian era.

This 12th century madonna has extravagant sleeves, and a tucked and fitted bodice that hints at the human form underneath.

In the 13th century, plagues and Crusading disasters encourage the body to retreat again under shapeless gowns. Blousing dolman sleeves conceal sex.

But in this 14th century sculpture, the virgin swings her hips, hugs her child and displays flesh at her shoulders.

This sculpture of a saint indicates that religious inhibitions seem to have been abandoned in the late 15th century. The Renaissance is blowing up from Italy.

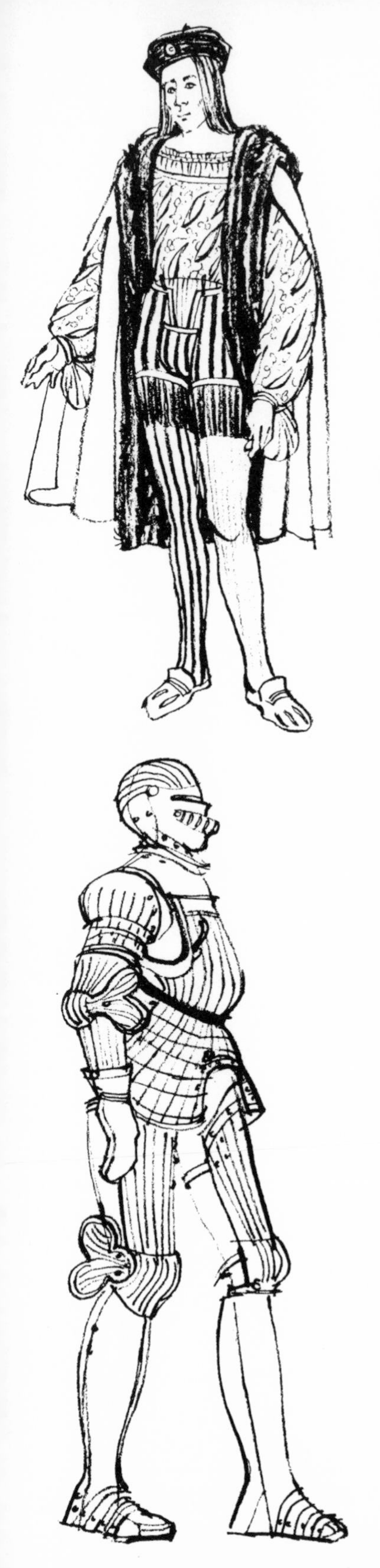

and the laws didn't work.

A late 15th century statue of St. Barbara completes the story in the Cloisters collection. She looks windblown, worldly, and beautiful. Masses of golden hair fall over her shoulders. Her head is crowned with a chaplet of flowers. A deep, square neckline and tightly fitted bodice shows off a very shapely figure. And St. Barbara's skirt is so long that it has to be attached to her wrist and lifted so that she can walk without tripping.

One glance at a picture or statue of a man of St. Barbara's time tells more about the Renaissance than any summary of cold facts. The true Renaissance man had ripped off centuries of long tunics. He had pulled himself free of the heavy coat-of-mail, which some diehard knights were still desperately patching with plates of metal to withstand gunshot. The Renaissance man was stripped down to what had been the knight's underwear—doublet and hose. (His trousers had disappeared under his armor, giving way to hose. And the fitted hip-length doublet had protected his skin under his hauberk.) He had shrunk his doublet and slashed its sleeves, letting his linen undershirt blouse out at waist, neck, and slashes. Further, he had taken the practical triangle of cloth that had covered his genitals before hose were sewn together into proper tights and had turned it into a display of male virility—the *codpiece*.

The sumptuous Renaissance silks and velvets of which the new male costume was made indicated that trade and diplomacy in cities and courts were the new scene for men of action.

The knight's day was done.

17

The medieval age might be dying in the West. But in the East it was still strong. Medievalism there was continually revitalized by invasions of semibarbaric horsemen, who forced the Byzantines to defend themselves and kept their knights active.

In the 10th century, the Turks moved out of the steppes and into Asia Minor and the Middle East. They spread east to India; and, bypassing Egypt, they spread west to Morocco. And they became Moslems in the process. As Moslems they adopted turbans and caftans. They added fantastic and real animal forms and human forms to the patterns that were woven into Persian silks. They used decorative armbands filled with Arabic script, but instead of using the static, upright shapes of early Arabic script, they used the cursive script. Its lively lines were a better expression of the wild spirit of Turkish Moslems.

They made their headquarters in Asia Minor, threatening Constantinople and giving Turkey its name. And under the influence of Mediterranean styles, their narrow steppe trouser gradually broadened into the balloon-like *chalwar,* the distinctive Turkish trouser.

The Turkish impact on Constantinople could soon be seen in the Byzantine Court's adoption of a long, belted tunic lined with beaver fur. It was added to the trousers and short Persian tunic Byzantium had already taken from the East.

In 1453 the fierce Ottoman Turks finally conquered Constantinople. And the Byzantium they took over was so Orientalized that they easily moved in and ruled. They wrapped the Turkish turban around the Greek skullcap to symbolize conquest.

The domination of much of the Islamic world by the Turks from the 10th to the 20th century was broken briefly but dramatically by the Mongols.

In 1206, a group of barbarian chieftains in a black felt tent at Karakorum in the Mongolian steppes made a young Mongol lord their *Ghenghis Khan*, or Universal Lord. At the same time they cut off tribute to the Chinese emperor, provoking him to war.

Still living up to the ancient steppe code of endurance, discipline, and mobility, and still dedicated to the horse, the Mongols had added heeled riding boots to the usual pants, insulating layers of tunics, sheepskin coats and metal-banded leather war helmets. Their women wore britches and rode astride like the men. And though the women didn't weave, they put a fine finish on felt by dragging it behind ponies.

Ghenghis Khan tried to hold his Mongols to a harsh code as they moved out of their own territory, conquering China and then venturing toward the west. Controlling his vast empire out of the black felt tents of his home base in Mongolia, he soon made the steppe costume all too familiar: fur-lined, knee-length, wrapped coat over a tight-sleeved caftan slit at the back for riding, trousers, heeled and quilted boots and fur cap. Fearing both luxury and the spirits of the streams, he forbade his men to wash their clothes. They had to wear them until they fell off in tatters.

Mongol coats often closed to the side instead of down the front. And although many outer coats had long sleeves, the typical Mongol coat had sleeves cut off at the elbow to keep the rider's wrist free and efficient. The tight sleeves of the caftan underneath provided the warmth he needed. Mongols often kept their fur hat even after they turned Moslem.

Mongol impact could be gauged by the spread of its

dress. Side-closing became a characteristic of coats and jackets throughout central Asia and most of the Orient. Outer sleeves were cut shorter in Persia and China. Heels were a step forward for horsemen everywhere.

Ghenghis Khan set up a courier and communications system that kept him in touch with the whole empire. His heirs, and especially his grandson Kublai Khan, linked East and West directly. They reopened routes the Turks had closed. Venetian merchants like Marco Polo could travel to China, taking back first hand reports of silk manufacture and fireworks. Chinese satins, brocaded cloud bands, lotus and peony blossom patterns and weaving techniques began moving westward again.

Enthralled by the splendor of the cities they had captured, the Mongols quickly lost their fear of luxury. Ghenghis Khan's heirs let caravans of cloth-of-gold and -silver, of sable and ermine and fox, of Chinese satins and Indian cottons pour into their camps. Soon the western Mongols became the legendary *Golden Hordes.* Though their coats kept their efficient fit and knee length, they were scrolled in gold arabesques. Gold turbans replaced shaggy fur hats.

Eastern Mongols showed a similar eagerness for Chinese dress. Kublai Khan wore the dragon robe; he made it his alone to wear and to award. And though his blue and gold robe was shorter than the T'ang robe, it had huge dragons writhing in the roundels that covered his shoulders. Its sleeves were wide enough to hide his folded hands.

As though, in turn, expressing the fresh vitality that had been brought in from the steppes, the Chinese Court took up side-closed Mongolian coats. The Mongols linked China to the world. They spread out by sea as well as land. And with her advanced technology, China could have had an overseas empire. But she didn't value commerce and progress enough to exploit her opportunity.

Medieval Asia from the Levant to China had a sense of balance that the West has never understood. It kept mind, body, and senses so satisfied that there was little desire for change. The balance between physical vigor and cultural refinement had grown naturally out of the conditions of life. Much Islamic and Oriental territory was basically hot

and harsh. Survival demanded toughness and endurance. In compensation, the oasis (courtyard, silk pavilion, caravan city, filigreed palace) provided refreshment with fountains and fragrant gardens, exquisite arts, and fastidious manners. The contrast between riding boots and harem silks, between battles and rose gardens, gave aristocrats the stimulation that holds men to a way of life.

Islam finally penetrated India too, though it took a mixture of Turkish and Mongol blood—the Mughals—to take the Mohammedan faith and Persian styles into India in the 16th century. Conversion was often superficial, though. The bulk of India stayed Hindu. And native dress gradually changed Mughal dress, rather than the other way around.

But the Mughal impact did bring to the upper classes throughout India the tradition of the long-sleeved, fitted caftan and the tapered Persian trousers that have developed (with some English influence) into the fitted, knee-length, high-necked "Nehru" coat and *jodphur* trousers of today.

Yet it still did not mean a denial of Indian dress. For loose *pajama* trousers had been worn with sleeved over-tunics for centuries in northern India, where there was continual contact with the steppe men. And the coat and trousers never reached the masses in draped cottons.

India has always seduced foreigners. And the dress of the Mughal rulers soon took on a sensual Hindu quality, a dreamy, gauzy look. Caftans began to be made of sheer cottons and silks; and the vivid colors of Persia gave way to soft blues, yellows, pinks, and greens. Caftan skirts took on the fullness of the *jamah* (the dress with gathered skirt) that was often worn underneath. And caftan girdles ended in a heavy spill of decorated cloth down the front. Trousers became full and soft. And the Indian love of tinkle and glitter led the Mughal lords to an unsurpassed use of jewels, pearls and ornament.

Islam confirmed India's own tradition of covering women, however gossamer the covering. The sari grew to a six yard long wrapping, which even upper class women began to wear over a full skirt and bodice.

When the relentless horsemen of Islam carried their faith and their dress west across north Africa, they carried them to a people not rooted so deeply in an ancient, distinctive and satisfying way of life, to a people who had simply worked out a way to survive under the most difficult of conditions. An ancient movement of peoples along the narrow northern coastal strip of Africa had left a band of swarthy Caucasians occupying the entire area. And as these people picked up the agricultural and herding skills of Egypt, hemp loincloths, skin mantles and massed ornament gave way to linen and cotton rectangles, oxhide tunics and sheep and goathair wraps.

The fertile strip these people held became a very desirable property in the Mediterranean world. Its grain, vineyards, olive groves, orchards and grazing lands were an unending lure. Its mysterious access to the gold and ivory and pelts from inner Africa drew traders and armies from all civilizations.

Conqueror after conqueror overcame the tribes hemmed in between the sea and the Sahara. And native chiefs who traded with the conquerors took on successively the dress of the Phoenicians, Assyrians, Greeks, Romans, and Persians. Finally, the whole area gradually took on sewn rectangular and T-shaped tunics, caftan coats and big draped shawls.

But life was not easy and the desert was the traditional place of escape from foreign domination. Berber tribes often fell back into the Sahara to gather their forces and harass their conquerors. Like steppe barbarians, desert warriors could hit and run back to safety. Then when they learned to use the camel, about 200 A.D., many moved right into the desert, where no one would follow them. Making their homes in the oases, they actively began to crisscross the vast Sahara along the very ancient caravan routes.

But the desert was a harsh master, too. Only complete adaptation to its conditions let the men of the desert survive. Yet its oases fed them and grew hemp, cotton and flax to mix with the wool and hair of their sheep, camels and goats. From these the Berbers wove insulating layers of

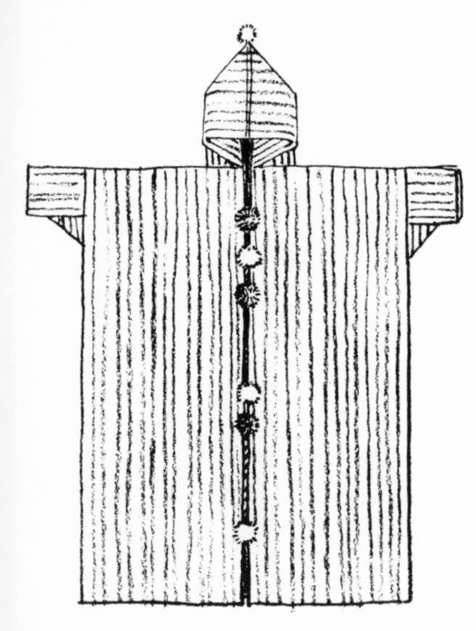

loose tunics and robes in simple, bold, geometric patterns, mainly stripes. They made rectangular head cloths and shawls big enough to seal in the head and shoulders and protect the body during sandstorms.

Berber garments suggest that the Romans had had more impact on north Africa than any other conquerors, though Roman-like garments are so right for the desert that they would probably have developed locally if they had not been brought in. The Berber shirt is like the rectangular Roman tunica. Wide-sleeved, dalmatic-like tunics are common. Algerian women still have ribbon clavii running down the front of their tunics. The Berber *djelaba*, usually of striped wool, is a big, hooded rectangular cloak very like the old hooded cloaks of Europe. The outer Berber wrap—often the fourth layer—is a monstrous rectangle, a voluminous blanket like the pallium. And the *burnoose* is identical in shape to the Roman paenula—the big, circular, hooded stormcloak that became the chasuble of the Church.

Islam arrived in Berber territory in Arab dress in the 7th century. The Arabic insulating layers of loose tunics and robes, with turban and trousers, had the same basic look of voluminous, undefined garments, the same flow of cloth back beyond the saddle that Berber dress had. It was dress the Berbers could adopt easily. And after a spirited resistance, most accepted Islam and let Islam's loose garments improve their own desert dress.

The Arabian trousers, essentially wide sacks with leg holes at the outer edges, adapted well to the Sahara. The turban merely formalized the headwrap Berbers had already found essential to desert travel. Islamic concealment of the body merely added moral significance to what was basically the same old layering of loose, protective clothing.

Berber women were already wearing the *haik*, a huge rectangle that could be draped and pinned and tied in as many ways as the Egyptian kalasiris. To obscure the body, as Islam dictated, they simply draped and pinned and tied their haik in the same way they had always arranged it for a standstorm. In public, they pulled the cloth across their face, showing only their eyes.

But changes in dress did not go only one way. The

Arab, in turn, adopted the burnoose as a graceful, body-concealing cloak. Islam restricted the white burnoose to the elite, and billowing white silk, gold edged burnooses soon clothed wealthy sheiks. Damascus steel swords and new trade with Islam let some Berber groups grow into a powerful silk-robed elite.

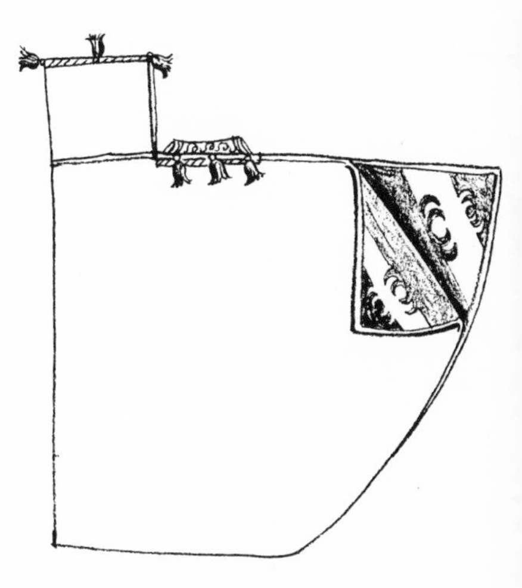

The burnoose and the haik have remained the basic look of the Arab–Berber world of north Africa. A large part of the strength of the burnoose is its suitability to the north African climate and way of life. Shadowing a man's face with its hood, it streams out over the back of his horse when he rides. And when he strides through a city, it flows back with grace and a look of power.

Today the burnoose is disappearing along with the pride in the old unprogressive ways it represented. In an article on the "stately cloak" in Morocco, the *New York Times* reported in December, 1969, that "almost nobody is wearing a burnoose today around the Rabat Hilton Hotel, where Arab leaders have gathered . . ." Though zeal to keep at least some of the old ways "prompts Morocco's young King Hassan II to wear a white burnoose over a traditional, ankle-length shirt on ceremonial occasions," he was wearing a "business suit and a sporty topcoat" for his meeting with King Hussein of Jordan. "Some lesser Moroccans feel a measure of scorn for their father's wardrobes," the *Times* noted.

Western business suits are replacing the burnoose symbolically in the cities, while trucks and airplanes are threatening it functionally in the desert. But the burnoose (paenula, chasuble) may prove too useful and too graceful to be allowed to die. "Some well-born Rabat women have taken lately to wearing burnooses as evening wraps," the *Times* reported.

18

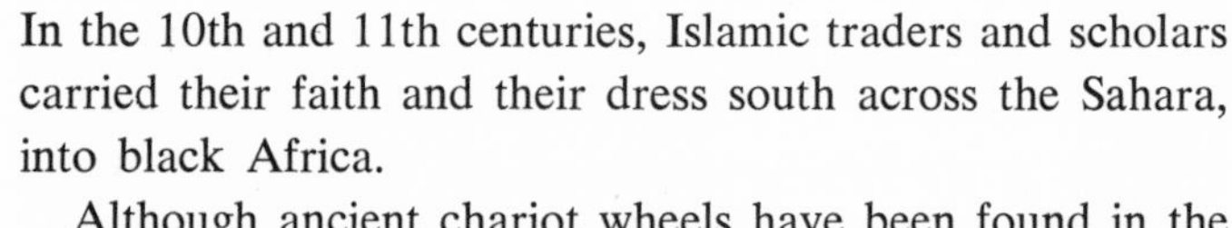

In the 10th and 11th centuries, Islamic traders and scholars carried their faith and their dress south across the Sahara, into black Africa.

Although ancient chariot wheels have been found in the Sahara, the Arabs seem to have been the first known aliens to penetrate deeply into Africa. Usually foreigners could get what they wanted without venturing into the continent itself. Grain, gold, ivory, jewels and animal skins always appeared on the north and east coasts of Africa from some remote source as if by magic.

To the ancient civilizations, Africa consisted of Egypt, a coastal fringe flanking Egypt on the Mediterranean and Red Seas and a terrifying region of black men and wild beasts beyond.

Even to Egypt, Africa beyond her borders was a wild and primitive world. The Egyptians revelled in the lion and leopard pelts they imported from such places, and in the gold and ostrich plumes and perfumes, in the ivories and ebonies and giraffe tails that came. But the animal elements in African dress and culture seemed to make Egyptians uneasy. In contrast to the gentle feather and flower patterns of Egypt, Lybians painted their oxhide mantles with bold splotches and stripes and zigzags that brought wild leopards and tigers and zebras frighteningly to mind.

When a Nubian princess and her retinue came to Egypt

to pay tribute, she came in Egyptian clothes. But 14th century B.C. wall paintings show a wild animal tail hanging from the caped sleeves of her new kalasiris. Leopard skins cover the Egyptian linen her men wore. And there are bold spots and stripes on the skin kilts and the wrapped skirts of her serving men and women.

Wild animals were part of the nature of Africa. Africans worked leopard, sable, zebra, giraffe, antelope, cowhide and other skins so beautifully that African furs and leathers were coveted like Chinese and Persian silks. But foreigners did prefer to pick them up at the coast.

Great east-west belts of land—coastal strip, desert, grassland, jungle—were part of the nature of Africa, too. They separated the continent into distinctive bands of territory, and strongly influenced native dress and its movement.

South of the Sahara, black skin took the place of clothes as a basis for display. It carried brilliant colors and pattern without being overwhelmed as a paler skin might have been. Instinctively making the most of their racial characteristics, Negroes played up their dark skin, their height and their frizzly hair. And they achieved stunning effects.

They exaggerated the darkness of their skin by applying contrasting, magic-making red and white paint. Their ivory bangles and ostrich plumes were a shock of white on black. And the white, yellow, red and intense blue geometric patterns on their palmcloth and cotton sarongs vibrated against their skin.

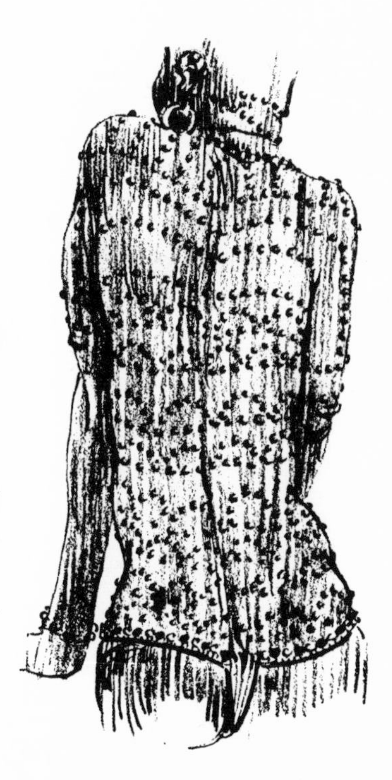

They oiled their skin to give it the luster of polished ebony. And just as the Chinese had raised a pattern of threads to capture the luster of silk, Negroes brocaded their skin with tattooes and patterned scarification.

They increased their natural height with lofty hair styles, plumes and high, wrapped headdresses. Rectangles were knotted at waist or shoulder to fall in long shafts of cloth. Heavy spirals of metal circled arms and wrists and ankles, marking slim joints. And some women made a cult of height, stretching their necks so high with permanent bands that they died of a broken neck if the bands were taken off.

Others extended both height and width, fattening them-

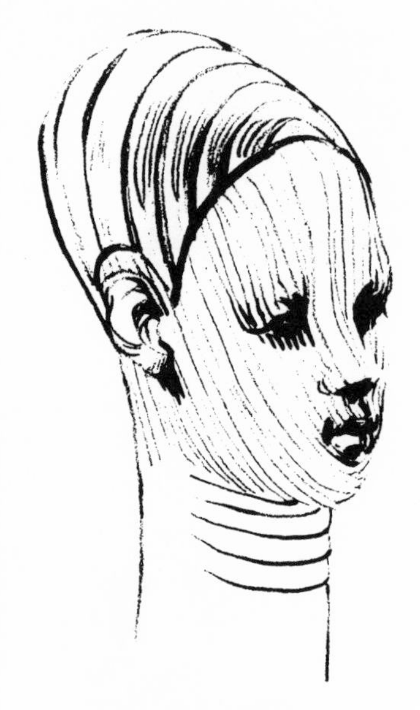

selves to a monumental size. Girls sipped sweetened milk in fatting houses and then put on layers and layers of skirts and mantles to look even better.

Black Africans sculptured their mass of hair, carving and controlling it into a variety of shapes, dictated by tribe, a rank or fashion. Since it didn't fall like Caucasian and Oriental hair, they exaggerated what it did do. Some worked it into tiny braids, which they oiled to look like stiff strings of black beads. Others cropped it short, leaving small tufts, which they worked with shells and beads into an intricately sculptured skullcap. Hair was carved into tiers of waves. It was shaped back from the forehead and up into a tall dome like Pharoah's crown.

Africa provided rich resources for achieving striking costumes: exotic pelts, cotton, hemp, palm fiber and oil, copper and gold that could be picked up in nuggets, precious and colored stones, shell and bone and ivory, feathers, ochre, indigo, saffron.

South of the Sahara, lying between the desert and the equatorial jungle, was the pleasant savannah belt of the Sudan. Negro tribes had always moved easily across the open Sudan. Ideas and techniques even flowed down from Egypt or in through the Red Sea ports and swept west. Five hundred miles wide and three thousands miles from east to west, this vast grassland invited movement, like the steppes. And because it did, origins of things like cotton are hard to trace.

But cotton, whether it originated east or west, was part of the Sudan. West Africans were cultivating it and weaving it thousands of years before Christ. And the knee-length, sarong-wrapped, cotton loincloth was, and is, a basic garment of black Africa.

West African indigo-dyed cotton was traded for ages across the Sudan and out of Red Sea ports, or picked up by camel caravans from the Sahara. It made Kano, a city of northern Nigeria, famous. Kano cloth still ranges from a delicate sky tint to a rich blue-black. And the complete range of color can be seen in some sarong cloths that have been tied into knots and repeatedly hand-dipped in indigo.

Others are decorated with an intricate batik-like process. Apart from the universal appeal of blue and the availability of the indigo plant, its continuing popularity is easy to understand. For the rich blues seem to glow against the glossy brown of dark skins. And the effect is magnificent.

Bazaar stalls in Ghana and Nigeria are still piled high with bolts of blue cotton. And a blue skirt cloth is still given to wives to celebrate the birth of a child. Berber Tuaregs still cross the desert to get the cloth, which has rubbed so much color off on their swarthy skins that they are known as "blue men."

Skins, with cotton, were basic to dress. In fact, thousands of years ago Africans were doing what our fashion industry is doing now—patterning short-haired cowhide to look like leopard or giraffe. In Africa, sable cloaks were common. The rarest and best furs marked rank and status. Men in full warpaint wore magnificent leopardskins on their backs. In a battle on Lake Victoria, reported by Dr. Livingstone, officers with snow white ostrich plumes on their heads had snow white, long-haired monkey fur or goatskin around their loins. Lances were ornamented with feathers and with rings of white monkey fur.

Because of the climate, the African use of fur and hide had more to do with magic and display than with warmth.

Even today, cowhide makes a tall Masai herder a dramatic shaft against the tawny gold of his East African landscape. His brown cowhide is cut and sewn into a lean wrap, knotted on one shoulder. Even if his wrap is a rectangle of cloth, it is heavy and often mottled with ochre to look like cowhide. His hair is dusted with red ochre. Huge copper rings hang from his ears and neck. And though his basic dress is as functional as a Greek shepherd's himation, the Masai's self adornment goes far beyond function. It ties him magnificently into his land.

South of the African savannah, pleasant wooded country gives way to a tropical rain forest. And south of this is a repeat, in reverse and on a smaller scale, of the belts north of the equator. In some of these belts, small pockets of people have managed to hold on to the original hunting, food gathering way of life. Displaced by the tall Negro as

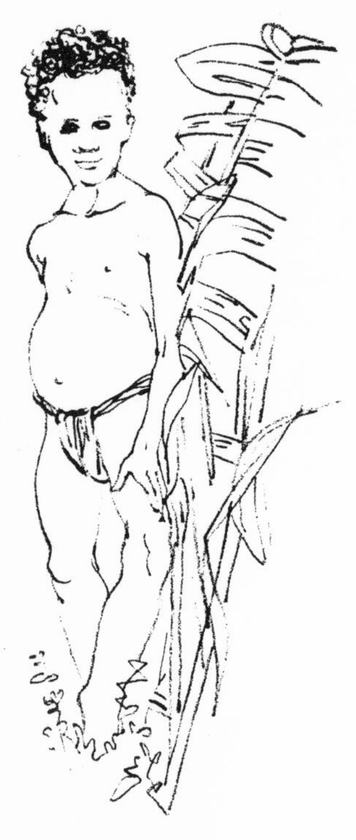

he expanded over Africa, naked Bushmen and Pygmies still show us what the other tribes were once like.

In a recent photograph, a Bushman's wife sits drilling a hole in an ostrich eggshell bead by spinning a sharpened stick between her hands. Hundreds of the tiny beads have been strung into her necklaces, into the narrow girdle slung low on her bare hips and into small circles hung from her ears and attached to her cropped hair so that they fall in white rings across her black forehead. More beads are twined with glossy leaves into armbands. She has no real garments. But an irregular piece of soft leather is wrapped around her shoulders and tied with leather thongs, leaving her breasts bare. And a large amulet hangs around her neck.

Like the earliest hunter's wife, she has taken what she needs from the simple things around her. And no doubt she draws magical protection, delight, dignity, tribal pride, and a feeling of beauty from her bits and pieces.

Highly tuned to his environment, her husband has intuition, delicate senses, speed, and hunting skills that let him bring down elephant and antelope with Stone Age weapons. He still lives with that sensitivity to nature that keeps him in harmony with his land.

But Bushmen are disappearing. As early as three or four thousand years before Christ, Nubians and Ethiopians in East Africa were pushing them inland and southward. And a great surge of Bantus (the dominant Negro race today) further displaced them after 500 A.D.

The people who displaced the Bushmen did much to change the ways and dress of Africa. Always in touch with Egypt and other civilizations, the eastern end of the Sudan early pulled ahead of its neighbors. One state, Meroe, was relaying eastern ideas west across the grasslands several centuries before Christ.

Nubia and Ethiopia grew into Christian states after Byzantines and Egyptian Copts came in with dalmatics and copes (hooded chasubles) in the 4th century. A 7th century Nubian church painting shows tunics with clavii and side-clasped chlamys mantles. Ethiopians claim their ancestors won battles by hurling cut-and-sewn gowns and beautifully wrought jewelery at primitive enemies to awe them into surrender. And even today Ethiopia has vestiges of chasubles, togas, dalmatics, and Persian-Byzantine trousers in its dress. A basic national garment, the *shamma,* a rectangle with colored borders, is draped with the massive dignity of a toga or pallium.

But Ethiopia was isolated and Nubia's Christianity was gradually swallowed up by Islam, so Christian dress did not sweep across the savannah. Dalmatics and palliums did quietly flow westward, though, enriching Africa's own developing dress.

In the western end of the Sudan, among Nigerians, Congolese, Ghanians, and their neighbors, dress had developed into well-structured patterns. There, the stages of life were carefully marked off and celebrated by the taking on of new garments. The nakedness of the infant gave way to the skin apron or the grass or bead girdle of childhood. A small loincloth and amulets announced puberty. A large skirt of cotton or palmcloth was put on with marriage. And layerings of cloth, massed beads and bangles, ceremonial robes and feathers marked the climb up the social ladder.

Unlike the Christians, these people were not ashamed of their flesh. Nakedness and bare breasts were common and comfortable. Sexual taboos and enhancement of fertility did cover up parts of the body and give tribal groups their own sense of modesty. But when Africans piled on layers of clothes, it meant status, not guilt. When a Congolese woman tied three tiers of palmcloth sarongs around her waist, it was to say that she was aristocratic, married, and wealthy. When she put on palmcloth bodices centuries before the Christian missionaries arrived, it was to lift herself above the bare-breasted masses.

Palmcloth was a step up from the early hunters' skin and grass girdles. An ancient, tropical, vegetable equivalent of felt, it was made by beating palm bark into a fabric that was often as soft as silk. Pieces were glued together into sarong lengths, much as tapa cloth is still made in the South Seas. Or the bark was beaten into net for airy mantles, which gave dignity without warmth. But even when they advanced to palmcloth, African men swung zebra tails from their shoulders. And over their genitals they suspended delicate little animal pelts: baby tigers, sables, martens, or civet cats.

Where cotton grew, north of the Congo, tribes gradually moved on to woven rectangles. But whether of cotton, palmcloth or coarse hemp cloth, African garments were essentially simple, draped rectangles. Yet, as Egypt and Greece proved, simplicity did not have to mean backwardness. Like them, Africa used the rectangle with imagination and flair. With it, they established tribal identities and the social ranks of rapidly complicating societies.

In the savannah, native dress may have reached its peak of development among the Yoruba tribes in the 10th to 15th centuries. Discovery of magnificent bronze sculptured figures at Ife, the center of Yoruba religious and cultural life, has made scholars realize how advanced Yoruba art was. It is ranked now with the great art of the world.

Yoruba costume on the sculptures shows a high state of social and technological sophistication. A king and queen wear single, knotted-on skirtcloths. The king's is wrapped around his waist. The queen's is tied up under her armpits. Both are heavily hung with beads, bracelets and anklets. It sounds very primitive, but it is not.

The cotton rectangles on the real king and queen were held up by sashes so elaborately knotted that they went far beyond function to become important display and rank markings. The heavy torque-like bands at neck, wrists, and ankles were of gold, copper, brass, or bronze, cast or wrought with great skill. Though some of the beads were of local red stone, many were of colored glass from a thriving native glass industry, in peacock, turquoise, deep green, red, olive brown. And ivory ornaments were so exquisitely carved that they still have few equals anywhere.

The effect must have been dazzling. But it was not a haphazard heaping on of glitter. Every knot, every ornament, brimmed with symbolism. Face markings on the sculptures may indicate the bead fringe that covered the faces of kings and isolated them from ordinary tribesmen. The figures carry symbols of authority: a beaded cowtail fly-whisk, a medicine horn. Small caplike crowns of tiered beads have knoblike insignia at the front. This king and queen represented the top of a big hierarchical pyramid, a pyramid supported by a wide base of naked slaves.

Islamic dress drifted into the Sudan with traders' camel caravans and with Arab scholars from about the 11th century, and it spread rapidly. As trade with Islam swelled the wealth, personal power, and worldliness of African kings, they began to adopt Islamic silks and wide flowing robes. The kings' court dressed in fine Egyptian cottons.

States right at the end of the Sahara trade routes were touched first. The men of Timbuktu quickly put on the flowing robes that were always the mark of the Moslem in black Africa. And Jenne, a little south of Timbuktu, became a center of Islamic culture and dress, dominated by Negro scholars.

A medieval splendor began to develop just south of the Sahara. Coats-of-mail were added to warpaint, and a glittering elite cavalry of semiprofessional warriors gave the kings the reliable armies they needed to keep their growing state under control. The sheik who commanded this cavalry wore layers of white muslin *tobes* (basic Arabian long shirts), a billowing white silk burnoose, and an Indian cashmere shawl wrapped into a turban. When his wives rode with him, they rode astride, swathed in silk burnooses.

But Moslem dress had not taken over. Glittering Negro knights in chain-mail tunics were trailed by foot soldiers carrying clubs and spears and dressed in only a goatskin belt.

And in Mali, a 13th century Berber visitor was aghast to see beautiful Negro Moslem women, free and unveiled, dressed only in sarongs of fine cotton. The king's daughters and his female servants were naked. His four wives and hundred slave girls were dressed in beautiful silk robes. Their silver and gold hair filets were hung with tiny silver and gold balls.

The arrival of the King was heralded by musicians playing gold and silver guitars, and by drummer boys in red

Nigerian dress continues its evolution up from animal skins and palmcloth. West African dress was rich with royal and tribal tradition long before Europeans arrived there. Even Portuguese doublets, Islamic silks and English hats have not halted its creative development.

This royal couple from 14th century Ife wears cloth skirtwraps, glass beads and bronze ornament.

In the 17th century, the old skirtwrap is almost hidden by the red flannel shirt derived from a Portuguese doublet.

An Itsekiri tribesman wears a combination of boater and buttoned shirt with beads and silk skirtwrap. But an Ibo man in massive agbada has taken only what he needs from desert horsemen, tribal tradition and from Europe.

woolen tunics and white skullcaps. Three hundred armed slaves escorted him. The king was brilliant in a red tunic and gold skullcap. And he held audience on a silk-carpeted platform, surrounded by silk cushions and shielded by an umbrella-like silk pavilion with a golden bird on top.

Before approaching him, subjects took off their court dress and replaced it with worn clothes. They replaced their turbans with dirty skullcaps. Then they approached with their baggy Arab pants raised knee high. They prostrated themselves before their king, knocked the ground with their elbows, and then stood with their heads humbly bowed. Whenever the king spoke, men took off their turbans and threw dust over their heads and bare backs.

Black African adoption of Islamic dress wasn't a wistful, awkward imitation. They changed the basic aba and tobe into a variety of garments. They gave the tobe a distinctively African shape by sewing together the narrow strips of indigo blue cotton that they had woven and sewn into larger rectangles for centuries. And as the most advanced states in West Africa began to reach the point of shift from top prestige for physical power to top prestige for physical inactivity—wealth, leisure, politics—the rich and powerful began to combine their own draped rectangles with the Islamic sleeved robe to achieve a big, weighty, suitably encumbering garment.

The medieval Sudan compared favorably with medieval Europe. For the average man, the standard of living was about the same. Iron tools cultivated the land. Progressive Africans pushed unprogressive neighbors out of the way. Knights kept the trade routes open and fought battles. And tribes consolidated into big states with central authority and well organized trade. In fact, a few great states were well on their way towards high civilization when the Europeans arrived.

But Africa relied mainly on Islam for the kind of outside stimulation Europe got from many sources. And after the 15th century, Islam began to settle back into reaction and orthodoxy. As a result, Africa, too, began to lag in progress.

Yet the continuing evolution of African dress—while Islamic dress stayed as it was—shows a progressive spirit. African dress moved on to garments like the spectacular *gbariye* and *agbada,* which Nigerian men still wear over loose shirt and trousers. Based on the old rectangles of sewn together strips, the gbariye achieved an immense spread of skirt by the insertion of pointed panels, or gores. And even greater mass was added by sewing on huge, flaring sleeves. The agbada had immense sleeves. which folded back onto the shoulders, piling up a great mass of cloth. As garments, both were far more highly developed than the Islamic robes that inspired them.

Late in the 15th century, the Europeans came to the west coast of Africa with sailing ships, overwhelming weapon power and an air of unquestioned superiority.

The familiar tragedy of culture contact took place. One group moved in on another, its superior weapons and technology subduing and awing the natives. And trusting its eyes, the less advanced group lost confidence in itself and in the ways it had developed to meet its own conditions. One of the first signs of demoralization was the eager search for bits of alien clothing, as though the clothes held contagious magic.

As so often happens, loss of pride in old ways resulted in a desperate scramble for new prestige. Negro kings and chiefs became eager accomplices in the slave trade the Europeans promoted.

There had always been tribal wars, and slave capturing had always been a sideline for tribal warriors. But suddenly it became big business. Africans may have captured fifteen million of their own kind and sold them into slavery on the plantations of the West Indies, and later the United States and South America. Coastal kings sold men for guns and dress goods and brass bangles. Greedy ambition threw many tribes into panic.

City-states like Benin grew powerful with the guns they got in payment for slaves. The Court of Benin decked itself out in finery from the holds of Dutch ships: cloth-of-gold and -silver, scarlet cloth, fine linens and cottons,

starched and flowered Dutch fabrics, lace ruffs, red velvet, violet embroidery silk, red glass earrings, gilt mirrors, crystal beads, brass bracelets and coarse flannel.

Islamic silks, light and loose and big had made sense for African ceremonial robes. But form-fitting velvet doublets and hose in heat-absorbing black or purple were out of harmony with the nature of Africa. So were stiff lace ruffs, tight at the neck. And traditional dignity began to give way to an unnatural pomposity.

Before, there had been almost universal awe for the majestic presence of black kings. But soon there were reports of barefoot kings in crowns shaped like Spanish helmets and in doublets with rusty gold and silver lace. There was amused contempt for courtiers who ate raw meat from gold plates while wearing doublets and breeches inside out and backwards, or while wearing brocaded discards from the Court of St. James.

Kings grotesquely exaggerated old marks of prestige. In Benin, the royal bead necklace grew so wide that it covered mouth and ears. A Bornu king carried the tradition of bulk to extremes by wadding his stomach and draping himself with a dozen layers of robes. He boosted his ego with an unnecessarily large, glittering retinue of courtiers and servants. He carried ritual isolation to absurdity by hiding in a cagelike pavilion that dripped with silks and satins. And he tried to outdo his co-ruler, an Islamic sheik, by keeping more women and by wrapping his head in an immense turban that turned it into a ridiculous globe.

Distortion of old styles and bizarre mixing of styles didn't extend much beyond the courts at first. And they didn't reach far inland. But the increasing need for slaves drove both European and Islamic slave traders inland. And as they took cheap cottons into Africa, they replaced the old handsome skirt cloths with slavers' shoddy versions of western dress. Though the majority of Africans kept their own tribal stateliness with their geometrically patterned cloths tied at the waist or knotted on one shoulder, the groundwork had been laid for the shift from African dress that came later with colonization.

Slave dress is a separate and even sadder story for the student of dress.

Like prisoners, slaves on the plantations were issued standard, cheap, shapeless cotton garments. Once a year the men were given overalls and shirts; the women were given calico shifts. Children were kept naked until they were four or five. Then they were given shifts.

For people accustomed to tribal ornament, beautifully worked skins, and stunning African pattern, the tasteless, standardized garments must have been as demoralizing as the whips and the hard work. Plantation owners exploited the Negro craving for better dress by offering hand-me-downs to men who learned specialized skills and to women who produced good slave babies, or who kept the plantation silver well polished.

In the 19th century, European colonial domination of Africa cut the continent into arbitrary chunks, with no respect for traditional boundaries. The great, open, living space of Africa was hacked up into political divisions that chopped tribes in half and threw ancient enemies together.

Colonial administrators, missionaries, and a new class of Africans, educated in Europe, completed the job of destroying much of Africa's pride in traditional dress.

Cotton plants from America replaced native plants. British Indian-woven cottons began to displace African cotton. Plaid and striped *Madras* was brought in, and *khaki,* the earth colored cloth the British Army adopted in India. These were a serious blow to the local handwoven cottons. The native cloth now began to seem coarse and crude in comparison with factory cloth. And except in villages, or for ceremonial wear, hand weaves started to disappear. Today, tourists searching for authentic African sarong clothes to take home, often wind up with cotton woven in England and printed in India in pseudo-African designs and colors.

In the 1950s, young Africans with western suits pushed Africa into westernized nation states that followed col-

onial boundaries. Yet this has brought a return to African dress. Narrow strips are handwoven and sewn into Yoruba gbariye or into a Ghanian *Kente cloth* (a huge rectangle worn like a toga). And they are worn with pride by most men on special occasions, and by diplomats.

But tribal dress fights a strong move towards the western dress that goes with westernized business and industry. Suits dominate the city streets. Nylon dresses have proved practical factory garb.

The conflict of old and new can be seen most vividly in Nigeria. There, the suit and western dress are thwarting an inventive development of native dress that survived the impact of Islam and slavers and colonialism. For Nigerians have continued to drape, cut, sew and embellish the rectangle in an incredible variety of ways. They have kept the headcloth, or *gele* (the long strip of cloth that has marked the married woman for centuries). The arrangement of the gele into a lofty pouff of color and pattern is spontaneous. Every time she puts it on, a woman can pour her taste and individuality into it. But this stately headwrap is threatened, like the *buba* blouse and skirt cloth. The loose, sleeved buba tucks into layers of skirt cloths. which have been wrapped and knotted into a permanent look of pregnancy. And such a display of pride in motherhood and matronly bulk is incompatible with the West's freedom for women and focus on youth.

Though industrialization and change seem inevitable, tradition continues. Berbers still ride into Kano to get their blue cloth. Indigo blue is still the national color. Pattern is still bold and geometric. Skirt cloths, bubas and the gele are still common. Men wear loose trousers, wide-sleeved shirts and the agbada. And in isolated areas, bead girdles, skins and red ochre body paint still cover nakedness.

Sometimes there is a mixture of dress: legs painted with white tribal patterns stick out of British-style, cotton shorts. And a member of parliament of the Itsekiri tribe moves like a divine king, with the far end of his thirty foot train—an extension of his wrapped sarong—knotted around a servant's neck. A loose tunic-shirt hangs over his sarong; but the shirt has a formal, tucked front and buttoned cuffs. His head dress is a straw boater topped by an ostrich plume. And a huge metal ornament hangs like an ancient amulet from a chain around his neck.

Traditional African dress is gradually becoming national dress, which means it is losing its functional purpose and is about to become folk costume. It is increasingly shaken out just for weddings, festivals, diplomatic appearances and ceremonial occasions. As Africa values western efficiency more, it values the weighty gbariye less.

But a tailored navy suit with tight collar and tie will never be comfortable in the African climate. And pink, rosebud-sprigged dresses designed for pale skin will never be right for black skin.

Over the centuries, Africans have always filtered out the unsuitable elements in alien dress, keeping only those that worked for them. So no doubt they will eventually Africanize even the business suit.

Whatever they do, the dress will be right only if it is appropriate to the nature of Africa and the nature of the African.

These three costumes tell the story of China: the action coat and trousers of the aggressive warlord; the leisured silk robes of the Confucian scholar who ran the brilliant courts; and the Manchu dragon robe which mixed traditional pattern and length with the conquering horseman's cuffs, collar and riding slits.

Subtle silk brocades of the French aristocrats gleaming in chandelier light were worlds apart from the simpler functional country clothes so popular in 18th century England. The silks were symbols of a fatal gap between aristocrat and peasant. England's plain wools were signs of respect for the land and indicated less class separation in dress.

Worn for centuries as work pants by peasants and sailors, the barbarian trouser returned as one of the fighting symbols of the French Revolution and remained in fashion, gradually replacing breeches. Above, dishevelled "sans-culottes," most of them in trousers, confront aristocrats in fashionable dress. Below, French women find an expression of freedom in the Greek chiton.

The puffed chests of the men in this advertisement, their tall hats and dark suits designed for work and travel, said clearly that this was an age of supreme male power. Nineteenth century women retreated under demure bonnets and impossibly limiting skirts, creating the greatest separation of male and female dress in history.

American Commander Perry broke Japan's isolation in 1853, opening the door for dark suits and industrialization. The pattern was repeated round the world in the 19th and 20th centuries. But at home, the dominance of Western men was threatened by women who, in the 1870s, were liberated from their restricting crinolines.

Clothes teach two things that are essential to an understanding of Japan: the high value placed on the warrior (samurai) as shown by his armor that went far beyond function with its enamelled metal, brilliant braid, embossed leather and gilded antlers; and the high value placed on nature, as seen in the creative spill of flowers across the simply cut kimona.

Africa has taken on the suit as a symbol of authority and progress. But will it ever have the beauty and integrity of her own costume? From Ife comes this royal regalia of West Africa's classical period (about 14th century); a splendid Medieval merger of Africa and Islam in chain mail and silk robes is worn by these Katsina horsemen; Nigerian herders illustrate the graceful use of handwoven rectangles and simple tunics.

Clothes can train a child for freedom as well as for adult responsibilities. You can feel the effect of clothing on the children in Winslow Homer's "Snap The Whip," and on the royal Stuart children who, in exile, take on the pomp and grandeur of Louis XIV's court.

Like the "sans-culottes," the young make their point with dishevelled alternatives to the status quo. Here, jeans are a wistful plea for change from mass production and obsolescence: The honest old jeans of cowboy and miner have been spontaneously embellished by the owner.

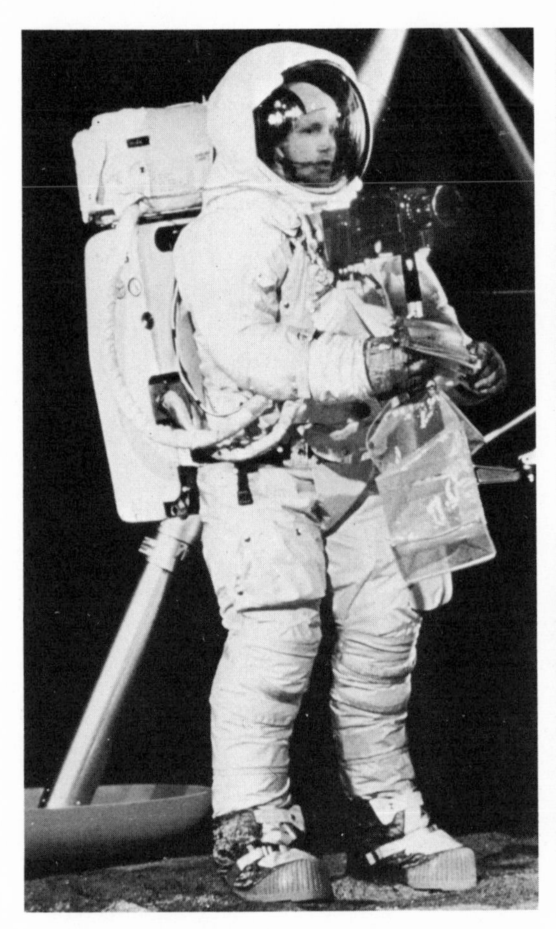

Costly research has produced the ultimate in functional dress—the moon suit; while institutionalizing the West's tendency to change has produced high-powered promotion of seasonal style changes. Here, all the svelte spectacle of a designer's show tries to impress the midi length on the public eye.

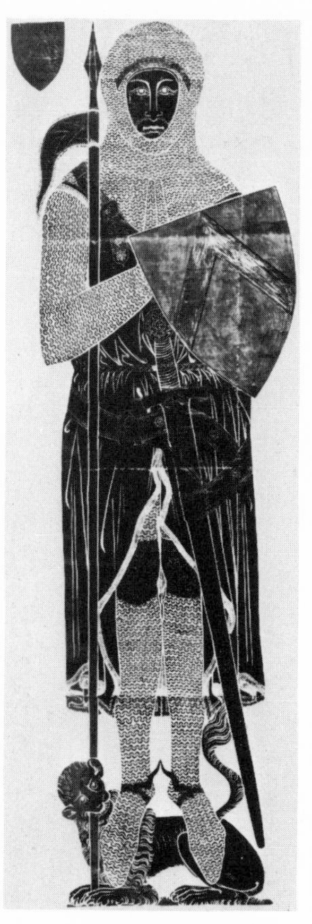

Chain mail and plate armor died when they could no longer do their job. If we begin to value the senses and self-expression more, can the super-functional business suit survive? The new mood is alive in today's chain mail, made of linked pull-tabs from canned drinks, showing pleasure in unfunctional display.

Hard hats watch, learn about the link between clothing and people, and make comments that, according to *Rags* magazine, are a form of complimenting the world and an attempt to make better human contact.

19

In the 15th century, Europe was pulling out ahead of Africa culturally. She even began pulling out ahead of the East. While Spanish and Italian dress expressed a bold new Western spirit, Islamic, Indian, and Chinese dress revealed a lessening of vitality, a slowing of creativity.

The Moors had been in Spain for over seven centuries and most of that time they had outclassed the Gothic knights in almost every aspect of the arts of peace and war. While Christian kings clanked about in unsanitary castles, Moorish princes reclined in breathtakingly beautiful palaces with blossoming courtyards cooled by fountains. Their wives wore gorgeously patterned Granada silks, with *tiraz*, decorative silk bands, exquisitely worked with inscriptions from the Koran.

Spanish Christians, determined to drive the Moors out, were expressing a stiffening of purpose in dress. The foundation of the unique Spanish style had been there before Islam. Because Spanish silver had been sought by all Mediterranean powers, Spanish clothing showed traces of Iberian, Cretan, Syrian, Carthaginian, Greek, and Etruscan dress. Barbarian torques and trousers had come in with the German invasions. And Visigothic kings had then taken up the heavy opulence of Byzantine Court dress, adding it to Spanish dress.

What Islam had added—apart from brocades and cloth-of-gold and -silver—was a proud erectness that seemed to express a standing up to the Moors. A rigid formality distinguished the Spanish style even when it was based, like the rest of medieval Europe, on tunics, mantles, girdles and swords.

The Christians borrowed much from the Moors, to help express their pride, their piety and their aristocratic militancy. They took black—one of Mohammed's symbolic colors—to look suitably austere. They protected their wives' virtue with veiling and seclusion. And before European heraldry developed, they wove their names and titles into tiraz bands to mark Christian nobles as visibly as Moslem nobles were.

When the Crusades threw all of Western Christendom into a Holy War on Islam, Spain drew new strength from Europe. Knights and pilgrims rode through, and the Spanish seemed to catch the new spirit that was enlivening the West. By the 13th century they had torn off the Islamic tiraz bands and replaced them with European heraldic design.

Heraldry, a development of the old family totem, often divided a knight's shield into halves and quarters by color. It also sometimes included a symbolic animal or flower. The decorated shield, surcoat and banner allowed a knight to be recognized when his visor was pulled over his face. *Parti-color* as well as the heraldic design spread to clothing as people began to cling to the familiar symbols of knighthood in a Europe that was turning to new ways of life. It seemed to ease the transition from medieval to Renaissance in the 14th and 15th centuries.

Away from embattled Spain, in the mainstream of Europe, the longbow, the gun and the changing social order were making the fighting knight obsolete, and a new merchant class was challenging his social position. As though reminding the world of his noble traditions, the knight began spreading his coat-of-arms over himself, his family, his servants, horses and equipment. He engraved and polished his new plate armor and topped it with towering plumes. In spectacular tournaments, he turned battle into a reassuring public ritual.

And the people, looking for stability in a changing time,

took up the familiar symbols of knighthood with enthusiasm. But they carried them to worldly excesses that expressed the new age pushing through. Wealthy townsmen also spread heraldic pattern all over their families' clothes and their servants' livery. And parti-color, which had once marked the merger of noble families, now gave men's hose one red leg and one green leg; it also cut women's gowns up into bold, geometric areas of color.

The fluid, open-sided surcoat that had covered the knight's chain mail and carried his identifying coat-of-arms, was distorted into an infinite variety of garments, most of them worn over the doublet and hose, and women's gowns. Deeply curved underarm openings on the *sideless surcoat* let a tightly-fitted gown underneath show through. And the front panel, the *plastron,* was decorated down the front with fur and jewelled buttons. Worn over a long-sleeved gown, it became a 14th century display of wealth.

The *houppelande* development of the surcoat widened the shoulders, swelled the chest, and pulled in the waist, exaggerating the male form. Its great, fur-lined sleeves were attached to the shoulders in a mass of gathers, and could be folded back and massed on the shoulders to display a rich fur lining. Or the sleeves could be so long that fur-edged slits let the arms through, while the sleeves hung useless. The body of the houppelande was sewn into tubular pleats that puffed out at the chest when tightly belted. It could be long to let a merchant show how wealthy and leisured he was, or very short to let a fashionable young man show off his legs. With typical 15th century extravagance, women's houppelande sleeves sometimes billowed out like butterfly wings as they moved.

But while other parts of Europe turned to towns and commerce, Spain stayed committed to battle. There, the obsession with throwing out the Moors kept the people more feudal, more hierarchical, more devout, and more intolerant than in the rest of Europe. While 13th century Europe was in loose bliaut gowns, Spain's firm waist-to-armpit lacings gave bodices the look of cuirasses. And Spain outdid all others in spilling heraldic design over clothing.

Velvet, the lustrous silk pile weave with weight and

warmth, moved Spanish dress farther away from Islam. And as Christian Spain stiffened for a final assault on Islam, the Spanish began to wear the *farthingale.*

Queen Isabella of Spain was wearing the new farthingale in 1492 when she drove the last of the Moorish princes out of Granada and sent Columbus off to find a trade route that would bypass Islamic-controlled routes to the Orient. Basically the farthingale was a series of hoops that held the skirt out into an architectural shape. This broke completely with the old Eastern and Mediterranean tradition of letting clothes take their shape from the body and from the fall of gravity. Instead of working with nature, the farthingale worked for power over it.

The waist seams of the 12th century bliaut had opened the way for further development of both skirt and bodice, and had been an important step away from the medieval tunic. The 14th century doublet and hose had stripped a man's body down to show what there was to build from. Then the 15th century farthingale came as a further stride into the constant innovations that had begun to characterize Western dress.

Inspired by Portugal's maritime adventures, Spain sent Columbus off. And with the silk industry of Granada finally in Christian hands, the nation also prepared to lead Europe into the elegant, stiff-necked silhouette that marked the age of exploration.

Meanwhile Byzantine officialdom had been fossilizing. The graceful tunics and cloaks of late Rome had turned into boards of embroidery and jewels. The chlamys had become so rigid that it had had to be slit up from the bottom to let the arm through. And the pallium had shrunk to a jewelled strip—the *loros*—which was slipped over the head like a narrow poncho.

As the Turks moved in, official Eastern Christianity fled to Russia. Moscow, still rough and feudal, became New Rome. The Russian border was the new frontier against Islam, particularly the Turks. And this shift to Moscow intensified the Byzantine character of Russian society and Russian upper class dress. As in Spain, militancy showed in dress and in rigid class distinction. Serfs were almost slaves. But not all of the Byzantine people went to Russian. Some went to Europe. And there they found a society that was far more alive than the one they had left.

Europe welcomed refugee Byzantine scholars. The classical manuscripts they brought with them spurred Europe's rediscovery of Greece, and strengthened the surge of interest in man that had already led Europeans to toss away encumbering long robes and strip down to the doublet and hose.

The Far East, too, contributed unintentionally to the new Western spirit, the new Western dress. Tales of travellers like Marco Polo stimulated Europeans.

Marco Polo had gone to China from Europe's richest, most colorful, most cosmopolitan city, Venice. Venetian furrier guild members paraded in ermine mantles; Venetian festivals of the sea blazed with jewels and cloth-of-gold. But even so the traveller from Venice was astounded by the palaces and parks and paved streets of Chinese cities. He was amazed by the thousand carts of raw silk rolling daily into a silk center. And he was stunned by the sight of twenty thousand nobles in jewelled cloth-of-gold robes paying tribute to Kublai Khan on his birthday.

Venice was already rich because it had a western monopoly on Mediterranean trade. The people of Venice were already enchanted by the Persian-style silks that were being shipped over from Sicily and carried home from the Crusades. But the inspiration of China spurred them on to manufacture their own silks to fill the growing demands of Europe. And Venice's silk techniques spread over Italy and then over Europe to dress the men and women of the Renaissance.

Italian silks tended towards bold floral designs, based on curving Chinese tendrils and flowers. But European weavers also developed a distinctive style in silks, creating looms that perfected the new silk pile, or velvet, weave. Velvet, which became the characteristic cloth of Renaissance Europe, let even silk increase the gap between East and West.

Gunpowder, printing and the compass had also come west with silk. And Europe exploited them as China had not done.

Travellers like Marco Polo brought more than things back to Europe. Their reports on silkworm culture, jade mining and beautifully caparisoned elephants sent other men travelling. The adventurer's ship began to replace the horse, and the vigor that was being frustrated by hollow tournaments and inactive city life shifted from castles and towns to the sea.

With the movement to the sea, trousers began to revive, worn along with coarse versions of breeches and hose; for sailors, like farmers, needed good, sturdy, functional, working pants. And that is what trousers had become. Skintight hose may have been the garment for men of leisure, but working men needed more practical covering.

From that time on, change was the one constant in Western dress. The merchant class was restless and competitive always pushing the aristocrats on to find new ways to proclaim their hereditary status. And a feeling that everything could be improved generally turned a small thing into a big thing. A bit of shirt ruffle at the neck grew into a high, stiff cartwheel of a neck ruff. The farthingale led skirts from a discreet cone to a sixteen foot wall of brocade; it led to panniers, hip rolls, bustles, hoops.

An opposite force, the force of reaction, was at work in the East. Any stimulation that might have flowed from the West to the East was stopped by the Ottoman Turks.

The Turkish sultan, Suleiman the Magnificent, negotiated as an equal with Henry VIII, Francis I, and Charles V when he moved into European politics. His bulbous turban and his rich layers of long, fur-lined and silk-lined caftans, tied with a wide silk sash, gave him a mysterious and disconcerting power in eyes of men accustomed to visible arms and legs. But actually, the austere, orthodox, Ottoman Turks were a wall cutting the rest of Islam off from Europe and the activity of the Renaissance. And their militancy blinded Europe to the loss of vitality in the rest

The East and West draw apart in dress. By the 16th century, the essential differences between the Orient and the West were dramatically visible in dress. The East covered the body, reclined, and tried to keep humans in some sort of harmony with the rest of the universe. The West displayed the body, stood erect, and tried to dominate the environment.

The recumbent harem woman in layers of light rustling silks is worlds apart from the erect Spanish lady.

Henry VIII, with codpiece, exaggerated width and blazing gems, is a statement of male challenge.

16th century Spanish women wore black velvet, high-necked ruffs, and rigid farthingale skirts and bodices to proclaim that they were pious and aristocratic.

of Islam.

Behind the wall, a loss of toughness could be detected in dress. There were fifty yard turbans, which only a leisured man had time to put on and only an inactive man could balance. Caftans were lengthening. And horsemen often wore two full-length caftans over their trousers. The horseman's sleeve, once tight and efficient, was sometimes so long that holes had to be cut near the top to let the arms through.

In India the Mughals wore sheer flaring caftans over puffed trousers of delicate silk. And their sashes were as sensuous with decoration as the traditional Indian girdle.

In Persia, the vigorous old motifs were being replaced by roses and nightingales. Vivid colors gave way to the gentle colors of an effete society: "fog," mulberry, rose, lavender, persimmon. A revival of the old decorative armband expressed a reactionary spirit.

In the harem, perfumed women reclined on silk divans piled with pink and rose silk cushions, intellectually dormant and physically indolent. They smoked their cooling *shisheh*, and shuffled about in slippers that were always sliding off perfumed, juice-tinted feet. Silk harem pants billowed out below a knee-length silk tunic. And over the tunic a long vest, buttoned to the waist, floated open from the waist to the floor. An outer, open-fronted caftan, or *gibbeh*, glinted with gold thread and shimmered with bright silk embroidery. Sometimes a silk shawl wrapped the hips, over the harem pants. Always, veils were draped over luxurious black hair. And the silks and perfumes and indolent women were enervating, unlike old barbarian encampments.

While the West went off to sea, armed with gunpowder, men of the East piled decoration on horse trappings and on sword hilts. Theirs was a commitment to medieval ways, a commitment that let them lag in the development of firearms.

Right up into the 18th century, China remained a powerful influence. The patterns the Chinese had developed colored and shaped the silks, cottons, gardens, porcelains, paintings and decor of France and England. But China was not the China that had been. The humiliation of being ruled by the foreign Mongols shook Chinese self-confidence and taste in the 13th century. Silk manufacturers began to produce garishly colored silks for the Mongol trade.

Still, the old self-renewing cycle of warlord and scholar continued. And in the 14th century a native dynasty, the Mings, threw the Mongols out, though the momentum of Mongol expansion carried along for a while. A fleet of ten thousand men reached the coast of Africa. But the Chinese had never really respected trade. And in the 15th century, the Mings chose to pull China back into traditional isolation. They scrapped the ships and turned their backs on Chinese traders who had settled in southeast Asian colonies.

In the blossoming courtyards, silk robes widened. Mongol riding slits at the back and front of tunics were replaced by the traditional Chinese side slits. Short outer sleeves lengthened.

But the Mings were going back to the past. The beauty of their period was deceptive. It lacked the vitality of greatness. For what it expressed was a futile nostalgia for the old, great China of the Han and the T'ang. The Mings hadn't even the strength to keep the Imperial dragon for themselves. It began to descend into the ranks of the bureaucracy.

In 1644, the Manchus came in from Manchuria and took over. Their tightly wrapped coats were cinched in with wide leather belts. Long, funnel-like horseshoe cuffs and high collars protected their horsemen's hands and necks.

The Manchus forced their pigtail on all Chinese men. But they too fell back on the old distinctions of dress to enforce their rule. They broke up bureaucratic ranks into even more dozens of degrees than the Chinese had, codifying the different degrees in dress. The color and decoration of robes was decreed by law. Roundels—the symbol of

Heaven—on the emperor's robe were filled with his dragon. The square—a symbol of earth—appeared on each official's chest, with the insignia of his office on it.

Ranks were also marked by fancy knobs on the top of the Manchu headdress, a small domed cap with turned-up brim. A peacock feather whisk at the back of the cap marked special Imperial favor, with three grades of favor shown by one, two, or three-eyed peacock feathers.

But China's poetic taste and love of nature persisted. The prescribed costume for an officer of the Board of Music was still delightfully Chinese. The cut of the robe was standard Manchu—a wide-sleeved, shorter robe over a long, tight-sleeved one. Both robes were crimson satin. A golden oriole sang in a square on his outer robe. And an allover pattern of small golden sunflowers was spread over his under robe. The high rank of the colors—yellow and red—showed China's continuing devotion to the arts. A vertical plume of primrose yellow feathers fluttered on the officer's cap.

Under the Manchus, the dragon robe spread out more widely through official society. But its spread was controlled by laws that ensured that a man's precise social position could be read in the size, type, number, color and placement of the dragons on his ceremonial robe. Even the number of claws on the dragon's foot was restricted by law. Only royalty could wear five claws.

Greedy and ambitious men started wearing more and better dragons than they had earned. Three claw men had four claws embroidered on their robes. By the 18th century, Manchu emperors were forcing men, by law, to pull out the threads of any claws they weren't entitled to. And when, in the 19th century, the dragon robe was mass produced and sold to merchants and bankers, who had always been looked down upon, the integrity of old China was gone.

Everywhere in the East, the elite grew steadily more gorgeous while the masses tried desperately to cling to what little they had. Right up into the 17th century, the wealth and splendor and beauty of Eastern dress almost hid the fact that, under all the shimmer and the glitter, the basic shapes had not changed. There were no real innovations. It was the people of the West who were making the innovations.

When castles and knights gave way to towns and merchants and exploration of the seas, people were caught up in a new age. They tried to hold on to the familiar medieval forms, but the Renaissance was bursting through. The whole mood of Europe began swinging into worldliness, into independence from the Church, and a new craving for beauty began expressing itself spontaneously in clothing.

The Renaissance claimed to be a rediscovery of the classical Greek past. But the extremes of the 14th and 15th centuries moved dress irreversibly beyond the peplos. Clothes distorted the body shape instead of glorifying it.

Sleeves ballooned out. Shoes stretched into ridiculously long pointed toes. The cone-shaped *hennin* thrust a yard long spire up from a woman's head.

Italy led the Renaissance in dress. Never as concerned with heraldry as the rest of Europe, always richer in trade, more wrapped in Oriental silks and colors and more aware of the classical heritage, the Italians broke easily with medieval tradition. While English women of the 14th century were still columns of layered cloth topped by a bandaging of wimples and gorgets, Italian women were experimenting with a low-cut gown and a tight-fitting bodice. Their hair was flying free.

As they became less and less bound up in feudal thought, the people of the Italian peninsula discovered sheer human enjoyment in glowing reds and blues. The rest of Europe was still carrying color symbolism to such extremes that a man couldn't wear green in public without embarrassment. (Green had moved on from meaning *new love* to meaning *cuckolded.*) The Italians were even breaking purple out of its ancient royal and religious symbolism.

Cloth-of-gold changed. And the way it changed expressed a new commitment to hard cash. Woven from threads wrapped with real gold wire, the cloth lost the suppleness of the dyed Eastern fabric and turned men's minds from the symbolic value of gold to its real value.

Diplomacy was rising out of medieval pageantry, especially in Italy where city-states became a laboratory for new life styles. Like everything else that led to modern systems, diplomacy had to fight its way through the extravagances of late medieval and renaissance pageantry and ego. When ambassadors made their "solemn entries" into cities, fountains still spewed wine and banquets still served room-sized pies with flocks of birds flying out.

But Italy was not alone. At the Field of Cloth of Gold, the newly crowned Henry VIII and Francis I, King of France, met more for personal competition than for politics. They came to outdo each other with a blinding display of mock castles, banquets and cloth-of-gold doublets, horse trappings and pavilions. Henry VIII's costume brought male dress to its highest level of display. A jaunty plumed hat glorified his head, which was made more powerful by a square-cut beard that bristled against a touch of white lace ruffle—a sign of leisure. Padded doublet sleeves were slashed to show rich satins under the cloth-of-gold. A huge, puffed-sleeved coat, or *chamarre*, had fur-lined lapels thrown back over his shoulders, extending his body into a powerful bulk and making him a massive square set on two well-muscled legs. Even the jewels in the massive gold collar slung around his shoulders were square cut. The alternating strips of silver and gold cloth gathered into the *bases* (skirts) of his doublet swelled his hips. And a magnificent, slashed and brocaded codpiece focussed attention on his male sexual power. All his surfaces glowed and glittered.

In Spain, power was concentrated in monarchs who dressed with traditional Spanish grandeur, but now there was a difference. With exploration, a new age had begun. And dress had taken on the feeling of a fresh start, and a simplicity that Henry's dress did not have. The Spaniards kept their dress dark and lean. Colors were black and gold. Spain was very pious, very aristocratic, very militant; and it was becoming very rich.

Even American gold didn't relax the feeling of threat Spanish nobles had built up during the centuries of Moorish occupation. Their passion for pure Spanish blood blinded them to balance. And during their greatest days of wealth, power and confidence, they ruthlessly threw out the Jews and the rest of the Moslems, though both were vital to the nation's economy.

As the 16th century progressed, any soft medieval lines that might have remained in Spanish dress took on the stiff look of armor. The woman's bodice and the man's doublet were both rigid with gold-shot velvet, heavy brocade and jewels; both stretched down to a point in front, flattening the chest like a cuirass. Long bands of rich braid on sleeves, skirts, doublets, capes, especially down the center front, seemed like military decoration. *Bombast* (stuffing) swelled sleeves, doublet front and breeches to the firmness and smoothness of metal. (When hose had gone about as far as they could go in erotic display of the body, they began to be covered at the top by brief *breeches.*) Necklines rose. And the tiny ruffled edging above the shirt's drawstring grew to a stiff, wired *ruff* that held the neck straight and the chin high. The farthingale made women's skirts rigid, and the overskirt was slit down the front to accomodate it, showing a triangle of gold-encrusted underskirt. Knitted hose fit in a way bias-cut cloth never had. Short, swinging velvet and brocade capes (grown out of old circular storm capes) had a military dash the chamarre and the houppelande lacked. Women got the same cape silhouette by slitting the huge, stiff, flaring sleeves of their outer robe.

Spain's prestige carried her dress all over Europe. But when the rest of Europe began putting some of the lusty, reckless exhuberance of the age into stiff Spanish shapes, Spain watched its own splendor fade. She still had a huge empire. But the gold was running out. The best business men, farmers and craftsmen had been banished and there was no middle class to replace them.

Drawing away from Europe, Spain settled back into the disillusioned living with the past that Cervantes caught in *Don Quixote*. Coats-of-arms were most important; though they were often worn with frayed lace and tarnished gold braid. The farthingale skirt stretched out into a distorted wall of brocade, sometimes sixteen feet across. Spain's dress, like its empire, kept up appearances until the 18th century. But the creativity that had produced elegant innovations like the farthingale was spent. Isolated from progress, Spain and Spanish dress became an anachronism in a Europe that was moving towards swashbuckling cavaliers.

Henry VIII's daughter, Elizabeth I, turned Spanish dress into something that let the daring of the age come through, while still achieving the most regal image in Europe. She kept the rigid stomacher, puffed sleeves, and huge skirt; but she cut the pious Spanish neckline so low that her breasts were exposed. She replaced the farthingale with the *drumroll*, a hip bolster that gave her skirt a wide, almost square shape. She split the Spanish ruff to fan out behind her head. She added huge, wired, lace wings behind the ruff. In white satin, with her great spread of skirt, sleeves, ruff and wings, she moved through public processions like a stately ship under full sail. Almost bared breasts, red hair and flamboyant jewels simply added dash to majesty. She was a Queen dressed to please people who still loved spectacle.

With even women beginning to see themselves as individuals, it's not surprising that children, too, began to exist, as children. Until the 16th century they had been just small adults who probably wouldn't live to grow up. They were tightly wrapped in swaddling clothes—bandage-

In the late 15th century, the Renaissance Italians bared the throat with a tiny shirt ruffle.

In aristocratic Spain, the ruffle rose to cover the throat.

The ruffle soon left the shirt, becoming a separate ruff that held the head even more erect.

In late 16th century Spain, the ruff was wired out to an impractical wheel of expensive lace.

The changing spirit of Europe can be seen in the growth of the ruff. As gold from a new empire poured into Spain, a shirt ruffle evolved into an enormous wheel of lace.

In England, Elizabeth I split the Spanish ruff to display her bosom, and framed her head with a huge wired veil.

Even in the 17th century Spain clung to the closed ruff now rigid with starch.

like strips of cloth—for at least a year, then put into small copies of women's clothes. (Boys stayed in female dress until they were toilet-trained.) And the prevailing death rate seemed to numb people into a fear of making much of their children.

Then, with a growing confidence in life expectancy, parents began to make their children a special class. Boys were the first to feel the change. Instead of adult clothes, young upper class boys were put into the long robe that was still being worn by churchmen and scholars. The robe was replaced by doublet and hose at about seven or eight. The threat of being put back into the robe kept boys under control.

It was a vigorous age, full of the religious passions that had already split the Catholic Church in two. Protestant Elizabeth's magnificence and Catholic Spain's rigid glitter stood inflexibly against each other. And simple Puritan dress stood against both.

Puritan dress grew out of Dutch burgher dress, which tended to be somber, conservative, and quite Spanish because of Holland's ties with Spain. But the Dutch ruff expressed the basic difference. Turned into a white wheel, framing plump, scrubbed cheeks, it seemed to speak of the virtues of cleanliness, industriousness and bourgeois respectability.

Puritan dress was the beginning of the end of public spectacle. For stark, black, Puritan dress represented moral reform, which threw out color, emotional ritual and the splendid hierarchy of the Church. It replaced them with plain, practical values.

Puritan attitudes and dress strongly affected both northern Europe and young America. In fact, it set the standard for the northern American colonies early in the 17th century. And the tradition of the plain, hard-working, non-aristocratic man still sits heavily on the shoulders of the man in the business suit.

All of this was offset in Europe, though not in America, with the coming of the *cavalier*. Cavalier dress was built of lace, leather, plumes and military swagger. As if they were eager to be knights again, men took to big boots folded down into a cuff, with lace sometimes flopping over the cuff. Unlike the knights, they dressed mixing war with luxury. They slung sweeping military cloaks over one shoulder, below big, rakish, plumed hats. Their doublet skirts, slit and overlapping, flared out comfortably over breeches that now reached down to the knee. With their huge swords hung from baldrics, they clanked through houses in great style.

The most significant symbol of Spanish rigidity, the ruff, began to sag down onto the shoulders early in the 17th century. Called the "falling band," it spread out over the shoulders in big, lace collars. And the easy, loosened doublet and breeches of the men were matched by the softening and widening of women's dresses. Necklines fell away, exposing throat and shoulders. Rigid skirts collapsed and fell in big, easy folds. Sleeves and hair puffed out at the sides to complete a blowzy effect.

By the middle of the 17th century, a new calmer age was beginning. The Thirty Years War, which had torn Europe religiously, politically and economically, ended in 1648. Strong nations and strong kings rose up—France and Louis XIV in particular.

Louis claimed to rule by divine right. And like the sun, his emblem, he cast a golden glow on everything around him, shrivelling those who got too close. The leather-booted, sword-swinging cavalier came to Court to serve as lackey to the king. Nobles just home from war had to settle for the job of handing the king his shirt in the morning. And competition at Court became so intense that men vied for jobs like this.

With the new luxury and leisure, doublet and hose and breeches were beginning to die. But as they did, they became more elaborate. The lacings that had tied a man's breeches to his doublet became a frenzy of loops, bows, rosettes and spaghetti-like fringes that spread to neck and sleeves, and to the garters that held the breeches in at the knee. The doublet shrank to a bolero. The shirt bloused out below it. Breeches widened until they looked like frilly skirts festooned at the waist and the hem with banks of looped ribbons. These were the *petticoat breeches* of the mid-17th century.

Ballooning petticoat breeches and flapping bows and ruffles were the death rattle of the old doublet, hose and breeches.

A young Dutch couple in 1669. The shirt puffs through slashes in the doublet sleeves and at the waist.

But already some men were suggesting that fantasy was no way to solve problems or get at the truth. They deplored poetry, superstition, fancy breeches and any other products of the senses and emotions. Reason was their goal. And their search for truth and for nature's order began to strip off some of the gorgeous decoration and to eliminate the doublet that had lost its function. They were replaced with the *coat.*

At the time, the coat was a sensational new fashion. It arrived as a knee-length, fitted, sleeved garment that was essentially the Persian horseman's caftan. And it came double. There was an outer coat and a long inner vest cut just like the coat. Together they almost hid the breeches.

The vest, most visible indoors when the coat might be removed, was usually more richly embroidered than the coat. It was eventually shortened to the waistcoat.

As early as the 14th century, a coat called the *caban* had come in from the East, through Venice. And early in the 17th century, a few daring Englishmen had worn the caftan and the Indian cotton pajama suit of sleeved, buttoned tunic and loose trousers; for diplomats and the great trading companies had begun to put them in touch with East Indian and Islamic dress. The French military had worn a plain warm coat for years before the coat became a Court sensation. So it was not really new, just newly fashionable.

Though essentially a foreign style, the coat was in the old Germanic tradition of the cut-and-sew, lean fit and functional action garment. And the West's innovating spirit went to work on it almost at once. While the East's caftan remained unchanged, Europe's coat went through a steady evolution into the businessman's suit jacket, and as the coat changed so did the rest of men's dress.

First, the high neck and collar of the coat forced a change in the shirt collar, which had already evolved from tiny shirt ruffle to wired ruff to starched ruff to big flat lace collar. Now the lace was all pushed to the front, to the neck opening. And neckwear was on its way towards the *cravat*, towards the collar and tie.

The coat came in with a revolution of the mind, a revolution fought quietly at first by intellectuals searching for order and discipline. It took time to filter through society, and Louis XIV held on to many of the old trappings for a while. Looped ribbons still clustered on his right shoulder, neck, and waist. Big bows still held masses of lace at his neck. His breeches even ballooned for a while longer. But they were squashed by the straight skirts of the coat he did adopt. And gradually the balloons were narrowed into trim knee breeches.

Louis combined the old trimmings and the new coat in such a way that his personal display raised him well above his people. His reds and golds blazed regally. The turned-back cuffs of his coat and vest luxuriated in lace, brocade and gold braid. The handmade lace at his neck indicated wealth and aristocracy. And, with the spirit of imposing man's will on nature, wigs began to distort the shape of his head with a piling up and a spilling down of curls.

As he settled into Versailles near the end of the 17th century, Louis displayed his personal interpretation of the philosophical revolution. He went to extremes in imposing order on nature. In gardens radiating out from his palace, he disciplined plants into geometric rows. But he went too far. He carved shrubs and trees into unnatural shapes. He controlled every court move with rigid etiquette, turning even the simple act of getting dressed in the morning into a prolonged and pompous ceremony.

What was swelling in Louis was not just royal ego, or Renaissance love of spectacle, or even a new philosophy. It was France's growing awareness of itself as a nation. The Sun King's splendor was the wealth and power of the French nation, newly dominant in Europe. His dress displayed the state controlled silk and lace industries. The nation's trade alliances with Islam, which still controlled most of the trade coming out of India and China, were visible in his Indian and Chinese print cottons, or *Indiennes.*

France's colonies sent in wealth. French bureaucracy brought in taxes. And it all reached a concentration of splendor at Versailles, where a massing of taste, money and craftsmanship lifted the glory of France farther and farther out of the reach of the average Frenchman.

Peasants paid taxes but had no stake in the land, no sense of involvement in the nation's glory. They wore the coat, too, but in poor, undecorated versions that made it a functional garment.

Court artifice reached its peak in the full-bottomed wig. Though wigs had started as a natural looking supplement to real hair and had stayed moderate in size early in the Sun King's reign, they made no pretense to naturalness by the 1680s. Instead they massed curls up on the head and over the shoulders, letting them fall in heavy hanks down the back and front, framing the cravat. Such wigs glorified the head at a time of growing intellectual excitement. Their topheavy pompousness matched that of the Court. And their cost, care and impracticality made them hard for the lower classes to own. As Louis aged and the Court creaked with even stiffer protocol, the big wig began to be dusted with white powder.

Women's dress was little changed by the coming of the coat. The beginnings of the new age of reason also passed women by. Their gown stayed basically unchanged. Though it had stiffened and softened, narrowed and swelled with the years, it was essentially the dress that had started with the Spanish farthingale. In simplest terms, it was still a doublet attached to a skirt.

There were some changes, of course. A train sometimes added grandeur. And instead of wearing wigs, women stretched lace up into a tall structure, the *Fontage,* which shot straight up from the forehead like a partly-opened fan. The high morals of Louis' second wife, Mme de Maintenon, brought new rigidity to dress. Female curves were disciplined with *stomachers,* which flattened the chest like a board. And even gowns lavished with delicate French lace managed to take on a prim stiffness.

When Louis died, the Court moved into soft silk. It was tired of grandeur and precision. Subtle colors and soft watery silk replaced blazing gold and red. Ruffles, bows and lace blurred outlines and covered up the pointed stomacher of women's dresses. The Fontage collapsed and

women turned to boudoir informality. They put on the *sacque*, which fell loose and unfitted, front and back, making them fluid masses of silk when they settled into a sofa.

Then, finally, the gown split right down the front and spread to show the inner bodice and petticoats. The fit at the back of the bodice gave way to deep, inverted pleats, which hung loose from shoulder to floor. These are known as *Watteau pleats,* after the man who painted them so often. Formal gowns still featured a stiff stomacher; but now it was softened by a ladder of bows.

Order and symmetry were rejected. The delightfully random nature patterns of Chinese silks and porcelains were rediscovered and set up as models. And the French silk industry developed vaporous silks with infinite gradations of color and shifting highlights.

The intimacy of the salon began to replace the formality of Court protocol. And in the elegant salon, French women began to come into their own. They became adroit at moderating the conversation of brilliant men. This boosted the mature Frenchwoman to a level of prestige she has never lost. And women's clothes, for the first time, began to overtake men's in lavish display.

The Chinese silks that inspired 18th century elegance were the product of thousands of years of patient study and mystical devotion to nature. But French flower garden silks were fleeting fanciful diversions for a Court that was far removed from nature. The flowing lines of the sacque were as close as 18th century France came to the Chinese robe. And it soon gave way to skirts stretched out to an unnatural width by side hoops, or *panniers*. The Court was incapable of Chinese simplicity.

In spite of temptations, men held on to the basic cut of their coat. Its skirts did take on a lively flare after Louis' death. And it did borrow some of the subtle Chinese color and embellishment. But more change was coming. The rational, stripped-down minds that had created the climate for the coat were becoming more influential. And they were finding allies in England.

Things looked fresh and simple across the Channel. Nature wasn't second hand to the English. Farmers still had a stake in the farms they worked. And a prospering commerce meant that the government didn't have to drain farms with taxes. Country life still had such prestige that merchants and bankers bought estates as soon as they could afford them. And the parliamentary government was vigorous enough to keep a firm check on the king and prevent him from establishing Louis' splendid isolation from the people.

English country coats at all levels of society were plain colored, sturdy, beautifully fitted, and cut from fine English woolens, which stretched and gave with movement as silks did not. They were slit at the back and cut away in front for riding. Leather breeches were tucked neatly into riding boots. The vest was cut short so it wouldn't get in the way. And instead of a mass of lace at the throat, Englishmen knotted plain white linen. Leaving a discreet curl over each ear, they pulled their hair back into a knot to accommodate the high-crowned, small-brimmed hat that protected their head if they were thrown from a horse.

Compared to the French ladies, the English women were like a breath of country air. Never having had the restraints of a Louis XIV, their dress didn't have to react with Watteau pleats or the sacque. English women had simply gentled and simplified the old gown. Keeping it fitted at the waist, they let its skirt fall in graceful gathers. They crisscrossed white linen *fichus* on their chests. They did swell their heads with a powdered mass of curls, but the effect was more of tufted clouds than of rigid sculpture. Sashes were wide, girlish ribbons. Colors had the clear delicacy of wildflowers. And English women developed such a passion for the light, brilliantly flowered Indiennes, that English weavers started printing their own.

By the 1760s. England was beginning to seem an ideal land to almost every class in France. To the large, dissatisfied peasant class, it was a place where peasant dress still represented dignity. To intellectuals, its unimbellished wool coats and plain breeches were a symbol of equality.

And to the jaded Court, English dress was a relief from a superfluity of refinements.

English country clothes and the unsymmetrical English garden (based on the Chinese garden) moved across the Channel just as the writings of Voltaire and Rousseau were exposing the inequities of the French system and were crying out for a more natural, uncorrupted society. And the simply cut coats of pioneer America strengthened the trend.

The clothes of most Frenchmen had adjusted to the idea of social revolution twenty years before it finally came. But the Court didn't understand. It clung to the precious artificial world that had given it such power in the 18th century. It took simple English gowns and Polish aprons and turned them into fantasy. The Court ladies hitched skirts up above their ankles and pulled overskirts up into Bo-Peep pouffs on their hips. They tucked modest linen fichus into voluptuously low necklines.

Marie Antoinette, Louis XVI's queen, delighted in playing milkmaid at a miniature farm created for her at Versailles. But it was all make-believe. For the awkward pannier hoops, miles of handsewn ruffles, and embroidered brocades persisted. Female heads were built up into aristocratic fortresses, with frizzed hair massed up over horsehair pads, powdered heavily, and topped with plumes, huge mob caps, flower gardens, and even sailing ships.

The Revolution burst out in 1789. The shopkeepers and laborers who attacked the old regime in the streets took up the tough trouser of farmers and sailors. They made their *sans-culottes* the visible symbol of the Revolution. And anyone caught in *culotte-dorees* (the gold embroidered breeches of the aristocracy) was beheaded. They also adopted the red liberty cap—the old, flop-topped Phrygian cap that had been worn as a symbol of freedom in Greece and Rome. Revolutionaries replaced powdered curls with dishevelled hair.

In the raging intolerance that followed the Revolution, people lived or died, depending on what they wore. And breeches, hose, and brocade were very speedily shed.

When the terror had passed, breeches did come back,

with restrained use of embellishments and silks. With Napoleon, even rich color and imperial elegance came back into dress.

But there had been permanent change in French dress. The simple English cut had become basic fashion, not just a symbol of equality. And the lowly sans-culotte did not drift back to sailors and farmers. Instead, it was gradually adopted by the middle class and aristocracy, replacing breeches almost entirely early in the 19th century. The things it now represented—hard work and equality—had gained the prestige formerly reserved for leisure and privilege.

Class distinction did spring up again in dress, of course. But it was more subtle. The perfection of the fit, the quality of the cloth, the immaculate whiteness and elaborate arrangement of a man's neck linen (a sure sign that he was personally above dirty labor) were clues to his status.

Setting the pace in the early years of the 19th century, Beau Brummell, in a perfectly fitted, plain, dark coat, contrasting trousers, and snowy cravat, was a visible expression of the power shift that had taken place. The English, not the French, were now the leaders in men's fashions. While the French had been fighting their Revolution, the English had been revolutionizing the production of textiles with their new, steam-powered spinning jenny. Since England's power was built on democratic government and technology, innovations that did not inspire lavish display in the upper classes, simplicity was the rule.

As England moved into the 19th century, chests swelled, stiff cravats forced chins higher, tophats reached high, tight fit checked "vulgar" action and dark colors restrained emotion. The men of the British Isles were girding themselves to the earnest responsibility of running the world. Before the end of the century, they ruled one quarter of the earth.

The French lady looked to Greece for a way of expressing her sense of freedom after the Revolution. And by 1800 her high-waisted, chiton-inspired gown was setting the fashion over most of Europe and inviting pneumonia with

its sheer cotton, tiny puffed sleeves and very low neckline. Its immodesty would have shocked Athens. But its simple charm made it very suitable for little girls, who adopted it, too.

In France, taste, hand skills and luxury textiles continued to be lavished on gowns; and then, after the middle of the century, a new species of French designer took control of women's fashions. The *couturier* gave an aura of exclusiveness to French gowns that assured the survival of the tradition of taste and beauty. He made French female fashion a valuable national resource. But he didn't bring money into France as factory-made cloth and clothes brought it into England.

Englishwomen tried to follow France. But most bought English merchandise and it was clear that English factories increased efficiency and supply at the cost of beauty. Chemical dyes were garish compared to subtle vegetable dyes. Sewing machines gave a cruder fit and finish than hand sewing. And as an insecure new class worked to entrench its position, it trimmed with a heavy hand. The fringes, flounces, ribbons, beads and embroideries piled on Victorian gowns lacked French finesse.

Then as Englishmen moved confidently through a mobile age of empire and industry, their wives' skirts began to spread out at the bottom and pull in at the waist. Shoulders slumped, and sleeves swelled out below them. By the middle of the century, women were gasping in the corset cage that constricted their waists, and were fainting in the prison of petticoats that held out their immense skirts. With small hairdos, matronly shawls, and bell-shaped skirts, they had the silhouette of a teacosy; and they were as housebound. (Restricting velvet suits and lace collars were a step backward from freedom for their young sons, too.)

It was a trapped, frustrated age for women, an age of extreme sexual inequality. The rustle of petticoats and bared shoulders for evening were seductive and provocative; yet, the overall effect was prim. Women's escape into billowing skirts and delicate pallor seemed a retreat from the vigorous practicality expressed in male dress of the time.

In fact, the only obvious benefit the industrial revolution brought the mid-Victorian woman was the steel hoop that lightened her load of petticoats. And it manipulated her into an even more unnatural shape.

But by 1870, things were obviously changing. Women were beginning to free themselves from their huge skirt. First they pushed its fullness towards the back. Then they bunched it up into *bustles*. Then, as the century closed, they narrowed it all around.

As the 20th century came in, women's dress was still stressing the bust, waist, and hips of the dependent woman. It was still lavishly embellished. But it was starting to express the liberation of women.

For day wear, men had cut their coat off squarely at the hips, producing the modern suit jacket. (They had shortened their waistcoat long before.) And they were wearing jacket and pants in the same dark color instead of in the contrasting colors worn earlier. The last touches of color were disappearing as men took on the symbolic, spartan dress of the new religion of work and science.

In England, though, the persisting lure of country life let men keep contrasting colors for riding clothes, yachting blazers and flannels, and in checked knickers. Instead of staying at the factory, improving efficiency, English industrialists still scurried off to their country estates and to the sporty trappings of the traditional gentlemen.

Power slipped gradually across the Atlantic, to the United States. There, there was nothing to keep the suit from its plodding evolution towards plain function.

After women's dress passed men's in lavishness in the 18th century, it changed more and more rapidly. But men's dress stayed almost static. Any last, lingering urge towards plumes and brocades was nipped off by Darwin. For in the middle of the century, he shattered man's last illusion of a central position in the universe. Man was not as special as he had thought. He was an animal descended from other animals. And this threat to his superiority pushed him on to even greater emphasis on the machines and the science and the suit that marked his uniqueness in a world of animals.

Since the first velvet-doubleted Portugese ventured down the coast of Africa, cultural exchanges have tended to run in one direction. From the West to the non-West. The Portugese did not return to Europe in indigo sarongs. Convinced of superiority, the West has been all but impervious to the dress and ideas it has encountered.

And no one has surpassed the 19th century Englishman in oozing confidence in his system. The puff-chested, stiff-collared, upright Victorian strode through the world. Even in the most remote and primitive land, he knew that his best defence was his British bearing, backed by gunboats, rifles and the wealth and power of the entire Empire. When extreme heat forced him to compromise, he did it awkwardly with shorts and short-sleeved shirts which exposed legs and arms to a blistering sun and the tsetse fly. He never understood the secret of the aba or the summer kimona. Joining him in hot colonies, his wife strangled in high-necked, corseted gowns. And in the Crimean War, Lord Cardigan led his Light Brigade off to annihilation while, according to Cecil Woodham-Smith in *The Reason Why,* "the bright sunlight lit up the brilliance of cherry colour and royal blue, the richness of fur and plume and lace," inviting both heat prostration and cannon fire.

But the net result of the staunchly upright Englishman was to make those who saw him begin to doubt their own ways. After 1850, even the oldest, strongest centers of culture—Islam, China, India and Japan—were losing confidence in what the robe, the dhoti, the turban, and the kimona represented.

21

The effect of Western Man on the prestigious cultures of the Old World has been staggering.

But his effect on the less advanced cultures of the Americas and the South Pacific is a truly tragic story. For trade beads, cheap cloth, blankets, liquor, guns and disease replaced feathered cloaks and headdresses, bison and sea otter robes, tapa sarongs and confident identity.

The destroyers thought they were getting rid of the gaudy dress of heathen savages. But they were really wiping out sensitive and beautiful responses to territory. A passion for feathers was shown in Aztec mosaics of shimmering, varicolored feathers sewn to cloth. And this passion for feathers was a wistful response to a land with few birds. The Peruvian Inca's feather warbonnet and armor supported his vision of himself as a great bird of prey.

The deerskin, quills, and muted browns and blues of the Plains Indian showed that he was still drawing his inspiration directly from the prairie and the woods. But notable independence of nature was revealed in the Inca's storehouses full of woolen garments, in his sophisticated gold necklaces worked with pearls and turquoise, and in cloth as finely woven as any in history. He had reached a high state of civilization.

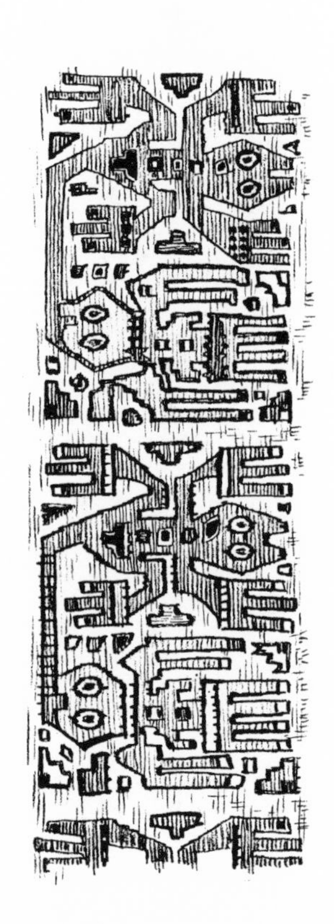

When the Spaniards came, the Incas faced the crisis in their finest clothes. For they believed that the gods would respond to a proud display of confidence. But it didn't

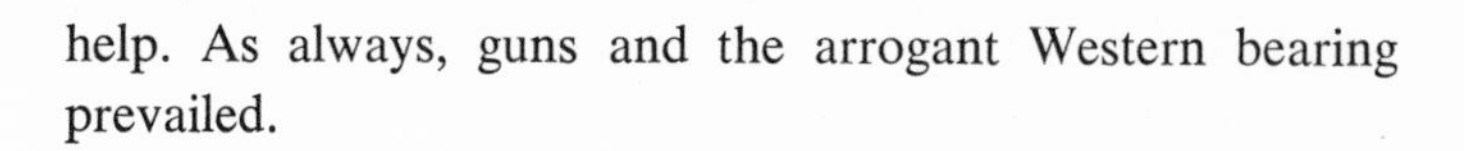
help. As always, guns and the arrogant Western bearing prevailed.

Everywhere the suit has become a symbol of progress. When an Arab sheik first put it on, he was probably wistfully identifying himself with men who could produce machines and good crops. Turkey, sitting right on Europe's border, felt the pressure of the West so strongly by the 1920s that her progressive leader broke the old spell of the Orient by force. In 1925, Kemal Ataturk brought his country into 20th century dress by decree. He understood that clothes were much more than a facade. He had felt humiliation as a youth when he had worn his *fez* in the West. Originally a Greek hat, the brimless fez had been adopted in a 19th century revolt against the turban. But over the years it had become as conservative a symbol as the turban.

Planning his campaign carefully, Ataturk put on Western clothes, shocking act for an Islamic leader. His biography, *Ataturk,* shows how he quieted gasps with a statement that Turkey could be civilized only "with boots and shoes on our feet, trousers on our legs, shirt and tie, jacket and waistcoat—and, of course to complete these, a cover with a brim on our heads. I want to make this clear. This head covering is called *'hat'*." He limited the turban and robe to professional religious men. For a climax, he danced publicly with a woman at a ball, bringing Turkish women back into society.

In 1928, Persia followed Turkey's example in giving up the symbolic dress of Islam.

But even the most ruthlessly progressive Easterner felt the tug of tradition. When President Eisenhower visited him, the very Westernized Shah of Iran laid down miles of carpet under his visitor's wheels—an extravagant gesture straight out of medieval Asia. And even after nationhood in 1947 ended the power of the maharajas in India, princes gathered for a wedding in orange and vermilion turbans and a subtle range of silk brocade coats: pale peach, green, cream, gold, biege. Pink and gold saris and jewels sparkled against the background of a white palace, filigreed arches, and cool, tinkling fountains. State elephants were caparisoned in silks and cloth-of-gold for the wedding procession. It's hard to let go of a gorgeous past.

In China, the dragon robe persisted with the Manchus until 1911, when both it and the Manchus were thrown out by a people's revolution.

Then, almost overnight, the old, symbolic, upper class dress disappeared. Western suits came in, and Western style military uniforms. But many elderly men, forbidden the brilliant ceremonial dress, continued to wear the standard, casual dress of the Chinese official, an unadorned, short black silk jacket over a long, wrapped and belted, dark blue silk robe.

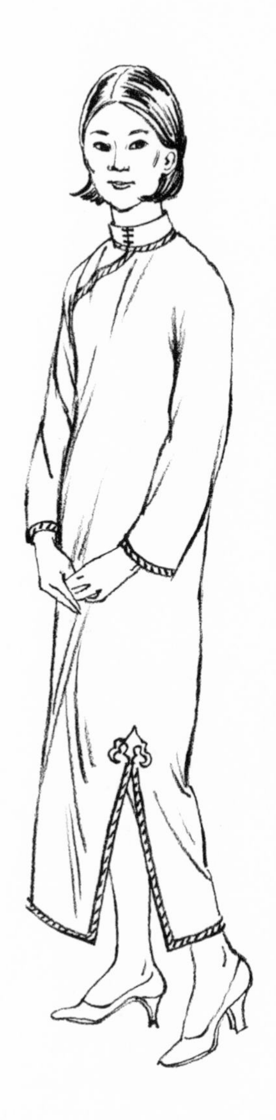

Women found a compromise between the old and the new in the *cheong sam.* Essentially the long, straight *p'ao* tunic with a standing collar, worn by Manchu men and women, the cheong sam displayed the body by means of darts, which fitted it to the figure. Its hem moved up, and its side slits revealed the wearer's legs. A fluctuating hemline allowed it to follow Western fashion trends. And shorter lengths, combined with the slits, gave unprecedented freedom to Chinese women, whose ancestors had once shuffled along in bound feet.

Women also discovered the potential in the peasant's jacket and pants. Slimmed pants and high-necked, side-closed jackets, made of silk, gave women a young, willowy look that was appealing even to Western eyes.

Both were comfortable and flattering. But both were banned after the Communist takeover in 1949. The graceful cheong sam remained only in places like British Hong Kong. The blue and black mandarin robe and jacket found refuge in Taiwan.

Communism came out of the West. It came to China in Western military uniform and peaked cap. The customary drabness that comes with industrialized, standardized, mass production of garments, was intensified in China by a commitment to hard work and equality. Leaders set an example by wearing a harsh yellow-green uniform based on Western military dress. Workers joined the all out effort with dark blue cotton jackets and trousers, quilted in the

winter. Details such as collars, buttons, pockets, were different from traditional peasant dress; but for the masses in China, dress had not changed much. Yet, for the first time, they were considered important to China's future. The uniformity of their blue rallied them like a flag, helping them accept the abrupt stripping away of four thousand years of tradition.

By the mid 1950s, the Chinese were restless in their drab uniform, and attempts were made to bring individuality and color into Chinese dress with state-sponsored fashion shows of state-approved, committee-designed cotton dresses based on the outdated fashions of eastern Europe. But clothes designed for matronly East German and Russian women were a disaster for the small Chinese woman. The current tensions between national commitment and the urge to display often lead young women to throw a cotton dirndl skirt over rolled-up trousers.

Japan had a long tradition of learning from foreigners that eventually made it easier for the Japanese to accept Western ideas and Western dress.

In the beginning, Japanese dress was borrowed from China. When T'ang culture flooded over to Japan from Korea in the 6th and 7th centuries, the Japanese Court adopted T'ang costume; it kept observers at the Chinese Court to study dress and manners. The Japanese began layering their robes, like the Chinese. They used color in hats and ceremonial robes to mark off graduations in rank.

But as the T'angs declined, the Japanese began to outstrip the Chinese. And their Court carried layering and width to extremes, wearing up to twenty layers of different colored robes as though to proclaim the superiority of 11th and 12th century Japanese culture.

Building on the Chinese model with vigor and creativity, the Japanese began to find their own style. And the Mongol conquest of China in the 13th century accelerated the move away from Chinese culture. For Japan defeated the Mongols, and Japanese confidence soared. Their own distinctive characteristics began dominating their borrowed

Chinese ones. Respect for the warrior (samurai) class and a passion for nature and for simplicity took over.

Even before the victory over the Mongols, warrior lords called the *shoguns* had taken the real power away from the emperor, and the samurai class was highly respected.

The discipline and simple tastes of the soldier touched every aspect of Japanese life, balancing a high refinement. Zen Buddhism, instead of burdening a man with philosophical studies, let him contemplate himself and nature. Tea drinking became an ascetic ritual that "cleansed the senses."

Even the court began to shed its layers of silk. And *hakamas*, the loose trousers that had always been worn under the wrapped, sleeved robe, moved outside (even on women for a few centuries). Men slit their basic robe from shoulder to waist to get their arms out quickly. They cut sleeves off other wraps. And their wives tossed off layers of robing, stripping down to the simple, wrapped white *kosode* they wore next to their skin. The kosode was made of big rectangles with sewn-on rectangles for sleeves; it was wrapped across the body, and held on with a simple sash. To avoid buying formal, expensive Chinese brocades, the Japanese devised inexpensive ways of dyeing and decorating the basic white kosode. Their devotion to nature and simplicity and individuality led them to develop it into the art form of the *kimona.*

The essential difference between China and Japan could be seen in the dragon robe and the kimona, the classic robe of each country. Both of silk, both patterned with nature forms, both long unfitted wraps evolved from the simplest coats of sewn-together rectangles, the dragon robe and the kimona were natural, human responses to different situations.

In a land where flowers and birds were scarce, the Japanese found delight in a single twig, blossoming against a blue sky, in the random beauty of their landscape. And each kimona became an individual expression of that delight. Bamboo forms, pine, clouds, birds, streams, flowers—especially cherry blossoms and plum and wisteria—were splashed boldly and asymmetrically across the kimona.

Where a Chinese floral motif would be lost in endless repeats, a single Japanese blossom stood out clearly.

The kimona itself stayed unchanging, just rectangles sewn together and sashed. But the sash, the *obi,* eventually went far beyond function to become an important part of the art of the kimona. And the same combination of lively creativity and clinging to tradition turned the hakama trousers into huge culottes, which gave the feeling of long, voluminous robes without hindering an active man.

While China gave honor to the scholarly bureaucrat, Japan gave it to the warrior. His armor became a display of pride in skill at arms, and obsession with rank. Instead of following body lines as Europe's armor did, the samurai's armor was a series of big flaps that gave him an impressive breath. Breastplates carried totem-like insignia and designs dyed and printed on leather, or etched on metal. The flaps were made of enamelled and lacquered metalplates laced together with bright braided cord. And his patterned silk kimona showed through in places, adding even more texture and color. He topped his helmet with stag antlers and covered his face with an iron mask, carved into a ferocious snarl. He carried it all to war in a wooden chest.

By the early 19th century, Japan had surpassed China in the range of colors and in the variety of effects that could be achieved in silk production. The uniquely Japanese techniques of stencilling and block-printing were what permitted this. And the work was done by a commercial middle class unknown in China.

But the samurai, like the outmoded European knight long before, still had an important role to play in a changing society. In 1867, a faction supporting the emperor and opposing the shoguns, led by appointed (not hereditary) officers, defeated the followers of the shogun in battle. The samurai disappeared, but the samuri sense of class distinction, spartan personal ethic and hatred of ostentation and waste moved on into the business world. Bowing continued undisturbed, and with it formality between classes. Stability was maintained.

The armor, the silk hakama culottes and the kimona were officially retired from active duty, for men at least. And the

Western suit, the symbol of progress, began to move in.

The suit was a drab replacement for the exquisitely decorated kimona. But at least its plainness suited the samurai code of austerity, and its stiff white collar did mark the gentleman off from the laborer. Like the kimona itself, it represented radical change without complete abandonment of tradition.

The kimona has not disappeared. Though rarely worn now in public by men, it is having a revival among women, especially for important occasions like weddings. And alert Western observers are watching it with great interest.

22

Figleafing through history, exploring why who wore what, we discover that even the strangest clothes made sense. They said, in effect, "Look! This is what I am."

The strangest clothes are still making sense. They're still revealing what we value, confessing what we wish, admitting what we cling to.

The Westernization of "underdeveloped" countries continues to spread like a sooty smog. Dark suits move in with factories and skyscrapers. And bursts of pride in native dress may be more wishful thinking than confidence in old ways.

If the whole world were to adopt the suit, at least we'd have an international language of dress. North Americans would no longer misunderstand the "feminine" long robes of an Iraqui sheik. American tourists wouldn't be closing kimonas to the left—as Japanese do for a corpse.

But the thought of a world of men in charcoal gray and navy blue suits is appalling. The loss of all the saffrons and embroideries and batiks and indigo turbans would leave the landscape as bleak as a charred forest.

The suit grew out of a chill, cloudy Europe. It was right for its time and place. But when men work in the searing heat of Kuwait on the Persian Gulf in secondhand, pinstriped suits shipped in by the bale from the U.S.A., it seems sad.

Even if the power to spread dress shifted from the U.S.

to, perhaps, Japan, it would prabably still be the suit that was spreading. For though Japan still bows and clings to formality between classes, she has all but buried her own brilliant, blossom-strewn kimona under Western dress. The kimona is worn now mostly for special occasions, at-home comfort, and by country women.

We have made the suit so sacred that it's not going to die easily. But it is under siege. It's being openly attacked from without by the unconventional dress and grooming of the young. It's being broken down gently from within by designers like Bill Blass and Cardin, who inject color, pattern, and innovation in cut into the familiar form. And the change is made as painless as possible by men's boutiques and wide press coverage of seasonal collections of men's fashions. The suit is being weakened even by the suit-wearers, on whom it lacks the confident commitment it had on the men who brought it to its peak.

The mid-nineteenth century man made the suit a clear expression of what he was. Though plain and somber, it conveyed his distinction with a small waist and expanded chest, a rigid white collar that held his head high, and a top hat that emphasized his uprightness. Its coat and trousers tied him to a tradition of work and action. But its white collar and tight fit said that he was *not* a laborer.

He met his male friends in clubs. He drew his power from heavy, blackened, masculine things like steam engines, coal, big machines, cargo ships, trains, steel. Like the Greek aristocrat or the Renaissance banker, he was part of a lively, largely male world that gave him variety and stimulation outside the home.

The suit seemed to lose some of its distinction when power shifted from the age of steam and empire to the age of technology. Shoulders narrowed. Chests deflated. The cut of the jacket relaxed. And the formal vest all but vanished.

Some of the changes were drawn from sports and from the brief vacations the business man took to recharge his batteries for work. Here he indulged himself in color, a bit of pattern and extreme casualness. It all affected his suit, but didn't alter it deeply, because modern Western

Man found his real identity in the work that kept progress and his family going.

Women's dress in the meantime has become steadily shorter and less restricting. Feminine flutter has been replaced with men's shirts, slacks, blazers, brimmed felt hats, fiitted wool overcoats, cardigan sweaters and chunky, low-heeled shoes.

Given a boost by the mobility and heavy work forced on them by two world wars, women—especially in the 1920s, 1940s, and 1960s—spurted on to emancipation with short skirts that allowed free movement, and unfitted clothes that de-emphasized childbearing and the female body.

In spite of lapses after wars and during the Depression, the general trend to short, free, mobile, multipurpose clothes has continued, reaching a peak in the '60s in pared-down, skimpily cut, unembellished dresses, coats, and suits that made the body a boyish shaft. With everything coordinated and matched, women's dress began to approach the bland uniformity of the business suit.

In the mid-sixties, a space age look crept in with shiny plastics, chrome hardware, geometric bands of color, boots and helmets and shorter and shorter skirts. And it all made the older woman look terrible. Liberation for women had suddenly become dominated by the young. And the young were most dominant in the U.S. and England.

Suddenly Paris was like Spain when the rest of Europe left her behind in her farthingale. For French couture was still dedicated to preserving the mystique of the matron—a mystique that dated back to the 18th century women who had dominated the politics and culture of France from their salons. The essence of couture clothes was womanly elegance, built up by complicated inner construction of seams, darts, bias-cut cloth, hooks and ties, and corsets. For, though the designer Courreges joined the move to space-age fashion, most of the French couture was still dedicated to expensive, beautifully hand-finished clothes made for an elite group of women with good taste. Paris fashions still supported France's reputation as a repository of culture and the arts.

But the easy *shifts* of the '60s undermined inner construction. The miniskirt and limp hippie dress—both initiated by the young—all but abolished elaborate detail by the end of the decade.

Paris tried to adapt to the youth cult and mass production. Many designers began producing lower priced collections for retail boutiques. But it was no surprise to clothes watchers that it was Paris that offered an alternative to the miniskirt—the mid-calf *longuette*—and sent it over to the United States on a chic, mature woman, Mme Pompidou, wife of the French president.

The mini came out of England; hippie dress, out of America. Both marked the arrival of a new class in power—youth.

With a pioneer tradition of hard work and informality, American children had gained a taste for early independence and functional clothes. They got more of both after World War II, when adults, eager for home and families again, devoted themselves to the comfort and wishes of their children. They were put into blue jeans, which quickly became the clothing symbol of the young.

Made first for the California gold rush by a merchant named Levi, blue denims had been taken up by cowboys, who for years got them to fit better by jumping into a horse trough and letting their new jeans dry and shrink on their body. Then, right after World War II, suburban America skyrocketed them to national popularity. Coming on as rough, tough cowboy pants, blue jeans represented much that Americans valued: a link with the frontier past, plain function and comfort, cheap mass-produced availability and expendability.

The Levi, and its mass-produced, nonshrink, fadeproof, perma-pressed, zippered variants gave children a new freedom. But it failed to give them a few things the old habit of wearing adult lace, velvet and styles had given—things like variety and aesthetic satisfaction, and a sense of the preciousness of things. Instead of helping to ease children into the responsibilities and values of the adult world, jeans and shirts became a uniform that set children apart from adults in suits and high heels. In retrospect, the

plain sameness of children's coveralls and jeans were a logical product of the standardized suburban environment. Classless, sexless and unadorned, jeans gave the young a taste more for freedom from restrictions than for their parents' values. And their neuterness may have given children a taste for freedom from sexual stereotypes as well.

At any rate, when the children grew up, many rejected the drip-dry society. They came out of the suburbs vaguely dissatisfied. And their clothing began to express a yearning for a more worthwhile self-image than suburbia had given them.

They took jeans with them, preferring the honesty of the authentic old Levis that shrunk, faded, and closed with buttons, over neat synthetic slacks.

Some young rebels broke completely from society and created their own communal life style. They took the dress of groups who seemed to have been closer to the earth and to one another: Indian tribes, pioneers. They discovered the baubles and flamboyance of the gypsies who squatted free on the fringes of society, and the robes and incense of Indian holy men who seemed to have a mystical harmony with nature and the universe.

With long hair, beads and fantasy costume, the young began to involve their senses and emotions in dress. Building up a communal counterculture around revolt against their parents' culture, they brought clothes back to handcrafts and nature. They wove headbands and ponchos. They tie-dyed cloth by knotting it and dipping it into dye. They worked leather into sandals and fringed vests. They revelled in textures and tactility: velvets, thick moustaches, suedes, nubby hand weaves.

Although their visible statement was drawn from the past, it was saying something new. It was expressing a new commitment. In his prediction for *The Year 2000*, Herman Kahn suggested that we are already moving into the post-industrial age. We are already heading for a devaluing of the work ethic, and for a fuller use of the senses, for more leisure and less deferment of pleasure. We're shifting prestige away from the banking and corporation executive. A more sensual, more humanistic age does seem to be expressing itself everywhere. Men's dress is coming alive. Hair has begun to creep down around the ears and neck of bankers and lawyers. Women are picking up the hippie idea of dressing up, of putting themselves together with spontaneity and imagination.

The new way of dressing that is spreading out from the counterculture has even been dignified with its own fashion magazine, *Rags*, created in the spring of 1970. It promoted $14.95 parachute boots from the Army and Navy surplus stores instead of couture clothes; it encouraged readers to make their own tie-dyed and leather clothes; and it urged the saving and recycling of the newsprint the magazine is published on to prevent waste of natural resources.

But millions of men still climb into their grey suits every morning. Habits are hard to give up. And so are the obvious benefits that the suit-wearer's work and science have brought us: longer life, freedom from drudgery, and theoretical equality, just to name a few. His society has conditioned people to the convenience of easy-care, inexpensive clothes. Science's synthetic fibers have even brought the wig—one of the most ancient, aristocratic, and satisfying means of altering your image—within the reach of everybody.

Right now, science could probably put us into clothes that are molded instead of woven; clothes of totally man-made materials, with built-in heat, cold, and communications. But the human demand has not yet been strong enough to turn clothing research away from its concentration on industrial, space and military clothing. Only a few designers, have projected their thinking into genuinely new clothing forms.

We cling to the familiar needle and thread, the woven rectangle, ancient fur, cotton, wool, linen, and silk. We use synthetic fibers to make "fake fur" the way ancient farming societies used new skill to make "fake fleece" kaunakes. We try to make dacron look and feel like cotton and silk because we're not ready yet for the look and feel of plastics and inflatable micro-environments. We hesitate. Turn back to old styles. And in our homes we hover between space age shapes and materials and the reassuringly familiar furniture of 18th century France, colonial America, Victorian England.

But much of the confusion in contemporary dress is more than a clinging to the familiar. There's an attempt to somehow avoid what seems inevitable—the ruthless march of science at the expense of the individual and the total environment. As technology takes us farther and farther away from a state of nature, some people return to original nudity, hoping that neuroses and hang-ups will fall away with clothes. But we are not simple children of nature. We need clothes now. And it is because we are a society emotionally and economically committed to clothes that nudity can be an effective shock tactic in the current social revolution.

The hippies' escape into costumed ritual has been compared to the tribal rites of initiation into adulthood. But theirs is a rite of passage without the passage. Unwilling to move on into a society they don't admire, many stay in the regalia instead of putting it away for adult garments. It gives them group identity and the courage to keep up their confrontation with adults. Their turning to the past is one of the oldest means of escape from reality. And it doesn't usually do much to halt history.

Women escape, too, into longer skirts (one of the most ancient marks of the dependent and limited woman), into fantasy costuming picked up from the hippie culture, into wigs.

When the mid-calf length skirt was splashed across women's pages in the spring of 1970, many thought it was an egomaniacal plot by *Women's Wear Daily* to prove its power to twist fashion around its finger. The major publication of the garment industry, *Women's Wear Daily* is very influential. But it's unlikely that it has the power to stop or start strong new movements in dress.

The longer hem and more matronly silhouette seem to be a drawing back from current change, a vote for tradition in the face of a frightening disruption of old values. Women are hesitating on the brink of almost complete liberation from the old limitations, even from childbirth. The modern woman has the contraceptive pill, social acceptance of small families, and even the possibility of test tube babies. The miniskirt was leading her out of skirts that have hampered her since cave women cut theirs out of leather. And though the drive to liberation is being given muscle by a determined women's liberation movement, most women may not be quite ready for it. The hemline crisis said that some women may want to hold on to the old role. They may even prefer dependency. They may still prefer mystery and romance to the aggressive candor of the miniskirt. In a mobile age, though, hampering skirts are unrealistic. And longer skirts are met with resistance and confusion. The 1970s may turn out to be a decade of hemline confusion that many will blame on the whims and instability of women. In reality, women will be responding to the conflicts and tensions of the times far more sensitively than suit-bound man.

While some women escape, others are fighting constructively with clothes.

Unisex clothing—identical clothes for both sexes—is new to the modern West. And it may be just what we need right now. Worn by the young, pants, navy pea jackets, and long hair are blurring the old sex images, breaking down a lot of barriers to frank communication. For babies are not born with the concept of pink-blue, skirts-trousers, submissive-aggressive. These are things society teaches as it trains children for their role in life.

Our society has trained girls for frills, dolls, coy seduction and brassieres to turn breasts into architectural monuments. It has trained boys for the opposites. And the stereotype hasn't suited everybody. It has set up a lot of romantic marriages based on dishonest relationships.

Now we know that men and women share many of the same traits. The casual sameness of much dress seems to be saying this. Many young women have thrown away brassieres as seduction traps. And publications like *Rags* try to counter the contrived boy-girl cliches that still flood most media.

But unisex clothes could also be the beginning of a gen-

eral desexing of society, a slowing of interest in sex, as looser morals make it more easily available, and as an abundance of babies becomes a threat—rather than a necessity—to the survival of the species.

A new concern for the environment may be changing dress, too. It may be altering the very ancient status symbolism of furs. As militant groups protest the wearing of threatened species like leopards, more common furs—rabbit, perhaps—may become the most acceptable furs to rich and poor alike. And this would be a remarkable reversal of the old habit of putting top value on the rarest, most expensive things.

Environmental concern may also make us begin to look at clothes the way we're beginning to look at billboards and treeless tract housing—as part of the total landscape. It may lift the aesthetics of dress up from being a purely personal thing to being part of a general concern with man-made ugliness.

Hippie dress, in spite of its fantasy and nostalgia, is helping to direct us to a fresh look at the almost forgotten qualities of natural, earthy costume materials.

The dress of the young blacks is a confident new assertion of Negro identity. Abandoning the hair-straighteners and skin-whiteners that tried to blend them into the white world, they reach back beyond slavery for a new expression of their own innate dignity. Afro haircuts, tribal print cotton shirts and headwraps give them the dramatic presence blacks have always had when they stayed true to their natures. And if it helps to train the white man's eye to see black as a color instead of a symbol, the young blacks will have won a social revolution as significant as the Renaissance, which turned purple from symbol to color.

But one of the most dramatic breaks with the *status quo* is the new dress of the Roman Catholic Church. Many priests and nuns have thrown off the medieval gowns and starched headdresses that set them apart and above. They've stripped themselves of the symbolism and the special privileges it gave them, and put on dress that lets them get involved with their flocks on a more human level. Like the blacks, they are sick of being faceless symbols. And this is the essence of what all the young rebels are fighting for with dress—a breaking down of our society's barriers to human communication. This is very new. It is also very old. For the monks who hitched up their peasant homespuns to get involved made the Church real and important to the struggling German tribes of the early Middle Ages.

Revolutionary dress always goes to extremes to make its point. And when the crisis has passed, it always eases up. In France, the "sans-culotte" eventually stopped guillotining men in breeches. The crisis for our time is not over yet. In fact, the battle of values seems only beginning when construction worker's hard hats can become the rallying symbol of men who support American tradition and who oppose the long-haired young. But at the same time, groups of students and professors have had their hair and beards symbolically cut in an effort to bridge the gap and reestablish communication. Hair may be worn short again. And some of the super function of the moonsuit may even creep into hippie dress.

If the suit is knocked down in the fight between feeling and function, its vestiges will no doubt hang on, just as the 18th century riding coat hangs on in white tie and tails. Very few of even the most violent rebels will want to give up all the good things the suit-wearer has brought. They know it's largely science and technological efficiency that can give them the leisure to return to handcrafts and to a development of the senses. And trousers still make sense for active people.

If the suit disappeared overnight, it would be a terrible shock to everybody; the men who find their identity in it would feel confused. But if the suit and the headband joined forces, we might go into one of the great ages of dress. For the tools of science could do fantastic things to open up the senses and serve individual expression. Color could be made to respond to mood. New surfaces might take tactility far beyond fur and velvet. Artificial amber could glow with real warmth.

We could put on a psychedelic blend of sound and color to face the world, or retreat into the serene isolation of self-contained garments. Group garments could bring friends together. Personal climate controls and mini-environments could let us travel freely over the earth. Or the moon.

Clothes could reach super function for work and travel, super sensuality and individuality for home.

The combined forces of natural and synthetic, hand-crafted and machine-molded materials could let us express our "intrinsic worth" to our world in the richest clothing vocabulary the world has ever seen.

Selected Bibliography

The Classical world, Egypt, and the West since the Renaissance have been heavily documented in history, art, and costume books. The specific references in this brief bibliography will attempt to guide the reader into the less well-documented areas.

Costume—General Reference Sources

Boucher, François. *20,000 Years of Fashion.* H. N. Abrams, 1966.

Davenport, Millia. *The Book of Costume.* Crown, 1948.

Payne, Blanche. *History of Costume.* Harper & Row, 1965.

Hiler, Hilaire. *From Nudity to Raiment.* E. Weyhe, 1929.

Bruhn, Wolfgang and Tilke, Max. *A Pictorial History of Costume.* Frederick A. Praeger, 1955.

Laver, James. *Taste & Fashion.* Dodd, Mead & Co., 1938.
Costume. Hawthorn Books, 1964.
The Concise History of Costume and Fashion. H. N. Abrams, 1969.
Modesty in Dress. Houghton Mifflin, 1969.

Von Boehm, Max. *Modes and Manners* (4 volumes). J. B. Lippincott, 1932–35.

Weibel, Adele Coulin. *Two Thousand Years of Textiles.* Pantheon Books, 1952.

Birren, Faber. *Color, A Survey in Words and Pictures.* University Books, 1963.

Journals: *CIBA Review* (chemical company journal with excellent articles on textiles and costume)

National Geographic Magazine
Women's Wear Daily, newspaper of the garment industry
Rags, clothing magazine of the counter-culture

Psychology of Dress

Flügel, John Carl. *The Psychology of Clothes,* Hogarth, 1930.

Roach, Mary Ellen and Eicher, J. B. *Dress, Adornment and the Social Order*. Wiley, 1965.

Langner, Lawrence. *The Importance of Wearing Clothes.* Hastings House, 1959.

Anspach, Karlyne. *The Why of Fashion.* Iowa State University Press, 1968.

Bergler, Edmund. *Fashion and the Unconscious.* Robert Brunner, 1953.

Ryan, Mary Shaw. *Clothing: A Study in Human Behavior.* Holt, Rhinehart & Winston, 1966.

Winick, Charles E. *The New People: Desexualization in American Life*. Pegasus, 1968.

Maccaby, Eleanor E. (editor). *The Development of Sex Differences.* Stanford University Press, 1966.

Portmann, Adolf. *Animal Forms and Patterns.* Schocken Books, 1967.

Strauss, Erwin W. *Phenomenological Psychology.* Basic Books, 1966. (Includes essay on upright posture.)

Roszak, Theodore. *The Making of a Counter-Culture.* Doubleday, 1969.

Aldridge, John W. *In the Country of the Young*. Harper's Magazine Press, 1969.

McLuhan, H. Marshall and Fiore, Quentin. *War and Peace in the Global Village*. McGraw-Hill, 1968.

Kroeber, Alfred Louis. *Style and Civilization.* University of California Press, 1963.

Kahn, Herman and Wiener, A. J. *The Year 2000*. Macmillan, 1967.

Court, Catherine. "An Interview with Marshall McLuhan: Mini Skirt Tribalism." *Rags,* October 1970.

Grene, Marjorie and Portmann, Adolf. "Beyond Darwinism." *Commentary,* November 1965.

History

A few examples of how rich history can be when clothing is taken seriously:

Huizinga, Johan. *The Waning of the Middle Ages.* Longmans Green, 1924.

Aries, Phillippe. *Centuries of Childhood.* Knopf, 1962.

Brundage, Burr Cartwright. *Lords of Cuzco.* University of Oklahoma Press, 1967.

Reichwein, Adolf. *China and Europe: Intellectual and Artistic Contacts in the 18th Century.* Knopf, 1925.

General Reference Sources

McNeill, William Hardy. *The Rise of the West.* University of Chicago Press, 1963.

Singer, Charles, Holmyard, E. J., Hall, A. R. (editors). *History of Technology* (5 volumes). Oxford University Press, 1954.

Toynbee, Arnold J. *Civilization on Trial.* Oxford University Press, 1948.

The Cambridge Ancient History. Cambridge University Press.

The Cambridge Medieval History. Cambridge University Press.

Shepherd, William R. *Shepherd's Historical Atlas.* Barnes and Noble, 1964.

Specific References

Earliest History

Breuil, Henri and Lantier, R. *The Men of the Old Stone Age.* St. Martin's Press, 1965.

Leroi-Gourhan, André. *Treasures of Prehistoric Art.* H. N. Abrams, 1967.

Braidwood, Robert J. *Prehistoric Men.* Chicago Natural History Museum, 1967.

Steppes, Persia, Islam and the Orient

Bhushan, Jamila Brij. *The Costume and Textiles of India.* Taraporevalo, 1958.

Piggott, Stuart. *Prehistoric India to 1000 B.C.* British Book Service Ltd., 1962.

Basham, A. L. *The Wonder That Was India.* Sedgwick & Jackson, 1954.

Hambly, Gavin. *Cities of Mughal India.* G. P. Putnam's Sons, 1968.

Grube, Ernst J. *The World of Islam.* McGraw-Hill, 1967.

Rugoff, Milton. *Marco Polo's Adventures in China.* Horizon Caravel Books. American Heritage, 1964.

Schulthess, Emil. *China.* Viking, 1966. (Photos of mainland China.)

Cammann, Schuyler. *China's Dragon Robes.* The Ronald Press, 1952.

Scott, A. C. *Chinese Costume in Transition.* Theatre Art Books, 1960.

Goodrich, L. Carrington. *A Short History of the Chinese People.* Harper Bros., 1959.

Minnick, Helen Benton. *Japanese Costume and the Makers of Its Elegant Tradition.* Charles E. Tuttle Co., 1963.

Benedict, Ruth. *The Chrysanthemum and the Sword: Patterns of Japanese Culture.* Houghton Mifflin, 1946.

Phillips, Eustace Dockray. *The Royal Hordes: Nomad Peoples of The Steppes.* Library of Early Civilizations, Stuart Piggott, editor. Frederick A. Praeger, 1965.

Rice, Tamara Talbot. *The Scythians.* Ancient Peoples and Places Series. Frederick A. Praeger, 1957.

Jettmar, Karl. *The Art of the Steppes.* Crown, 1964.

McGovern, William Montgomery. *The Early Empires of Central Asia.* University of North Carolina Press, 1939.

Artamanov, M. I. *Treasures from Scythian Tombs.* Thames & Hudson, 1969.

Rudenko, Sergei I. *The Frozen Tombs of Siberia.* University of California Press, 1970.

Dalton, O. M. *The Treasure of the Oxus.* Trustees of the British Museum, 1964.

Tilke, Max. *Oriental Costumes, Their Designs and Colors.* K. Paul, Trench, Trubner & Co. Ltd. (London), 1923 (Brentano's, 1957).

Houston, Mary. *Ancient Egyptian, Mesopotamian and Persian Costume and Decoration.* A. & C. Black, 1954.

Frankfort, Henri. *The Art and Architecture of the Ancient Orient.* Penguin, 1959.

Ghirshman, Roman. *The Arts of Ancient Iran.* Arts of Mankind Series edited by André Malraux. Golden Press, 1964.

Persian Art: The Parthian and Sassanian Dynasties. Golden Press, 1962.

Godard, André. *The Art of Iran.* Frederick A. Praeger, 1965.

Rubens, Alfred. *A History of Jewish Costume.* Valentine, 1967.

Culture Contact

Bad Heart Bull, Amos and Blish, Helen H. *A Pictographic History of the Oglala Sioux.* University of Nebraska Press, 1967.

Levenson, Joseph R. *European Expansion and the Counter-Example of Asia 1300–1600.* Prentice-Hall, 1967.

Burland, Cottie Arthur. *The Exotic White Man.* McGraw-Hill, 1969.

Haring, Clarence H. *The Spanish Empire in America.* Harcourt, Brace & World Inc., 1963.

Oliver, Roland. *Africa in the Days of Exploration.* Prentice-Hall, 1965.

Fagg, William Buller. *Afro-Portuguese Ivories.* Batchworth Press, 1960.

Africa

Wilcox, Ruth Turner. *Folk and Festival Costume of the World.* Charles Scribner's Sons, 1965.

Schulthess, Emil. *Africa.* Viking Press, 1964.

Lhote, Henri. *The Search for the Tassili Frescoes: The Story of the Prehistoric Rock Paintings of the Sahara.* E. P. Dutton, 1959.

Hintze, Fritz & Ursula. *Civilizations of the old Sudan.* B. R. Gruner (Amsterdam), 1968.

Hodgkin, Thomas. *Nigerian Perspectives, an Historical Anthology.* Oxford University Press, 1960.

Davidson, Basil. *The Lost Cities of Africa.* Little, Brown, 1959.

Willett, Frank. *Ife in the History of West African Sculpture.* McGraw-Hill, 1967.

Dark, Philip and Forman, Werner. *Benin Art.* Paul Hamlyn, 1960.

Murdock, George Peter. *Africa, Its Peoples and Their Culture History.* McGraw-Hill, 1969.

The Americas

Hiler, Hilaire. *From Nudity to Raiment.* E. Weyhe, 1929. (Chapters on Peruvian and Mexican costume.)

Du Solier, W. *Ancient Mexican Costume.* Ediciones Mexicanas, S.A., 1950.

Blacker, Irwin and Eckholm, Gordon. *Cortes and the Aztec Conquest.* American Heritage, 1965.

Brundage, Burr Cartwright. *Lords of Cuzco.* University of Oklahoma Press, 1967. (Last days of the Inca, excellent on costume.)

La Farge, Oliver. *American Indian.* Golden Press, 1960.

Mason, Bernard S. *The Book of Indian Crafts and Costumes.* The Ronald Press Company, 1946.

Diaries and Chronicles

Authentic journals can be the most vivid and accurate source of costume information:

Froissart, Sir John. *The Chronicles of England, France and Spain,* translated by Thomas Johnes. E. P. Dutton & Co., 1961.

Herodotus. *The Persian Wars,* translated by George Rawlinson. Random House, 1942.

Diaz del Castillo, Bernal, edited by Shirley Glubok. *The Fall of the Aztecs.* St. Martin's Press, 1965. (Journal of the Cortes expedition to Mexico.)

Gregory of Tours, edited by Ernest Brehaut. *History of the Franks.* Octagon, 1965.

Quant, Mary. *Quant by Quant.* G. P. Putnam's Sons, 1966.

The West

Bark, William Carroll. *Origins of the Medieval World.* Stanford University Press, 1958.

Fichtenau, Heinrich. *The Carolingian Empire.* Barnes & Noble, 1957.

Duby, Georges. *Rural Economy and Country Life in the Medieval West.* University of South Carolina Press, 1968.

Pirenne, Henri. *Mohammed and Charlemagne.* W. W. Norton, 1939.

Medieval Cities. Princeton University, 1925.

Munz, Peter. *Life in the Age of Charlemagne.* European Life Series edited by Peter Quennell. G. P. Putnam's Sons, 1969.

Trevor-Roper, Hugh. *The Rise of Christian Europe.* Harcourt, Brace & World, 1966.

Morley, Charles Rufus. *Medieval Art.* W. W. Norton, 1942.

The Year 1200 (2 volumes). Metropolitan Museum of Art (New York).

White, Lyn, Jr. *Medieval Technology and Social Change.* Oxford University Press, 1962.

Evans, Joan. *The Flowering of the Middle Ages.* McGraw-Hill, 1966.

Oldenbourg, Zoe. *The Crusades.* Pantheon Books, 1966.

Mattingly, Garrett. *Renaissance Diplomacy.* Houghton Mifflin, 1955.

Chamberlin, Eric Russell. *Everyday Life of Renaissance Times.* Everyday Life Series. G. P. Putnam's Sons, 1965.

Panofsky, Erwin. *Renaissance and Renascences.* Almqvist & Wiksell (Stockholm), 1966.

Picture Credits

"Adam and Eve," painting by Albrecht Dürer. The Metropolitan Museum of Art, gift in memory of Johnston L. Redmond, 1967. Frontispiece.

Detail of Fresco of the Hunters. From *The Search for the Tassili Frescoes,* by Henri Lhote. Photograph by Henri Lhote. Page 56.

Detail of The Shelter of the Children. From *The Search for the Tassili Frescoes,* by Henri Lhote. Photograph by Henri Lhote. Page 56.

Sumerian Cylinder Seal. The Metropolitan Museum of Art, lent by Rev. Paul Moore, Jr. Page 57.

Statuette of a Man. The Metropolitan Museum of Art, Rogers Fund, 1950. Page 57.

Wall Painting: Isis Leading Nefret-iry from the Valley of the Queens. The Metropolitan Museum of Art. Page 58.

Greek Statue of a Woman in a Chiton. The Metropolitan Museum of Art, Rogers Fund, 1944. Page 59.

Procession of the Family of Augustus. Alinari. Page 59.

Gold Torque with Two Mounted Scythians as Finials. Photograph by Werner Forman. Page 60.

Assyrian Relief from Palace at Ancient Nimrud. The Metropolitan Museum of Art, gift of John D. Rockefeller, Jr., 1938. Page 60.

Persian (Sassanian) Silver Plate. The Metropolitan Museum of Art, The Cora Timken Burnett Collection of Persian Miniatures and Other Persian Art Objects, bequest of Cora Timken Burnett, 1957. Page 60.

Empress Theodora and Companions. Alinari. Page 61.

Detail of a Mosaic Ceiling from the Archepiscopal Chapel at Ravenna. Alinari. Page 61.

Equestrian Statue of Charlemagne. The Louvre. Photograph by Réunion des Musées Nationaux. Page 62.

The Virgin Enthroned. The Metropolitan Museum of Art, gift of J. Pierpont Morgan, 1917. Page 62.

The Journey to Emmaus and St. Magdalen and Christ. The Metropolitan Museum of Art, gift of J. Pierpont Morgan, 1917. Page 63.

"Showing of the Helms Before the Tournament," from *Traitie de la forme et devis comme on fait les tournois,* by Rene of Anjou. Bibliotheque Nationale. Page 64.

Detail of the Adimari Wedding Procession. Alinari. Page 64.

Painting of the Infanta Isabella Clara Eugenia with Magdalena Ruiz, by de Leano. The Prado Museum. Page 65.

Painting of the Archduke Rudolf of Austria, by Sanchez Coello. By gracious permission of Her Majesty Queen Elizabeth II. Page 65.

Portrait of Shah Jahan on Horseback. The Metropolitan Museum of Art, gift of Alexander Smith Cochran, 1913. Page 66.

Detail from Ceramic Dado Panels of Persian Ladies Entertaining a European Merchant in a Garden. The Metropolitan Museum of Art, Rogers Fund, 1903. Page 66.

Detail from Door Jamb of Yakshi Figure (of a Woman). Center of Asian Art and Culture, The Avery Brundage Collection, San Francisco. Page 67.

The Sen Sisters, painting by Frank Owen Salisbury. The Metropolitan Museum of Art, gift of the Artist, 1953. Page 67.

Pottery Statuette of Kneeling Man. Center of Asian Art and Culture, The Avery Brundage Collection, San Francisco. Page 168.

"Whiling Away the Summer," Chinese Painting by Liu Kuan-tao. Nelson Gallery–Atkins Museum, Kansas City, Missouri (Nelson Fund). Page 168.

Manchu Dragon Robe. The Metropolitan Museum of Art, Rogers Fund, 1942. Page 168.

Detail of Etching "L'Assemble au Salon," by François N. B. De Quevauviller. Achenbach Foundation for the Graphic Arts, Palace of the Legion of Honour, San Francisco. Page 169.

Colonel George K. H. Coussmaker, Grenadier Guards, painting by Joshua Reynolds. The Metropolitan Museum of Art, bequest of William K. Vanderbilt, 1920. Page 169.

Etching of French Revolutionary Sans-Culottes, engraved by Jean Duplessi-Bertáux. Achenbach Foundation for the Graphic Arts, Palace of the Legion of Honour, San Francisco. Page 170.

Print from *Observations sur les Modes et les Usages de Paris,* 1827. The Metropolitan Museum of Art, Harris Brisbane Dick Fund, 1938. Page 170.

Lithograph Advertisement for "Sayce's Patent Travelling Coat." The Metropolitan Museum of Art, Bella C. Landaur Collection. Page 171.

"Delivery of the American Presents at Yokohama." The Metropolitan Museum of Art, Whittelsey Fund, 1947. Page 172.

"A Sketch at the Bazaar." The Metropolitan Museum of Art, Harris Brisbane Dick Fund, 1928. Page 172.

Japanese Print "Daimo Procession Game," by Kiyomitsu Torii. The Metropolitan Museum of Art, Frederick Charles Hewitt Fund, 1911. Page 173.

Armor for an Officer of a Daimye of Sakai. The Metropolitan Museum of Art, Rogers Fund, 1904. Page 173.

Oni of Ife in Full Regalia. Photograph by Frank Willett. Page 174.

Katsina Horsemen, Nigeria. The Consulate General of Nigeria. Page 174.

Hausa Herder, Nigeria. The Consulate General of Nigeria. Page 174.

Index